T0265809

Praise for *Across a Waking Land*

'This book is an open-hearted, humble and gritty adventure with a deep love of nature at its heart. It takes courage to walk alone across the land, and it takes passionate curiosity to find out what lies behind the green fields of Britain. Roger Morgan-Grenville possesses these qualities, they shine through every page. *Across a Waking Land* is a masterful interweaving of personal endeavour with the big conservation challenges of Britain today. I loved it.'

MARY COLWELL, author of *Curlew Moon*

Praise for *Taking Stock*

'Funny, insightful and hugely informative ... a charming book'
Daily Mail

'Tremendous ... We all need to take stock, and this is the ideal starting point. I learnt a lot from this book and laughed a lot too.'
Rosamund Young, author of *The Secret Life of Cows*

'Stylishly locates the importance of the cow in absolutely everything from finance ... to future food. [A] first-prize rosette for this paean to the wonderful cow, Man's other best friend.'
John Lewis-Stempel, *Country Life*

'A lyrical and evocative book'
Daily Express

'No cow could ever hope for a better appreciation of its truly unique worth.'
Betty Fussell, author of *Raising Steaks: The Life and Times of American Beef*

'An epic story told with warmth, wit and humanity. Will make us feel differently about these long-suffering animals.'
Graham Harvey, author of *Grass-Fed Nation*

Praise for *Shearwater*

'This charming and impassioned book meanders, shearwater-like, across a lifetime and a world, a rich tribute to an extraordinary bird drawn through tender memoir and dauntless travel.'

HORATIO CLARE, author of *A Single Swallow* and *Heavy Light*

'*Shearwater* is sheer delight, a luminous portrait of a magical seabird which spans the watery globe'

Daily Mail

'This is wonderful: written with light and love. A tonic for these times.'

STEPHEN RUTT, author of *The Seafarers: A Journey Among Birds*

'What I love about Roger Morgan-Grenville's writing is the sheer humanness of it ... Bravo – a truly lovely book.'

MARY COLWELL, author of *Curlew Moon*

'*Shearwater* is a delightful and informative account of a lifelong passion for seabirds, as the author travels around the globe in pursuit of these enigmatic creatures.'

STEPHEN MOSS, naturalist and author of *The Swallow: A Biography*

'A captivating mix of memoir, travel and ornithological obsession ... A book not just for seabirders or island-addicts, but for all who have ever gazed longingly out to sea and pondered vast possibilities and connections.'

BBC Wildlife magazine

'A beautiful mix of memoir and natural history ... entirely infectious.'

Scottish Field

Praise for *Liquid Gold*

'A great book. Painstakingly researched, but humorous, sensitive and full of wisdom. I'm on the verge of getting some bees as a consequence of reading the book.'

Chris Stewart, author of *Driving Over Lemons*

'A light-hearted account of midlife, a yearning for adventure, the plight of bees, the quest for "liquid gold" and, above all, friendship.'

Sunday Telegraph

'*Liquid Gold* is a book that ignites joy and warmth'

Mary Colwell, author *of Curlew Moon*

'Beekeeping builds from lark to revelation in this carefully observed story of midlife friendship. Filled with humour and surprising insight, *Liquid Gold* is as richly rewarding as its namesake. Highly recommended.'

Thor Hanson, author of *Buzz: The Nature and Necessity of Bees*

'Behind the self-deprecating humour, Morgan-Grenville's childlike passion for beekeeping lights up every page. His bees are a conduit to a connection with nature that lends fresh meaning to his life. His bee-keeping, meanwhile, proves both a means of escape from the grim state of the world and a positive way of doing something about it. We could probably all do with some of that.'

Dixe Wills, *BBC Countryfile magazine*

'Both humorous and emotionally affecting ... Morgan-Grenville's wry and thoughtful tale demonstrates why an item many take for granted should, in fact, be regarded as liquid gold.'

Publishers Weekly

By the same author

Taking Stock: A Journey Among Cows
(Icon, 2022)

Shearwater: A Bird, An Ocean, And a Long Way Home
(Icon, 2021)

Liquid Gold: Bees and the Pursuit of Midlife Honey
(Icon, 2020)

Unlimited Overs (Quiller, 2019)

Not Out of the Woods (Bikeshed Books, 2018)

Not Out First Ball (Benefactum Press, 2013)

Across a Waking Land

Across a Waking Land

A 1,000-Mile Walk Through a British Spring

Roger Morgan-Grenville

Published in the UK and USA in 2023
by Icon Books Ltd, Omnibus Business Centre,
39–41 North Road, London N7 9DP
email: info@iconbooks.com
www.iconbooks.com

Sold in the UK, Europe and Asia
by Faber & Faber Ltd, Bloomsbury House,
74–77 Great Russell Street,
London WC1B 3DA or their agents

Distributed in the UK, Europe and Asia
by Grantham Book Services, Trent Road,
Grantham NG31 7XQ

Distributed in the USA
by Publishers Group West,
1700 Fourth Street, Berkeley, CA 94710

Distributed in Canada by Publishers Group Canada,
76 Stafford Street, Unit 300
Toronto, Ontario M6J 2S1

Distributed in Australia and New Zealand by
Allen & Unwin Pty Ltd, PO Box 8500,
83 Alexander Street, Crows Nest, NSW 2065

Distributed in South Africa by
Jonathan Ball, Office B4, The District,
41 Sir Lowry Road, Woodstock 7925

Distributed in India by Penguin Books India,
7th Floor, Infinity Tower – C, DLF Cyber City,
Gurgaon 122002, Haryana

ISBN: 978-178578-976-2
eBook: 978-178578-977-9

Typeset by SJmagic DESIGN SERVICES, India

Printed and bound in the UK

CONTENTS

LIST OF ILLUSTRATIONS

15. The author at Cape Wrath, 11 kilos lighter.
16. Members of the Save Danes Moss Action Group, Macclesfield, Cheshire.

All photos by the author, with the exception of 1, 2 and 14 (Caroline Morgan-Grenville), 9 (Hamish Robertson, Tweed Forum), 10 (Kit Hollins) and 15 (unnamed graduate from Sheffield University!).

ABOUT THE AUTHOR

Roger Morgan-Grenville was a soldier in the Royal Green Jackets from 1978–86, serving all over the world. In 1984–85, he led the first expedition that successfully retraced Sir Ernest Shackleton's escape across the sub-Antarctic island of South Georgia. After leaving the British army, he worked in, and then ran, a small family company importing and selling kitchenware. In 2007–08, he helped to set up the charity Help for Heroes, and in 2020 he was a founding member of the conservation charity, Curlew Action. He jointly set up a roving cricket team in 1986 (The Winchester Hunters) and lives in West Sussex. This is his seventh book. His earlier titles, *Taking Stock*, *Liquid Gold* and *Shearwater*, are also published by Icon.

DEDICATION

To Caroline, for getting it from the start

And to the people who inspired, taught, fed and entertained me along the way

PROLOGUE
Cam Fell

'A ship is safe in a harbour, but that is not what ships are built for.'
WILLIAM FEATHER (AMERICAN PUBLISHER)

By lunchtime, it is snowing hard.

High up on a Pennine fell, I am sheltering in the lee of a dry-stone wall, watching driven snow scudding across a copper sky over my head, feeling it insinuate itself in icy shards through the little gaps in the stonework behind me. I watch it gathering on my pack, in tiny ball-like grains, feel it on my neck and cheek. A few metres to my right, an old Swaledale ewe lies tight to the wall, lumps of frozen snow gathering in her fleece. She is eyeing me sullenly and she is going nowhere. I have come fifteen miles across the moors this morning to be here, and have another five to go for the more permanent shelter of Hawes. Walking on in these immediate conditions is not a good idea for many reasons, so I stay put. For a few minutes, I nibble on a cheese and pickle sandwich through gloved hands, and wait for the storm to abate, because they all eventually do.

Only this one doesn't. Instead, it intensifies for a time, noisily buffeting snow and strands of fodder above me and out into the invisible wastes of the valley below. Some kind of crow cartwheels downwind through the wild air above me. My core temperature is fine, but I know that I am very exposed out here on the lonely hill. I am well equipped, but I haven't seen a forecast for days, and have no idea what is to follow. I am expected down in Hawes later in the afternoon, so I know that someone is aware of where I am coming from, and the route that I am taking. I remove my right glove and take out my phone to see if it has any bars of signal, so that I can check the local forecast. It doesn't – and for an instant, the isolation that this implies thrills rather than alarms me. Right now, it is about resilience, about the decisions I make and, above all, about the comforting presence of the 300-gram survival bag in my backpack. Whatever the weather throws at me, I can lie out the worst of it inside it if I need to, like a vast orange caterpillar.

I don't even know what day of the week it is. Far to the south, my friends are in offices, on farms, at desks and in warm kitchens. This is an adventure whose details have been shared with them, so they know roughly where I am and what I am doing. We are mostly of an age where a break from routine, which is what this snow is, counts as a holiday in itself. At my age, you take situations like this wherever and whenever you find them, before the curtain of decrepitude sweeps them elegantly from your view.

'Lucky idiot,' they are probably thinking, as they rinse their morning coffee mug under the cold tap.

And they are right. Out here in the uncertain embrace of a British spring, I am indeed a lucky idiot.

*

What follows is the story of that lucky idiot's adventure. It is a long nature walk, just shy of a thousand miles, that I undertook mainly alone in the spring of 2022. I was 62, and Vladimir Putin had just invaded Ukraine.

These days, what we once called nature we now call biodiversity, whose accumulated losses sit rather too quietly for their own good in the shadow of its louder sibling crisis, climate change. Ironically, for the developed country with by far the highest per capita proportion of conservation group membership in the world, we are also the one with by far the worst record on species loss. But I didn't want to see how bad it was – we know all that already – so much as what was being done about it in this, the most nature-depleted developed country on earth, and whether I was entitled to be hopeful. Hope, after all, is not just the preserve of the starry-eyed young.

Besides, I needed an adventure. We all need adventures, whether we know it or not.

I chose to go on foot, because any other form of transport would be just too fast for observation, too hasty for the gradual process of arriving at a settled view; even my slow old bicycle would pass roadside hedgerows too quickly to catch that nervous blackcap, or that tiny group of cowslips on the bank. Then I selected a route that zigzagged the length of my island home from the gentle shoreline of the Solent to the towering cliffs of Cape Wrath up on the northern coast. I found a mix of wildlife restoration projects more or less close to my route, varying in habitat, size, method and intent, and then organised to pass through them, to see how they were going. From a tiny allotment in Sheffield to the vast sweep of the Trees for Life project in the ancient Caledonian Forest, from the shaggy four-footed biodiversity engineers grazing the Malham limestone pavement to re-meandering work on a tributary of the Tweed, I walked my inquisitive way through a Britain that I scarcely knew existed.

I saw what I saw (and what I saw was only the tip of a huge iceberg of our nature) not as a trained ecologist or career conservation worker, but just as an interested observer and listener. By the time I reached Cape Wrath, grubby and 10 kilos lighter, any conclusions I had reached were probably more visceral than scientific, but I would also like to think that they were tested continually along the way, and with hundreds of people whose job it is to know more than me, and with plenty more who just had an opinion to share, and were honest enough to be conflicted themselves. Often, I reached no conclusions at all. And, as I walked, I kept tripping over related things of which I was previously only half aware, like the direct link between nature and mental health, my own very much included, and the overwhelming whiteness, maleness and middle-agedness of Britain's outdoors population. To be honest, at times it was like walking towards a mirror.

But it was an adventure, pure and simple, one in which I tried to hop off the merry-go-round of daily news and commitments, and I started to find for the first time since my boyhood trips to the local common, that I had the time and the headspace to see and hear the natural world properly, and just about imagine my planet quietly breathing in the background. Ironically, and perhaps inevitably, after two years of avoiding it, Covid had the time and the headspace to come and find me somewhere in the Cotswolds. Of course it did. That's how planning works.

But beyond the endless miles that I was inflicting on a body that probably felt it was long past that sort of thing, it is of course the people that I will remember with most clarity. While there were professional naturalists, conservationists, ecologists, landowners, academics, farmers, campaigners and gamekeepers among them, many were just volunteers trying to do the right thing, and then to do it again and again and again, without expecting pay, let-up or thanks. If you only take one thing away from this story, make it the wonderful web of mycorrhizal strands of human inspiration and effort that is being made every minute of every day, often unpaid, unseen and unheard, on behalf of your nature. The list of acknowledgements at the back of the book does not begin to express properly my gratitude for the thousand random acts of kindness I found along the way, or to the people I never even met who, maybe decades ago, fought to make the land of my walk accessible to me, and to keep it as vibrant as it just about still is.

As I wrote, I found myself in subconscious dialogue with a younger version of myself, politely asking why he seemed to have cared so little in the past about something so critical to his own survival, and to that of his fellow humans, as the biodiversity around him. In a way, I suppose that this is just a long letter back to that younger self. But, like a prayer wheel spinning away on a Himalayan hillside, two unavoidable questions kept passing in and out of my brain as I walked, and wrote: If not me, who? And if not now, when?

Just as the hope continues to glimmer out of the darkness, so do those questions. Meanwhile, the clock is ticking.

RTMG
Petworth
August 2022

PART 1

Birth of a Journey

1. A CURLEW AND A ROUGH POPPY

'It was the best of times, it was the worst of times; it was the age of wisdom, it was the age of foolishness; it was the spring of hope, it was the winter of despair.'
CHARLES DICKENS, *A TALE OF TWO CITIES*

I can date the birth of my walk to a precise evening in early June, nine months before it actually started.

I can pinpoint it to two fields, a hundred or so miles apart, both of them beautiful.

The first is in the Severn Vale. I am with an 80-year-old conservation field worker. It is mid-morning, and we are looking for signs of breeding curlews. It is, he says, a giant Lammas meadow,* as old as the churches we can see in the distance, and by a mile the best field he has ever known for nests. No silage† is taken here; instead,

* A floodplain meadow, generally managed communally, and so called because grazing animals were not allowed on before Lammas Day (now August 1st).

† Silage is green grass, cut early and stored anaerobically, as winter forage for livestock.

the field will eventually be mown in strips for hay, as it has for more than 500 years, but not before the young birds have had a chance to fledge, and therefore escape the flailing blades and crushing wheels. Time was, he continues, when you might have found upwards of fifteen nests over the area and, above them, a concerto of parent birds bubbling out their beautiful anxiety at his approach. Some of those chicks from the previous millennium would not have made it to adulthood, as is the way with nature, but the general health of the population would be protected by the number who did, in the bountiful equilibrium that preceded industrial man.

This year, however, has seen a catastrophically wet May during which the nearby Avon had burst its banks twice and washed away most of the nests, so he knows that there will be fewer of them. And it's not as if this year is an outlier; the same lack of success has attended just about all of the last dozen seasons, albeit for a cocktail of differing reasons, and the effect on numbers is starkly visible. In the event, we find four, which he counts as something of a result, though it turns into three when one of the nests is found to have been predated by a passing fox. Two weeks later, he emails me to say that two of the other three had gone that way as well and that, for the first time in his 60-year memory of that 500-acre meadow, there would be maybe only two fledged curlews in the entire field. Just two. The parents have simply given up for the year, he adds, and are already back down on the Severn estuary, feeding as if in midwinter.

When you see breeding curlews down by the sea in June, it is not a good sign.

The curlew, besides being just one of the 574 different bird types that have been identified in Britain, is also an indicator species, which means that it provides strong clues about the overall health of its own ecosystem, and the other species it shares it with. Thus, as for the highly visible and gloriously audible curlew, so for the less charismatic lapwing, corn bunting, skylark, yellowhammer and other ground-nesting birds; and as for the ground-nesting birds, so for the insects below, and the raptors above them in the food chain. Indeed, so for the whole ecosystem. This is the twelfth bad year in succession on the meadow, and the curlew population is starting to crash. Across the border in Wales, the situation is even worse, and over the Irish Sea, some reports suggest that they are down to just over 400 pairs on the entire island.

The field worker tells me that he reckons we have no more than twenty years to save them as a breeding species in the southern half of Britain, thirty at the outside. Half a century of relentless concreting over of their habitat, of early-season silage making, of intensive forestry, of agrichemicals, of dog walkers and of uncontrolled predators, not to mention a neighbouring country that still regularly tries to licence them to be shot,* has brought the breeding population of Britain's

* France, to be clear.

largest wader to its knees, and is starting to consign that most beautiful of all songs in nature to a collective memory on some digital tape.

When the curlew falls silent, the two of us agree, so does a part of us.

*

Eight hours later, and high up on the South Downs above Arundel, on my way back to my car in the dusk after an early evening meeting of local farmers, I spot a single rough poppy. I have deliberately left my car half a mile away so that I can walk back through that field, and find that poppy.

I am not a good enough botanist to spot it on my own, but I have been shown how and where to see it by someone who is, and as part of a project that we are both working on. I know that these days it is a vanishingly rare summer flower of these margins, a survivor from the chalky seed bank that has recently been disturbed just enough to germinate it, maybe for the first time in a hundred years. In the same row, I spot cornflowers, some dwarf spurge and a single narrow-fruited corn salad. That last one even my parents probably never saw, back in the 1950s.

I stop to examine them, and hear beyond the tall hedgerow the tell-tale 'rusty gate' calls of a covey of grey partridges. At the far end of the 30-acre field, a marsh harrier slides down the evening breeze towards her woodland roost, momentarily catching the horizontal rays of the sun on her plumage; along a mown strip of headland runs a hare in the same direction. If I stay long enough, I might see as many as ten species of raptor in and around that field; if I am patient and clever enough, which I am not, I could count up to 500 different invertebrates. Indeed, if I wait a year, I will hear 'head-started'* curlews calling here maybe for the first time in centuries, brought in as eggs from a more plentiful habitat, and then incubated and released.

Little of this home-counties Eden was in evidence two decades ago, not even the hedge. Instead, this was part of a 100-acre prairie field of barley among whose barren contours the great ecologist, Dick Potts, had once reported on what he believed would be the final act in the extinction of the grey partridge as a bird of the Downs. Since then, the fields have been divided up, fourteen miles of hedges have been installed on top of new beetle banks,† and twelve-metre strips of wildflower mix, or bird mix, sown; dew ponds have been excavated and lined, and a patchwork system of farming reinstated, with a four- or five-year rotation that includes livestock. This is no organic farm, though, but an ambitious arable concern every bit as intensive and profitable as that old prairie, a quiet assertion that 're-naturing' linked

* Head-starting is the practice of removing eggs under licence from birds in an area where they are plentiful, and can be re-laid, to a sparser one where they can be incubated, fledged and released in the hope that they will return to breed.

† A beetle bank is a raised bank of grass and flowers that is run through an arable field to increase the insect life in the middle of it.

corridors rather than whole farms and areas could be the answer. The difference lies in what is in between those fields, in the 15% that was given back to nature. For a country that already consigns a third of its food to landfill, 15% of the farmland given back to nature doesn't seem too great a sacrifice. Dick Potts is sadly gone, but what he started here is now bursting out with new life. New life upon new life.

The lesson of the Peppering Project, as it is known, is in many ways as simple as the very first lesson of basic first aid: that is, first to remove the patient from the source of danger. By farming for biodiversity as well as yield, nature has been allowed to surge back at a rate that not even the most optimistic field worker could have hoped. In the first three years of the project, Potts reckoned that 30 years of decline had been reversed. Ten years on, and you would need to retreat by about a century to find the same volume and variety of life elsewhere. Some of the plants and insects being found these days haven't been in the regional guide books for half a century or more, if ever.

Nature is like that, if we only let her be. She bounces powerfully back. The famous camphorwood tree in Nagasaki and the 'Survivor' pear tree at the site of the 9/11 attacks in the heart of New York stand testament to the enormous underlying will of nature to live on in the most extreme circumstances.

Two fields, a hundred miles apart. Both beautiful, both loved. I could have taken you instead to a chemically-drenched sugar beet field on the Cambridge plain, and shown you no more than a couple of crows and a transiting pigeon, but that would have proved only what you should already know, which is that intensive monoculture is the death knell of biodiversity. What would be the point of showing you that?

Instead, the difference between these two equally well-managed fields demonstrates, first, the utter fragility of populations when they fall below a critical mass and, secondly, the rubber-ball resilience of nature if and when we stop messing her around.

Here, in the most de-natured developed country on earth, a rough poppy comes like the Nobel Prize for hope.

*

In the weeks that followed, I would occasionally find myself talking to friends about those two fields, and what they implied. Like a fly walking across a bedroom ceiling, they were a seemingly inconsequential part of my life that I somehow found impossible to ignore. Some people glazed over; some instantly got it, but a good number questioned why, with all the other and more existential problems of the world, climate change at the front of them, we should worry about a few wading birds, or some arable weed consigned to the seed bank of history. In a world of white noise, went the argument, how could we possibly have the mental bandwidth to think about biodiversity when there is so much else going on?

'Don't get me wrong,' was the gist of what they said, 'I like wildlife as much as the next man. But the disappearance of a few hoverflies isn't exactly going to kill us, whereas rising sea levels just might.'

One of the premises of my journey is that we need to worry about species loss, if anything, even more than climate change. Knowing that I am not one of Britain's 22,525 professors[1] and that I sometimes struggle to keep up with all the developing science, I found myself retreating four centuries into history for a philosophical reason why I should be justified in being as alarmed as I am.

One afternoon in the autumn of 1654, in a Jansenist monastery some twenty miles south-west of Paris, a young mathematician came up with a theory about the existence of God or, more accurately, a convenient way not to have to worry about it. 'If God does not exist,' he wrote, 'one will lose nothing by believing in him, while if he does exist, one will lose everything by not believing.' Therefore, however unlikely the existence of a remote deity might have seemed to this brilliant student of science, it was simply safer to believe in the concept of God than not, which he then went on to do.

This philosophical position is known as Pascal's Wager and, as the years have progressed, I have found it a useful device with which to override the endless scientific arguments about the exact degree of trouble we are in.* It is simply much safer than not for me to accept

* After Blaise Pascal, French mathematician (1623–62). Sadly, he would go on to find out all too quickly whether he had been right or wrong in his wager, as he died a few years later of stomach cancer, at the age of 39.

the sixth Anthropocene extinction as a fact, just as I also accept man-made climate change, water pollution and soil degradation as facts, and concentrate the efforts of my struggling layman's brain on what I can personally do to help.* If I do this, I won't harm anything more than it is already being harmed, and I stand a reasonable chance of actually helping make things a tiny degree better. It also enables me to accept as read that unchecked biodiversity loss has every chance of killing us. After all, only a species as cocky as our own would collectively overlook the 40,000 plants that throughout history have kept us alive, well, clothed, housed, mobile and, just occasionally, high; or started replacing the 7,000 that are edible with processed imitations.[2] It helps to know that most of the oxygen we breathe comes from microscopic plants at the bottom of the ocean,[3] and that all the money in the world won't enable us to pollinate by hand once we have killed off the insects that currently do it for free.

In other words, I have stopped wasting time lying awake and wondering who is right or wrong. I have seen the evidence and I buy the wager. We are trashing our planet, and we simply need to find ways to stop.

*

A few weeks later, I lie in bed, still thinking about that Nobel Prize for hope, and about the contradictions

* To be fair, there is a lot more information and evidence available to support these positions than Pascal had to support the existence of God.

between those two fields. It beats English batting collapses, which is what I normally lie awake and think about.

That's an annoying thing about getting older, to add to the usual list of body parts working less well, namely the bouts of sleeplessness, and then the strange things that a brain contrives to fill those unwanted hours with, when it has given up trying to sleep.

I have come to this point in which my entire working life now appears to revolve around Latin names and ecosystems, from a world of guns and grill pans: guns for the nine years I was paid by the taxpayer to be a soldier, to wear a uniform and at least look as if I was protecting my country; grill pans for how I made my living in the housewares industry for the quarter of a century that followed. The soldiering had taken me, unusually, to every continent on earth including Antarctica, and had given me an abiding fascination with birds and their fragile world. Then, after years of patience from business colleagues who had sensed some time ago that my mind would wander off to some peat bog or other, or a sea-cliff nest in the Outer Hebrides, while they were vainly hoping I might help them make important commercial decisions, I finally took the plunge towards the end of my sixth decade and became a full-time writer and campaigner. Thus I took a tiny leasehold in a world I had previously only been able to peep at over the wall. Now I have scrambled fully over it, albeit to a place where most people that I spend time with seem to have PhDs, when I don't even have a degree in anything to wave back at them. The only thing that I have ever been formally trained to do is kill people.

Meanwhile, all around us are stories, and sometimes those stories just need to be told.

*

A word on biodiversity, the variety of life on earth.

Understanding what we have lost in nature is an inexact science, not least because we often don't actually know what we are starting with. Famously, a dozen scientists were invited as recently as 2007 to an already well-studied Swedish island to see if they could possibly find anything new; two weeks later, they emerged with no fewer than 27 brand-new species, of which thirteen were shrimp-like animals that turned out to be abundant almost everywhere.[4] There is a general view that there are about 8.7 million species on earth (plus a cheerful admission that it could end up being double or even treble that), and that the really scary thing is that we only started killing things off in earnest about 70 years ago, or one second to midnight on the 4.5 billion-year clock of our planet to date. It is the speed of what we are doing, thousands of times faster than the natural rate, that should be holding your attention, if you are drifting off.

We are causing these declines and extinctions in a number of ways that you don't really need to be a scientist to understand, of which by far the most important is habitat loss, and by far the most significant reason for that is agriculture. Whether in the clearings of a trashed rainforest in Brazil, or on the desolate seabed below a

British salmon farm, we are removing species' habitat at a rate that was already alarming 70 years ago, but is now sped up by what has been drily known as the 'great acceleration'. Just as they did it in the Midwest of the United States at the turn of the last century and were duly punished 30 years later by the dust bowls, so we have done it here in our vast chemical beet fields. Secondly, there is over-exploitation whereby, both legally and illegally, we are simply taking more out of the sea and the soil than they can sustainably give us: and from rare hardwoods to Atlantic cod, we just keep coming back for more. Climate change is a surprisingly distant third, followed by the effects of invasive species, pollution, persecution and disease. Overlay that template on the familiar but vanishing English hedgehog, for example, or the curlew, and it goes from being avoidably theoretical to instantly recognisable. Then again, sometimes even our scientists don't know why species are disappearing.

We inadvertently make ourselves feel better about this by shifting the baseline of time against which we measure that loss, and by talking about pure biodiversity (meaning the number of species) rather than what we should be discussing as well, which is 'bio-abundance'. The tacit agreement to use 1970 as one of the baselines these days ignores, of course, any losses that were incurred earlier than that, for example when the hedges and orchards were grubbed up in Britain after the 1947 Agriculture Act. But we have lost a lot, and what we have lost lies often unseen in the shadows of the more dramatic crisis of climate change. This is not surprising: we can predict almost exactly what will happen to overcome a Pacific island nation if the sea levels rise by a couple of metres, and we cannot duck its urgency; but we generally have only the sketchiest of ideas of the long-term consequences of the disappearance of nineteen out of every twenty acres of our own hay meadows. After all, 58 metres of potential sea level rise, locked in its new fragility in the Antarctic ice, is understandably going to grab people's attention more readily than a 40-gram snow bunting that has simply run out of space on the British mainland. Like a routine visit to the dentist, species loss never quite seems to make it to the top of the mental in-tray.

We tend to think of biodiversity as something good to have, like otters on a sandbank or goldfinches on a bird feeder, rather than something of life-giving importance to us. Perhaps there is no starker reminder of the cost of messing around with nature than Covid-19: whatever we choose to believe about how the virus actually started, it is odds-on that a raccoon dog or an illegally traded pangolin in a Chinese wet market was its unwitting conduit from bats to us. Not only is the pangolin heading for extinction as the most trafficked animal on earth,* but the collateral damage of its approaching demise seems already to be our own species' sickness.

* 206.4 tons of pangolin scales were confiscated from 52 seizures between 2016 and 2019, a figure thought to be dwarfed by what passed through undetected. Wildlife Justice Commission report, February 2020.

A recent report from the Natural History Museum[5] puts the United Kingdom in the worst 10% of all nations on earth for biodiversity loss, pointing out that we have lost around a half of it all since the dawn of the industrial revolution. To lead the decline in a world that has already lost such a percentage of its populations of mammals, fish, birds, reptiles and amphibians since 1970 is no mean feat; and, when faced with a beautiful farmland view out of the window of the car, it is sometimes easy to ignore, below the surface, the quiet and largely unnoticed pulverising of wildlife that has accompanied our industrial and agricultural development. We see and hear generally what we wish to see and hear and, if you have never seen a turtle dove, you aren't exactly going to miss it when it finally becomes locally extinct. You simply move on and watch the next thing, until that goes as well. Curlews, for example.

Onto this shrinking landscape, then, those remaining lowland curlews alight to try to breed each spring, unaware of what is lined up against them. They have lost half their population in the last twenty years alone, or around 5,500 birds a year that just disappear. Their Latin name, *Numenius arquata*, describes them as the 'new moon bird' (the gentle curve of their bills reflects the gentle crescent of the infant moon), and yet they live in the old moon shadow of what happened to their cousin, the Eskimo curlew, back in the 1960s. Reckoned once to be among the most numerous waterbirds on Earth, they were hunted to extinction on their annual migrations from South America to Alaska. The last known one was photographed in Barbados in 1963. Who talks of Eskimo curlews today? But then who talks of the once even more numerous passenger pigeon? The last one, where not long before there had been around 3 billion, was called Martha, who died in a Cincinnati zoo in 1914, and you can still see her stuffed remains in the Smithsonian. The great American conservationist, Aldo Leopold, wrote an essay about her relationship with us on the occasion of the opening of a monument to the passenger pigeon in 1947, from which the central paragraph still calls plaintively to us today about our connection to these extinctions:

> We who erect this monument are performing a dangerous act. Because our sorrow is genuine, we are tempted to believe that we had no part in the demise of the pigeon. The truth is that our grandfathers, who did the actual killing, were our agents. They were our agents in the sense that they shared the conviction, which we have only now begun to doubt, that it is more important to multiply people and comforts than to cherish the beauty of the land in which they live. What we are doing here today is publicly to confess a doubt as to whether this is true.[6]

I sometimes surprise myself by how much I mind about this stuff. At some point in the sleepless night, I get up and look out over the garden and towards the giant old oaks in the neighbouring park, brooding magnificently in the moonlight. On a whim, I grab some clothes and walk down the road to where I know there is a gap in the wall, through which I can access the oldest of those trees. There are no curlews here, but there are a million connections from the highest leaf to the most distant mycorrhizal filament, and a tree that is communicating with others as surely as I am breathing. New age sentiment or not, it is why I want to be here, this morning, at the start of my seventh decade. It is called 'biophilia', and it is our species' instinct to connect with nature and other living beings, the deep evolutionary need that even the most urbane of us have to bring the outside in.

I lie uncomfortably on my back on the grass and the exposed roots, looking up to the emerging dawn shapes of the branches above, and a ridiculous idea comes to me.

*

Annoyingly, by full daybreak, the idea is still there.

The idea is an adventure, an adventure for that nameless part of life that fits between middle age and whatever comes afterwards. It's a daft one, but it is born out of the reality that I am making many of these judgements about nature emotionally, and based only on a knowledge of a tiny bit of our country, and the small number of things I observe for myself, or read. Those curlews link to other habitats, other species and other geographical areas, and there are whole swathes of the land they cover that I have only really seen out of a train window, or from a slow-moving motorway. As migrants, maybe they have seen the pinprick lights of a Danish city far below them during a night flight from Finland, rested on a deserted Dutch beach, and fed on some Essex marsh at dawn. 'When we try to pick out anything by itself,' said the naturalist John Muir of all these infinite connections, 'we find it hitched to everything else in the universe.'[7] If this story is about anything, it is about those connections.

What if I took a very, very long walk from one end of the country to the other, from the Solent to the North Scottish coast, chasing a single season northwards? What if I saw these things for myself at walking speed, those things that remain unrevealed when you pass them on a motorway at 70 mph? What if I then dipped in and out of just a few of the thousands of biodiversity restoration projects small and large, from a hedgehog house in a tiny suburban allotment to the biggest natural forest-planting scheme in Europe? How much would my views change? Would I become more optimistic or pessimistic if I totally immersed myself in the realities on the ground for a couple of months? One thing is certain: I will quickly be too old to even think about doing such a journey in the future. Misquoting the words of the immortal Tom Lehrer, by the time he was my age, Mozart had been dead for 27 years.

As I brush my teeth I look in the mirror, and see in front of me many reasons not to do it, but the sight of them instead makes me a little bit more determined.

At breakfast, and to my surprise, my wife Caroline tells me that she thinks it is a challenging idea, but a good one.

'It's just a long walk,' she says, eventually. 'And you only ever regret what you don't do.' This may be code for: 'And you will never stop going on about it if you don't go.'

'Do you want to come along?' I ask, after a suitable pause, but into an eloquent silence. As I utter it, I can see that it's not a great invitation, and I'm not even sure that I want to put her through it. Anyway, the entire lower half of my own body would like not to come, so I understand anyone else who doesn't.

She smiles and gets on with what she is doing, so it is a walk that I will do alone, an idea that thrills and terrifies me in equal measure. But that is what adventures *should* do. And after all, tourists follow the progress of the cherry blossom over in Japan, so why shouldn't I follow the progress of greening oak trees here?

If I can make it happen, it will be a thousand-mile migration to find the light.

2. THE AUK AND THE RED KITE

'A journey is like a marriage. The certain way to be wrong is to think you control it.'
JOHN STEINBECK, *TRAVELS WITH CHARLEY*

'All levelled like a desert by the never weary plough
All vanished like the sun where that cloud is passing now
All settled here for ever on its brow.'
JOHN CLARE, 'REMEMBRANCES'

For all that this is a journey of hope, it is still a hope that starts in darkness.

It is a darkness that is well exemplified by the little-known Bramble Cay melomys, a rat whose tiny living was eked out in the shrubberies and sand of one small island at the top end of Australia's Great Barrier Reef, and who, in 2015, was declared extinct by the International Union for Conservation of Nature. It had been driven there by rising sea levels and storm surges, and is now the first known mammal whose loss can be blamed in its entirety on climate change. Bramble Cay may be 9,000 miles away from those curlews, or that rough poppy, but the fate of that little rat should stand as a stark warning for the rest of us.

After all, nature writers these days have of necessity become recorders of decline, at best trying elegantly to stitch the occasional colourful thread of hope into a tapestry of what is going, or already gone. From the petite Sumatran rhinoceros to the chestnut ermine moth, biodiversity continues to pay the price for our forgetting that there should be no separation between us and the animals, between how we live and nature. We *are* animals, and we *are* part of nature. Nature cannot be something that we 'go out' into. It is where anyone with humility is already living. When one of Britain's largest conservation charities,* and without intended irony, comes up with the strapline 'Giving Nature a Home', you can start to see the nature of the problem, if not the solution.

In our distant biblical past, when we were supposed to have been 'gifted' dominion over the animals, birds and fish of the earth, no one could have foreseen the wrecking ball that we would subsequently swing around our planet, and the extinctions we would eventually bring to bear on any species for whom we could not find a profitable use. These days, most of us tend only to invite nature into our lives on our own terms: the dogs in our houses are simply wolves that we have domesticated to operate entirely by our rules (or partly

* The Royal Society for the Protection of Birds (RSPB).

by our own rules, in the case of mine); the manicured parks and gardens in our towns and cities are islands of delight that we can pass through quickly and hygienically, like the footnotes in the pages of a busy life. We enthuse about the goldfinch that has come to our new bird table, but we ignore the dozen species of pollinating insect that no longer visit our unnatural flower beds. We lay down a plastic lawn to have the sense of green without the risk of untidiness.

Because our species thinks in numbers, conservation, or rather natural decline, has tended to become a branch of the statistics industry over the years, whose percentages are a boring but effective way of informing us of what is going on in our world. It doesn't help that many of these figures contradict each other, or that the news we read is routinely, even exclusively, bad, in spite of the islands of hope whose presence often remains unreported. While this story is manifestly not about statistics, allow me to offer just five British ones at the outset, and only in case you are tempted to dispute the start point. The first three relate to lost habitat which, as we saw earlier, is the dominant cause of species loss. 97% of our wildflower meadows have gone,[1] as have 98% of our ancient woodlands* and 93% of our natural peatlands.[2] Add to that 76% of the biomass of our flying insects[3] and over 40 million of our birds.[4] While none of this is

* And 85% of what is left still has no legal protection. (Woodland Trust)

new – the poet John Clare was writing about the biodiversity loss that followed the Enclosure Acts 200 years ago – what should startle and divert us is its intensification. It doesn't really matter where you set the baseline, or whose research you read: the way that we have trashed the nature that tries to sustain us is extraordinary, but the speed at which we have recently done it is scarcely credible.

This is further complicated because, in addition to wiping out a significant proportion of the natural life on our planet, we continue to view the remaining bits of that life through the prism of what is known as 'non-human charisma', through which we rank the popularity of other species by what we see as their charm and appeal to us. This is why the red squirrel, for example, attracts vastly more conservation funds and attention than the equally endangered wart-biter cricket. And why we often seem to prefer to watch a pride of lions 6,000 miles away on our televisions on a Sunday evening than observe the riot of life going on in the hedgerow just down the road. This matters, as we shall see.

The pivotal moment for all this was around 10,000 years ago, when we started to move from a mobile, hunter-gatherer lifestyle to a largely static agrarian one. This process brought with it a number of effects, of which just two have been instrumental in leading to where we are now. First, the act of staying in one place and of having stores of food directly available led to an ever-steepening boom in our population, to the point that we became by far the most successful mammal in earth's history. Back then, there were somewhere between 1 and 10 million of us; now, there are around 8 billion. There being this constant growth in our numbers led inexorably to the second issue, that of our relentless need to adapt the environment around us to our own needs, rather than ourselves to the environment. We are the only species to have done this to anything like the scale we have, and it is why scientists have called our time the 'Anthropocene' age, an as yet unofficial geological epoch defined by the direct impact that we have had on the planet's ecosystems and, latterly, its climate.*

We can steal a tiny bit from related science here, even if it looks at first sight to be uncomfortably boring and technical. Stick with it if you can. In a sinister echo of Georgyii Gause's 'competitive exclusion principle', by which no two species competing for the same resources can coexist in equilibrium for long (meaning that one must die off or adapt), we have always been the strongest in any given competition; Gause wrote his book[5] back in 1934, and he actually had single-cell paramecia on his mind at the time, rather than the humans who would actually go on proving his

* Anthropocene, the term and the concept, was coined by Dutch scientist Paul Crutzen in a lecture to a scientific conference in 2000. His prevailing point was that it will ultimately be human decisions that set the future course of geological history.

principle again and again, powerfully and indefinitely.[*] Very little in our natural world survives prolonged contact with us.

By the time the music had paused, if it ever did, 96% of the entire biomass of the earth's mammals was filled by just us humans,[†] our pets and our livestock; everything else, every last elephant, antelope, stoat and rabbit, now makes up the other 4%. If the pivotal moment was 10,000 years ago, the catalyst for uncontrolled acceleration came from a village in Derbyshire one day in 1719, when John Lombe heralded the unofficial start of the industrial revolution by opening his silk-throwing mill.

You can find statistics for what then happened to the planet's biodiversity wherever you choose, but let us instead restrict ourselves to the fate of just two species of bird, by way of illustrating the problem and the potential solution: the great auk and the red kite. Their respective stories will cast contrasting shadows across the length of my journey.

---

* For further reading, try *The Nature of Nature*, Enric Saka (National Geographic, 2020), an excellent primer for any layperson wanting to familiarise themselves with ecosystems and how they function. And, for an excellent and simple introduction to biodiversity, read Alexandre Antonelli's *The Hidden Universe*.

† To put this into more cheerful context, humans represent less than 0.1% of animal biomass (i.e. including molluscs, nematodes, fish, etc.), which itself represents a figure 200 times smaller than that of plants, and 35 times smaller than bacteria. ('Biomass Distribution on Earth', Bar-on et al., paper for *PNAS*, May 2018)

Unlike most extinctions, we can precisely date the demise of the last great auk to a specific place – Eldey Island, Iceland – a specific day – July 3rd, 1844 – and to two specific men, Jon Brandsson and Sigurour Isleifsson. Three, if you count Ketill Ketilson who found that he had lost the appetite for the kill, but 'accidentally trod on the nest that the auks had been tending, thus rendering its single egg worthless to a collector.'[6] They had been paid to bring back an adult pair for a museum collector in Reykjavik, and everyone involved probably knew before the event that these were among the last of these birds on earth. Known as the 'northern penguin', the large and flightless great auk had managed to live out a reasonably successful existence on both sides of the North Atlantic, compensating for its clumsiness on the ground and absence from the air with superb speed and manoeuvrability in the water. For most of their time on earth, they faced no bigger threat than the occasional orca or white-tailed sea eagle and, while they were sometimes eaten by first-nation American communities, it seems not to have been in sufficient quantities to upset the equilibrium. No, that would come later.

For the problem with the great auk was that it happened to have more than just one harvestable value to humans beyond its flesh; from oil for lamps, and down for pillows, through to eggs for collectors and pretty feathers for fine hats, the bird unfortunately had it all. There are reports of them simply being herded up gangplanks in their thousands, down into the bowels of fishing vessels where they could be slaughtered at leisure, and used to bait fishing lines, or salted for future food. By the time Great Britain banned the killing of the bird for its feathers in 1794, it was far too late. The introduction of rats to their remaining island colonies, again by us, led them inexorably to that Wednesday afternoon in Iceland half a century later. If you want to see one now, go to the Natural History Museum in London, or imagine what a little auk would look like if it were five times bigger and with a longer bill.

If there is a better example of the wilful destruction of a species by exploitation, I don't know of it.

A world away from the great auk, a red kite soars over my village. I can clearly see the 'fingers' of her giant wings, her downward head scanning the road for carrion, her forked tail twitching the intricacies of her precise changes of direction. She is an opportunist, a traveller, and a survivor from the very rim of the abyss.

Once, she, too, was history. When my father used to take me birdwatching around here as a boy, we would no more talk about seeing red kites than we would penguins. Persecuted by gamekeepers, limited by egg thieves and poisoned by DDT, they had already retreated into an effective state of extinction by the First World War, the 'shite hawks' of Elizabethan history no more than some disease-carrying collective memory of a nation that found at the time that it didn't much mind. Outside of the Upper Tywi Valley in south-west Wales, they were only birds of the imagination.

Then in the years following 1990, something extraordinary happened. A handful of Spanish birds had been released in the Chiltern Hills north-west of London, and, safe from persecution, egg thieves and the worst of the agricultural chemicals, they bred successfully. Being carrion-eaters, they slowly started to move out along the lines of the road system to other parts of the country. It took them two decades to drift the 60 or so miles south to my village, but drift they did, until one Sunday April morning when the huge shadow of one brushed momentarily over my body when I was putting the potatoes down into my little patch of Sussex soil. Now the UK has a tenth of the world's population and they are everywhere, 10,000 of them, sharply reminding the local buzzards who gets to eat the roadkill round here. In fact, and with almost circular irony, it was announced in June 2022 that 30 red kites would be sent from Britain to Spain for each of the next three years, to the very country from which some of our own kites had arrived back in 1990, and where they are now in decline.

Their story is well known and widely told, and you could very easily add other charismatic species such as the white-tailed sea eagle to the list. But there is also a deeper significance to their success, which was the eloquent case it made for the controlled reintroduction of other species, the beaver for example. It also gave the sense that biodiversity loss did not need to be a one-way process. Others followed, some straightforward like the marsh harrier in Norfolk, and some, like the white stork, which had been absent from British airspace for 606 years,* maybe blurring the distinction between 'introduction' and 'reintroduction' a bit more than others. They are even breeding coral in London laboratories these days, in a coordinated project to try to accelerate the repair of reefs that have been obliterated by the effects of the industrial revolution. The time may be nearing when we will once again routinely thrill to the sight of a giant European eagle owl snatching a goshawk from some night-time forest roost in the Midlands, or a lynx hunting down a secretive muntjac. Each species will have to journey through the fragility of genetic health that comes from being part of a small population, but, in short, it all gives us permission to dream.

The great auk and the red kite took two similar journeys with two very different destinations. The difference was that the kite was only locally extinct, and so the pump could once again be primed, whereas the auk had gone for ever.

Of course, there are eye-catching scientific projects going on all round the world to recreate lost species which, with science's talent for a lack of irony, are known as de-extinctions. In San Francisco, there is a team working to bring back the passenger pigeon; in Melbourne it is the thylacine, and in Wageningen, Holland the cow's ancestor, the aurochs. It is also a branch of research that is drawing in a great deal of money, and potentially making even more for its investors: in Texas, in

* The last recorded one was seen on Edinburgh Cathedral the year before the Battle of Agincourt.

early 2022, a fundraising round of $60 million was successfully completed in the quest to bring the woolly mammoth back to life.[7] You can find endless articles and brochures extolling the virtues of these old ecosystem engineers once again trampling the Siberian steppes, but I find myself not yet quite convinced. Whether any of these projects are actually realistic in the long term, or just exercises in academic enterprise on some charismatic megafauna that happens to be capable of attracting research funding and seed capital, we already know that it is far easier, cheaper and better to help keep a species alive than it is to reinvent it, and that nature has already 'invented' all the species it requires. Besides, as Carl Sagan said all those years ago, 'extinction is the rule; survival is the exception', just not at the rate we are forcing it; the history of our planet has been one of winners and losers, and the less we play god the better, particularly when that god ends up in the unpredictable hands of the profit motive. To my less tutored mind, all these new ideas, resources and talents could probably be better allocated to keeping alive what we still have, and that is the premise my journey follows.

In nature, as everywhere else, where there is life, there is hope. The aim of my walk is to unearth that hope for myself, and what better season is there to search for hope than the spring?

*

That annual grand inhalation of life and of light from the south that we call spring only happens because a huge body of matter known as Theia once struck our planet a heavy glancing blow when it was young, knocked it off kilter and left the biggest fragment from the collision as our moon. It is that disturbance to our orbital plane that gives us our seasonal changes and which, once a year, calls hibernating animals out into the open and migrating birds to fly to the cooler end of their ranges to breed. From late February onwards, and from many points of the compass, a giant pulse of birdlife is bearing down onto this group of islands at the end of the Eurasian peninsula. From the tiny sand martin flitting over the crowded sea lanes of the English Channel to the stubby puffin bustling its way over the Atlantic edgelands on its way from its winter rafts, the sky is thrillingly alive with life.

It is a time of regeneration for all but the most stony-hearted of us, and it is now calling beguilingly to me. 'It's only a walk,' it seems to be saying, 'and it will be full of siskins, and of squirrels and sunshine.' It doesn't mention the rain, the steep hills, the blisters or the loneliness, which is good, because if it did, I probably wouldn't go.

A century ago, spring progressed northwards through the infinite jigsaw puzzle that is natural Britain rather slower than it does now*. A 2014 study from Coventry University demonstrated, using various measures such as the arrival of swallows and the flowering of the hawthorn, that the season's average rate of travel northwards

* Research now shows that autumn's timings are changing too, with inevitable consequences on things as separate as hibernation and seed dispersal.

had accelerated from about 1.2 mph between 1891 and 1947 to about 1.9 mph in the last twenty years. Some things, such as the ladybird, were quicker, while others, like frogspawn, had stuck to the old speed. This lesser understood effect of climate change matters, and for many reasons, not least its effect on the widespread requirement of plants and animals to rest, and the timing of the arrival of migrants into already depleted food sources. 'A recent study by the Met Office,' writes Joe Schute in his study of the quickening seasons, 'estimated the growing season to be, on average, a month longer during the past decade compared to between 1961 and 1990.'[8] Later on, he describes a 2002 study that had found that the average first flowering date for 385 British plant species had advanced by a full 4.5 days in as little as a decade. Obviously, this is not just a local phenomenon: the meticulous records kept by Henry Thoreau at Walden Pond in Massachusetts a century and a half ago, for example, have allowed researchers to work out that average temperatures have risen by 2.4 degrees Celsius since then, and the average plant blooms a week earlier than it used to.[9]

One species from another survey[10] strikes me, though: the oak. In 2021, the first report of an emerging oak leaf came from Devon on March 26th, and the effect had arrived in the north of Scotland about five or six weeks later. Is it feasible that I can walk north through my native land on its byways, footpaths and tracks at the speed of the front edge of the greening canopy above me, and to use the oak as the natural architecture of my journey? I decide that it has enough romantic significance to be worth a try.

Happily, spring progresses through Britain from the south-east to the north-west, which allows me to avoid the longer and often unloved Lands End to John o' Groats route, and to start instead by working out with a piece of string the shortest possible straight line between the English Channel and the Atlantic Ocean north of Scotland. By this device, I persuade myself that I should start with my feet in the Solent (because I live near it) and finish at Cape Wrath (for no better reason than because I have always wanted to go there). That provides a distance, as the crow flies, of about 660 miles, which I will do my very best to keep to below a thousand by cunning map work that I last used as a soldier nearly four decades earlier. A theoretical thousand miles divided by around eight weeks, plus a few days off, suggests about twenty miles a day, possibly a couple more. Incredibly, a few months later, I will meet an 80-year old man on top of Kinder Scout who had walked virtually the same route when he, too, was 62.

'Best months of my life,' he said, under a patient stare from his wife. 'Apart from the rain, the midges and the cramp. It was so liberating and so simple. Each day, just one foot in front of another about 40,000 times.'

But, if you lived in my body, you would not want to inflict a thousand-mile walk on it at the rate of 40,000 steps a day.

It is the kind of body that is better suited to other things, like sitting at a desk, walking the dog round the block or an occasional sleepy game of social cricket. It is a body that prefers pasties to pain, and it tenses up at the prospect of hard graft. However, to ensure that I actually go, and don't back out, I have started to bake the adventure's inevitability into my life by telling my friends I will do this thing, and telling myself that I will arbitrarily do it at the speed of the progress of spring. After all, the journey can't just be indefinite and, anyway, I have a living to make.

The challenge is then to find one good example of each of the main habitat types in Britain to walk through, as close to that line as possible. For the purist, around 65 such habitat types exist, but a looser interpretation would say there were around a dozen, from freshwater to forest, from mountains to coast.* The point about my walking through different habitats, while potentially inconvenient, is important; for each one has its own biodiversity systems, its own suite of problems and its own range of possible solutions. Equally, each one has deep connections with the other habitats immediately around it. By seeing a broad range, I feel that I might better understand the issues that we face, and what people are doing about them. After all, it is those people who remain in the centre of this renaissance, even if our own species represents only one of the more than 70,000 that Britain hosts.[11]

* The full list that I decided on was: grassland, arable, peatlands, coastal, freshwater, mountain, urban, woodland, scrub and heathland, the first two of which account for three-quarters of our land area.

Beyond that, I now have about a hundred days to complete all my current work, get all my kit together, get fit for the road after years of relative lethargy, work out a route, understand where I am going to sleep each night and come up with any number of contingency plans. 'What could be easier?' I ask myself. 'Only four decades ago I was a soldier, and this sort of stuff is in my DNA.' This is clearly nonsense, albeit thinly disguised nonsense in a high-visibility coat that only I seem to be unable to see, but I am already waist-deep in the research phase of my project.

Bored one evening, I ask my search engine how many joules of energy I will consume moving 15 kilos of mass 1,500 kilometres of distance. I'm not sure what exactly I am trying to achieve, but I can almost hear it laughing at me, as some Indian university formula comes up with a figure so huge, so unfeasibly unlikely, that my calculator runs out of room to display it. Then I remember that I only asked about the pack, not the 88-kilo body underneath it, and I go the kitchen for a biscuit.

'As an endurance athlete,' enthuses one website that I consult on the question of what to eat on my journey, 'you should stick with a diet that is 70% carbohydrate, 20% protein and 10% fat.' I love that, and go into the kitchen to inform Caroline that she is now married to an endurance athlete. She looks at the huge baked potato and grated cheese that I am making for my lunch, and says that this is, indeed, good news, especially given the size of the potato. Thus it is that, after six decades on the planet during which I had never heard of them, I briefly enter a new-minted world of sports gels, energy bars and electrolytes. From now on, I decide, carbohydrates will be my friend, just as walking poles will be my constant companion. Or at least, that's the theory; in the event, the poles will last all of about six of the thousand miles. You are who you are in this game, and not necessarily who you aspire to be.

I make an appointment with the local physiotherapist to sort out a couple of troublesome bits of my body and I buy two pairs of new walking boots, on the basis that I intend to walk more than the 700 miles they advertise as their limit. In the same shop, I find myself looking at a comically large backpack.

When he catches up with me, the insultingly healthy-looking shop assistant takes a long look at me and asks through a lush forest of outdoor beard if I am 'sure'. There are many things about which I'm not sure, including the wisdom of the entire adventure, but then he tells me that he is only referring to the enormous pack. Buy a large one, is the gist of what he says, and the only certainty is that you will fill it, and then have to carry its extra weight every inch of your journey. Half an hour later, I cross the Rubicon and buy a 55-litre pack, rather than a 65- or 70-litre one. The distinction, and one whose benefit I will not be able to judge until I am 700 miles or so into the walk, is that wild camping is no longer an option; or at least comfortable wild camping isn't.

*

On New Year's Day, I declare a 100-day moratorium on alcohol. Alcohol and pies. The thinking is that this reduction of calories and injection of discipline will get me through what I laughably call the training period, and nearly up as far as Edinburgh. If I can get that far, it is only reasonable to allow Highland malts and local lagers to fuel the back end of my journey.

A week later, and by now only 50 days from the off, I add biscuits to the banned list, then snacks other than at the weekend, and finally chocolate. I figure that the only way I can drag myself and a 15-kilo pack from one end of the country to another is to lose as much of that extra weight as I can from the body that will be carrying it, if for no other reason than to protect my knees. Like warfare, this is easier on paper than in reality. My body has cheerfully grazed the excess food from the surface of this planet without let or hindrance for decades, and it is a hard habit to break.

Another week on, I fill the backpack with a 5-kilo bag of dried dog food and a 7-kilo bag of potatoes, and then carry it with me each time I walk the dogs anywhere, so as to inure myself to the essential suffering connected to carrying my home on my back. My neighbours lose no time in telling me that they think I have lost my marbles. I also become the world's first endurance athlete to be called back from a training outing because he has half the family's Sunday lunch among his equipment. Next, I buy some walking poles, the supposed 20% removal of pressure on my knees compensating, in part at least, for a lifetime of chuckling at people who use what look to be ski sticks on perfectly good roads. Then, bit by bit, I start putting together a route, based on the ruinously expensive purchase of all 30 Ordnance Survey maps that cover my journey.* I shall be a latter-day nomad, albeit one who is clad in expensive merino wool, and carrying a powerful mobile phone. All I need, I muse romantically, is to choose tracks and footpaths that head more or less due north.

Unfortunately, for a man who will come to grudge every extra mile, it doesn't quite work like that.

The reality is that many of Britain's 140,000 miles of public rights of way go round in ever-decreasing circles, and often seem to peter out into marshes and disused airfields, or join busy main roads, created, it seems, by mischievous people who had too much time on their hands and too little to fill it with. Very few of these paths go in convenient straight lines between two places that you might want to visit. Theoretically, I could do the middle 270 miles on the Pennine Way up the spine of the country ('Britain's toughest trail' is what the Ramblers Association enticingly calls it, having quite plainly never spent a single day on the Cape Wrath Trail), but the 350 miles or so either side would require poring over the detail of my maps, and selecting routes.

It will subsequently take me a hundred miles or so to fully understand the attraction of disused railway lines, canal towpaths, reservoir service roads and old drove roads, all of which aspire to be as close as they can to direct and flat. Ironically, and only because the Pennine

* See Appendix 1 for the day-by-day route.

Way and I will eventually get bored of each other, the most reliable long-distance path I will actually use will be large parts of the 137-mile-long Beauly–Denny transmission line in the Highlands, complete with its 615 pylons and controversial service road, which isn't officially a path at all. I have already been warned by a friend who has done a thousand-mile walk himself that I need also to carry some top-of-the-range trainers, as that will make it a lot less uncomfortable for the inevitable miles that will need to be spent on tarmac.

Worryingly for my family, I become utterly, even needlessly, obsessed with maps, and with all the minutiae of the tracks, roads and contour lines that they contain. I spend long evenings rolling a measuring wheel across the map on the kitchen table, working out days of roughly twenty miles each, and with as much northwards progression as possible. Even road atlases enthral me, as do those antique county maps that people tend to stick up in the downstairs toilet. From the clumsy route that starts to emerge out of the planning process comes a growing list of days with fixed end points, themselves cunningly designed to be near the houses of friends and contacts with spare bedrooms. The difference between full-on camping (involving tent, stove, sleeping bag and days' worth of food) and walking from house to house is around 7 or 8 kilos of weight on my back, which is probably also the difference between success and failure. I may have to wild-camp in the Highlands, but by then I am intending to be fit. Between now and then, I will stay with friends, friends of friends, bed-and-breakfasts, bothies and cabins.

Aside from that, it will take me many hundreds of miles to understand the creative tension between the purity of the route, on the one hand, and my personal comfort and safety, on the other.

*

Just before I leave, I go to see Satish Kumar, an old family friend and tireless campaigner for peace and justice, who once walked an 8,000-mile 'Pilgrimage for Peace' from New Delhi to London and on across the Atlantic to Washington. It makes my walk look rather small, which is one reason I have gone to see him, and he also did the whole journey without money.* A thousand miles through a single country doesn't look too onerous a trip against a journey halfway round the world, even if he was in his early twenties when he did it.

'Live in the day,' he smiles, when I ask him how I might keep my spirits up on my journey, 'and not in the destination.' This is easier said than done for me, but I understand exactly what he means. After all, the older I am, the happier I become to acknowledge my own fragility, not least to myself.

'Expect and embrace hardships,' he adds. 'Because that way you will be ready for them when they inevitably

* The story of this journey, which started at Mahatma Gandhi's grave on June 1st, 1962 and finished at John F. Kennedy's graveside at Arlington Cemetery eighteen months later, is told in *Pilgrimage for Peace* (Satish Kumar, Green Books, 2021).

happen.' Generally, I have a bad relationship with hardship, so this is pertinent advice.

'I would also try to avoid distractions like music, or the daily news, and just observe the nature that you are passing. Finally, let it be a pilgrimage in the sense of allowing yourself to be changed by the experience. Then, everything you undergo will be added usefully to your life.' I decide not to tell him about the test match series against the West Indies that will be starting the day after I leave the Solent; after all, cricket commentary is more of a life force than a distraction, even when it involves England.

Finally, I ask if I can call him if I find myself starting to unravel, and he tells me that nothing would give him more pleasure.

'I wish I was a younger man,' says the 85-year-old activist, wistfully. 'For then I would come with you for part of the way.'

'But we would have to beg,' he adds, mischievously. As it happens, not one day goes by in the coming months when I don't think of all four of his pieces of advice, little gems that manage at once to be utterly apt but in no way obvious.

*

Then I go home and, in a last act before departure that is pregnant with ceremony and significance, make and eat an enormous gratin dauphinois from the last of my training equipment.

Unbeknownst to me, I have accidentally left one large potato in a fold in the lining at the bottom of the rucksack, where it will remain until I find it there three weeks later, somewhere in County Durham, half a kilo of vegetable matter, alone, undiscovered and slowly rotting.

You can probably still find its remains on a compost heap behind a bed-and-breakfast on the west side of Market Place in Middleton-in-Teesdale.

PART 2

English Miles

MAP 1. ENGLISH MILES

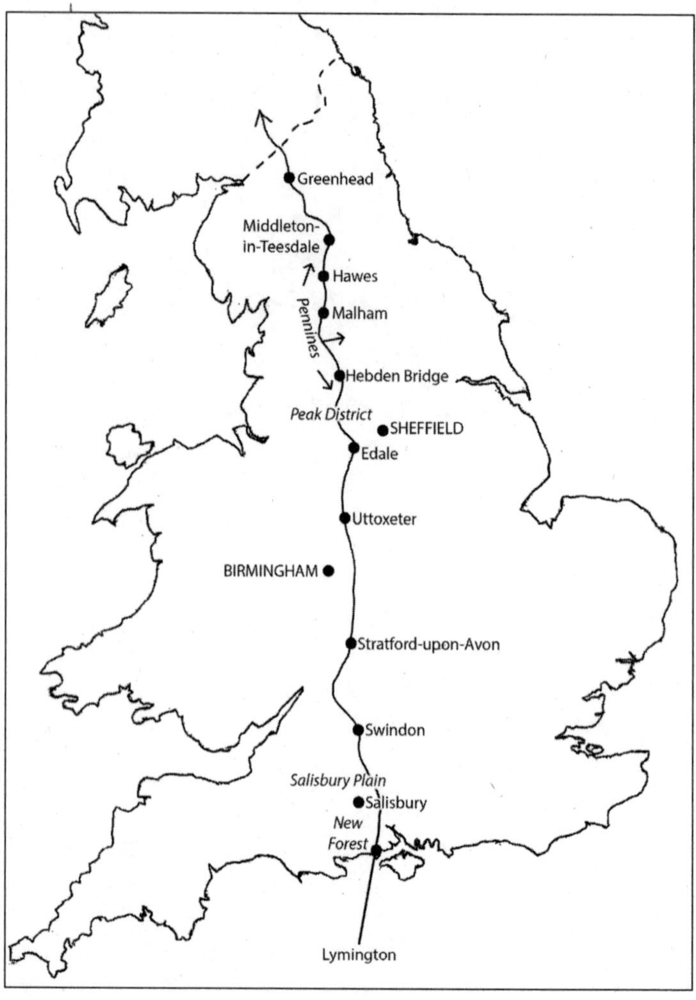

3. A FOREST AND A PLAIN

Lymington to Pewsey: 65 miles; three days
(PRINCIPAL HABITATS: LOWLAND DRY HEATH; LOWLAND CALCAREOUS GRASSLAND)

'Be careful what you wish for, especially if that thing is the end.'
SIMON ARMITAGE, *WALKING HOME*

Then one early March morning I am on the Solent, with a pack on my back, and my feet in the sea.

There is diluted sun on the water, and the ghost of Betjeman is seeping around the clinking halyards of the yachts at ease on the quiet, Monday morning estuary. Any magnitude of what lies before me is lost in the busyness of a town scratching itself awake for the working week. I stare at my reflection in a shop window and see not so much the hero I am looking for, but an awkward man with an unfeasibly large, black backpack. If I look very carefully, I can just about make out in his face the fear of failure, an old and unwelcome companion who has accompanied him on many an expedition before now. At this precise moment, no part of me actually believes that I can do this thing, but I keep that to myself.

Lao Tzu may well have talked about the journey of a thousand miles starting with a single step, but the first step of my own journey is straight into a warm quayside Lymington coffee shop. Then my second few steps are into the bakery next door, all of which suggests to me that the next 1,999,998 may be part of a slow, but comfortable, process. This is manifestly wrong, but I will discover that at leisure. I am also still blissfully unaware that the search for a decent flat white coffee will be an abiding trope of the journey, and that this one is the first of 68 in 54 cities, towns and villages that I will visit.* In the end, I will spend more on tea and coffee along the way than I did on my backpack and boots combined. Only much later in the journey will I come to understand that my daily search for what is in reality a double shot of 1,3,7 trimethylxanthine is an entirely natural thing for my body to want to do, blocking, as it does, the bits that make it sleepy and encouraging the bits that keep it enthusiastic and receptive. Also, it means that I will spend much of the next eight weeks 'intoxicated on sobriety',[1] which is kind of one of the reasons I am doing this thing in the first place.

Only when fully fortified by a mix of caffeine, sugar and a sense of general well-being do I head northwards

* The best one of all was in the Corner in the Square, Beauly, near Inverness. The worst will remain anonymous.

on the east side of the Lymington River, in a small but companionable mix of conservationists, friends and charity workers, all of whom have agreed to escort me through the New Forest for the first morning of my journey. The air is alive with those 'first syllables of spring',[2] the hearing of which is like the drawing back of the curtains of my soul, while the last traces of my late, unloved winter are skulking in the ditches and verges of Hampshire.

Ever since childhood, the idea of entering a forest has been an act pregnant with dark tension for me, something for which I would probably have to blame Hansel, Gretel, Little Red Riding Hood, Mole, or T.H. White. Forests are supposed to be full of dark places and unseen eyes, of paths less travelled and a world less understood. The New Forest doesn't quite work like that, partly because it isn't technically a forest at all, and partly because even the bits that are, aren't really. And, while we are on the subject, it isn't even new. Far from it; it is actually one of the oldest settled habitats in Britain. As I enter its southern boundary, the blue tits are what I notice first, which is great news for a surprising reason.

For the common old garden blue tit is the first of nature's indirect biodiversity engineers on my journey, co-evolving alongside the oak trees to devour the green oak tortrix moth caterpillar before the latter has time to breed in enough numbers to entirely devour the new greening oak leaves itself. That way, the blue tit chicks get their favoured food, and the oak keeps its greenery. The fact that they are here in numbers bodes well for the moment that the buds start to open and, at a time when the accelerating seasons are causing widespread problems, it is comforting to know that Britain's seventh most common bird is thriving.

All over Europe, the oak has been part of the architecture of our history, just as it is now part of the architecture of my journey. Beside the woodpigeon and grass, it is the only bit of nature that I am expecting to see most days. From its acorns we have made bread, from its tannins we have softened leather, from its timbers we have built ships and houses, and from its permanence the more sensitive of us have developed a sense of our own insignificance in the wide sweep of time. From within its branches, druids have cut mistletoe and around those so-called gospel oaks, preachers have spread the word; and even kings have hidden in them. Thousands of poems and songs (most truly awful, it has to be said) have been inspired by them, and our imaginations have produced a constant stream of stories and myths involving Green Men and much, much more. 'There is a powerful feeling of remembrance in the simple act of touching an oak,' is how one writer put it.[3] The oak also plays host to an astonishing variety of biodiversity, and the older it gets, the more it sustains; indeed, some of its most productive contribution to nature doesn't happen until it has been left where it lies after falling. Oaks have been around us for 2 or 3 million years, ebbing and flowing according to the status of the ice, and, in a lifespan that can last for a thousand years, they sustain over 2,000 life forms, 300 of them exclusively.

But the oak also carries more vital lessons for me in the interconnectedness of our biodiversity, as I travel north. For, if the oak had relied on its own devices to colonise northwards after the last ice age had retreated 10,000 years ago, limited just to the extent its furthest branches could drop an acorn, it would only have made it to the south edge of Salisbury Plain by now. But it didn't; in the humble jay it had a partner, each one of whom buried about 5,000 acorns each autumn in a wide area around, and then promptly left half of them in the ground to germinate. The result was that, in the evolutionary blink of an eye, the oak made it to all parts of the island, along with all the other species that relied on it.

Conveniently for the timing of my walk, I have discovered that the oaks in one place don't all break into bud at the same time. Far from it. Research done back in 1988[4] established that there could be as much as 24 days' difference between the greening of separate oaks in the same place, a difference based on age, position, water and a variety of other reasons. Whatever it means for the oak, it gives me unofficial permission to go just that little bit slower.

So I pat my journey's first oak appreciatively on its trunk as I walk past it just outside Lymington, wondering subconsciously how many more of the 120 million others in Britain[5] I will pass before I get to Cape Wrath. A grey squirrel in a neighbouring tree hurries away from me and up to the branches above.

He is an interesting case. His rapid ascent up the tree is a reminder that the previously idyllic life of the grey squirrel in those New Forest oaks has become markedly less so in the last decade. Thirty years ago, things were pretty easy for them, but when you discover the hard way that you are an average-sized meal for a goshawk by day and a pine marten by night, both recently arrived and currently successful local species, you will probably be forming your own views on the benefits of natural reintroductions, and they may not be charitable ones. Every step of the way this truth will echo and re-echo around my brain, the one that says you cannot look at any one part of this in isolation.

As we come into open ground to the south-east of Lyndhurst, we stop and listen for breeding curlews on the off-chance, but hear none. They will come, but probably not for another few weeks.

*

Less is sometimes more, and the complex plight of the New Forest curlew can perhaps be best seen through the prism of the success of its very distant cousin, the raven.

Like the red kite over my garden, the magnificent raven drifted back into the New Forest in 2003, to the general delight of the conservation community, and there are now at least twenty fiercely territorial pairs. The raven is an early breeder, nesting high on prominent features such as Scots pine trees and pylons; furthermore, he is a planner and he has an excellent memory. He is an early breeder for a very compelling reason.

Russell Wynn, lifelong scientist and director of the community interest company Wild New Forest, is walking me through his patch and explaining all this. He himself drifted back into the area after two decades as a senior scientist at the National Oceanography Centre in Southampton. At the age of 45, he figured that the maximum positive impact he could have on biodiversity would be to use the combination of his fieldwork skills and background of scientific rigour to work actively out on the ground for specific projects, of which the saving of the Eurasian curlew is front and centre. He and his business partner, Marcus Ward, are two of the increasing number of people who have sacrificed the income and trappings that go with a conventionally successful midlife career ladder to spend their remaining working lives actively conserving species. Neither has ever regretted it.

'Out there,' he waves his arm at the heath beyond the rise we are standing on, 'are normally five curlew nests, and this part of the New Forest holds one of the highest concentrations in the south. With just 500 pairs reported to be in the entire area south of Birmingham these days,[6] five nests on one area of heath is hugely important. We can isolate them from the public, but we cannot isolate them from those ravens, who have now joined the queue with foxes, badgers, carrion crows and buzzards, to predate any eggs or chicks, putting yet further pressure on them.' Over the last couple of years, in the silence of the empty lockdown forest, the ravens had fed well, and family groups were seen terrorising the local curlews in late spring. Russ reckons that there may be a holding capacity for a few more pairs of ravens before they reach saturation. Curlew egg clutches, on the other hand, are small at around four per pair, and all wastage is critical when numbers have declined by 70% in the last 40 years. The fragility of their current predicament is best emphasised by the lengths that conservationists go to protect them: a few months later, for example, two fledged birds were found dead on the same stretch of road after the local keeper had spent no fewer than 89 consecutive nights trying to keep them safe from predators. All the hard work had been done, but ultimately to no avail. Besides, they are nervy birds and will flush out and away earlier than many other ground-nesters. But among those other ground-nesters, the lapwing and the redshank, for example, the story is the same, and the challenge is as difficult.

The invisible goshawk who may or may not have been chasing that squirrel up the oak tree outside Lymington earlier in the day is another great example of this complexity within any given ecosystem. For this rare visitor from the edgelands of sanity, this predator of the air and ground of almost deranged effectiveness, of whom virtually nothing in the sky isn't terrified, cuts many ways in an ecological sense. On the one hand, she is an asset in the fight against our warming planet, owing to the large number of squirrels that she will eat, and who will therefore not go on to live long lives of stripping the bark off trees that then don't go on to grow to full size and sequester carbon. On the other, she cannot afford to discriminate over the relative rarity of what she catches, and her magnificent presence over the forest comes at a price for the local biodiversity, as is the happy way with nature. Ironically, the weaker a bird's situation, the higher number of them will actually go on to be killed by natural predators, rather than something directly to do with us. Then again, by eating the sparrowhawk (which she does), who would otherwise eat the little bullfinch, who himself voraciously eats the buds of fruit trees, for all we know the goshawk may well be indirectly damaging entire orchards.* Who knows? Nature doesn't stop at the limit of our eyesight and knowledge, which is why it is all so compelling and wonderful.

Russ and I agree that these are yet more examples of the 'no straightforward solutions' side of conservation, where nuance is king: one species' success is often another's failure. The price for uncontrolled seal numbers, for example, may be partly a decrease in salmon, just as more badgers tends to equate to fewer hedgehogs.† Most raptors have done exceptionally well since the turn of the century, to the delight of almost everyone who isn't still actively persecuting them; but a raptor has to eat and feed her family, and has no idea

---

* One of many fascinating examples of ecosystem engineering in Benedict Macdonald's book *Cornerstones*, Bloomsbury, 2022.

† Like most things, this is more complicated than we might think. Badgers are 'intraguild' predators, which means that they compete for the same food source with other species, but often just eat the competition anyway. However, it is the relentless loss of habitat, slug pellets, warming winters, busy roads and decline of earthworms that seem to have done for hedgehogs.

whether the bird she is stooping down on is on the red list of most concern. Indeed, a master thatcher I will meet later in the journey, and who runs one of the most competitive flocks of distance racing pigeons in the country, tells me in gory detail the mayhem that the resurgent local peregrines have wreaked on his birds. In the back of my mind I remember reading about an even more complex incompatibility, back when the wartime government ordered the shooting of all peregrines around the south coast, so as to allow the carrier pigeons safe passage as they went about their war work.* Even within the various New Forest authorities† there are many tensions, not least the impact of uncontrolled public access on protected habitats and wildlife, and the winners and losers from a regime of intensive grazing. The media coverage of these genuine tensions is a good example of our national resistance to having informed debates about any tricky subject to which there may be more than one right answer: if the newspaper sub-editor can't coat something on the front page as all good or all bad, total triumph or total disaster, it generally doesn't make the cut.

* Destruction of Peregrine Falcon Order 1940. The pigeons were used by Bomber Command crews to get a message back about their location if they were shot down.

† Natural England; Forestry England; National Park Authority; Environment Agency; the Verderers (the powerful group that regulates the New Forest's agricultural communing practices).

'There will have to be a trade-off, as another example,' Russ continues, 'between the national determination to plant trees and the number of curlews that we can aspire to. Curlews can't breed in forestry, and won't breed successfully close to it. It's a rare example of a head-on fight between climate change and biodiversity loss, in that the climate wants trees, but the curlew doesn't.' As a naturalist, he understands this, and does not take the easy option of pretending that it is simple. 'In the national interest,' he concludes, 'the curlew community will probably have to accept a slightly lower target than they would otherwise like.'

I ask him what steps he can take on behalf of the curlew. He is the right man to ask, as he is also the manager of the new national Curlew Recovery Partnership, and knows as much as anyone, particularly about these ones.

'It's a slow and indirect process,' he says. 'Legal predator control is challenging to deliver at scale in lowland farmland settings, and especially so in a busy national park and, anyway, much of the predation is by protected species. So, some of it is consultative stuff, such as advising Defra on curlew-friendly options within ELMS,* like pushing the cutting of grass fields holding breeding

* Defra = Department for Environment, Food and Rural Affairs; ELMS = Environmental Land Management Schemes, including Sustainable Farming Initiative, Local Nature Recovery and Landscape Recovery, that are part of the post-Brexit settlement for landowners and farmers.

curlews out from the end of May till mid to late July. Much of it is educational, explaining to local communities what is at stake, and empowering them to make the right choices.' We talk about protecting active nest sites with fencing, but he explains that this will only stop the ground predators, and may in fact draw attention to the nest in an otherwise anonymous landscape. Some of it is pure 'nudge' theory, such as the decision to close off some of the most curlew-sensitive car parks during the breeding season, and then quietly reopen them at the end of July. After all, we live in a land where the vast majority of us never stray far from our car, so the closure of the car park immediately reduces the local human disturbance, as well as sources of tasty picnic discards for opportunistic predators like foxes and crows.

With about 960 miles left of my walk to Cape Wrath, I am suddenly and uncomfortably conscious that we are now walking due south back towards the Solent. When we arrive at a little Bronze Age mound, I ask him if the fight for the breeding curlew is winnable. After all, this tiny corner of Hampshire is a beacon of curlew hope in a grim regional picture, even though, out of the 40 or so pairs of nesting curlews remaining in the New Forest, only about five chicks per year have successfully fledged in recent seasons, when what was needed for a sustainable population was closer to twenty.[7]

'Some days, I feel that they've simply got too many factors working against them,' he says, 'and that my generation will therefore be the last ones to hear that wonderful bubbling call over these lowland heaths.

Then there are other days when I feel that we are making real progress on this, when we might actually reverse the things that make them such unsuccessful breeders.'

We sit in silence for a minute, too far to hear the elegiac sound of a bubbling curlew from somewhere in the distance out on the tidal flats of the Solent, the fluting song that will soon be rising and falling among these heathers like the muted battle anthem of a war yet to be won.

For a minute or two, neither of us says a word.

*

In the afternoon, I move on, always northwards, alert for any signs of misbehaving limbs and joints.

I see the famous New Forest ponies and the occasional, fleeting fallow deer, not to mention the dark and oozing mire that continually insinuates itself into the tops of my boots. The ponies are not, as is popularly believed, wild, but owned by commoners who have the right to graze them and, each autumn, round them up and trade some of them. Their increasing numbers, now exceeding 5,000, have become an ecological challenge, with battle lines drawn between the powerful verderers and commoners, on the one hand, and some conservationists (including Chris Packham), on the other, who are concerned that the ponies are over-grazing the forest, stripping tree bark and preventing natural regeneration. The 1,200 or so fallow deer, brought in by the Normans in the eleventh century, create a slightly different version of the same challenges. There are two sides to this argument, and commoners would correctly point out that without grazing, the heaths and wetlands would quickly be swathed in scrub and 'unremarkable woodland' and the open landscape denuded of a number of specialist species such as the Dartford warbler and the smooth snake.[8]

Because I am with Russ, I become aware of things that I almost certainly wouldn't have noticed on my own: some black-tailed godwits on the estuary, the hidden but insistent call of a Cetti's warbler, a woodlark springing out of some conservation grazing outside Brockenhurst, and a tiny firecrest, a bird that is a hundred times lighter than a woodpigeon, flitting about in the undergrowth.* I am old enough to know this twin truth, that the best walk is the one illuminated by an experienced wildlife guide, and that the best wildlife guide is the one from the immediate area.

It has never occurred to me that you can walk twenty miles within the New Forest National Park and still be in it, which you can. Thus, sometimes we walk through residential areas, where Ukrainian flags droop, out of all local context, on rough-made poles, off post-and-rail fences, over the backs of garden chairs and outside community centres where passers-by are urged to donate to the cause. I see a woman walking in to one such centre

* The firecrest (*Regulus ignicapilla*) weighs the same as the 20 pence piece in your kitchen drawer. Go and pick it (the coin) up, and then imagine it migrating over the English Channel under its own steam. There you have the miracle of nature.

with a bundle of old sweaters and a yellow plastic tipper truck, and I try, for a moment, to relate their arrival in Ukraine sometime next week to the possible evisceration of Kyiv, Kharkiv and Mariupol by weaponry that the world had previously agreed over half a century ago never to use again.

By an old chair in an immaculate driveway on the edge of Lyndhurst, someone has lined a bowl with a large photograph of Vladimir Putin, along with an invitation to place dog shit in it. My old Jack Russell has come along for the first day, and I urge him to extrude one for the cause, but he doesn't find the timing convenient. I remind him of the many times that he seemed able to create something when it was least publicly wanted, but to no avail.

These may all just be thin pulses of defiance from a peaceful corner of prosperity, but they are pulses of defiance nonetheless, which is all we seem to be able to do, and important for that. It is also a stark reminder that all these battles for nature need to take their place alongside other, more immediate ones.

Meanwhile, we watch the various forest ecosystems, human and otherwise, trundle on. 'The Forest today is treated as a playground to be bent to the whims of visitors', observes a caustic local in an article full of the indignation of one who understands the value of what he has, but would rather not see it over-exploited.[9] And he is at least partly right. Next to the direct and indirect effects of climate change on the coast and the forest, population growth, continual development, the increased pressure on natural resources and the surge in 'car use and careless driving' are among the key concerns occupying the minds of the authors of a rather more balanced report by the National Park Authority,[10] where you can sense that there is a very real threat of this place gradually undergoing a death by a thousand unintentional cuts. After all, a quarter of the fast-increasing British population live within two hours of here, and it's entirely reasonable that they might want to come and share it just as I am now. In many ways, it is a microcosm of the challenge that many of Britain's national parks are facing: they play a vital role in the well-being of millions of people without everyday access to the countryside, and yet the more people who benefit, the more pressure the nature of the park will come under. In a country with the population density of Britain, and just as with the grazing ponies, I suspect that there is no easy answer.

But there is a small point almost hidden in the guts of the report that pulls me up short, as it will do many more times on my journey northwards, under the heading of 'Loss of Connection with the Natural Environment'. The way we live now has meant that, even for the children who are privileged to be brought up within walking distance of the forest, fewer than 10% of them play in wild places any more and their roaming radius has dropped by 90% in one generation. It turns out that we choose to make their physical risk assessments for them for as long as we can get away with it, content that they are safe taking their own digital ones instead, in the quiet of their bedrooms. The report goes on to say that half of all kids have been stopped from climbing trees.

What's the point of a forest, one might flippantly ask, if children no longer climb up its trees? More to the point, who is going to look out for tomorrow's curlews if today's children have never seen or heard one?

I love this place. I am sure its 15 million annual day-visitors do, too. And yet I am powerfully aware that the act of my walking across it can never be a neutral one. The best I can do is keep to the paths, and avoid, as much as possible, disturbing the wildlife.

Everything is connected to everything else.

*

Sometimes, the approaching season pauses for breath, for nature has no straight lines.

Halfway through the second day and under scudding clouds and a cold wind, the New Forest finally gives way to Salisbury Plain, with its wide horizons, chalk grassland and Iron Age hill forts – 300 square miles of natural wonder that most people only ever see from within a car in a traffic jam on the A303. I am still weeks from hearing a bubbling curlew or seeing a greening oak bud.

Secretly, I am rather pleased to have gained a few days on the oak, as it will now have to overtake me as it comes past, which should mean that I cannot fail to notice it. The verges are full of snowdrops and primroses instead, with the occasional flash of purple and yellow where a garden crocus has evaded its compost heap, harbingers, all of them, of a season that hasn't quite got its act together yet this year. A gigantic buff-tailed bumblebee queen drones heavily by, like an extra in a prehistoric film; she flies noisily, almost chaotically, past my boots on the path, wings seemingly restricted by the glue of her recent sleep. I walk past the hedgerows and copses of the southern plain to the endless but pleasing soundtrack of territorial great tits, exulting skylarks and Dylan Thomas' 'lovesick mooning woodpigeons'. Love them or not, the woodpigeon has proved a phenomenally successful exception to the tide of decline elsewhere, with a largely granivorous diet and a lifestyle that happens to dovetail very neatly with our own. There are about 5 million breeding pairs of them at the moment, which is around three times more than there were when I was a boy. In farmland, broadleaf woodland, towns and villages they are seemingly unstoppable and will quickly emerge, along with the mallard, the rhododendron and the plump, reared pheasant, as the true leitmotif of much of the first quarter of my trip. You could also add corvids to that list. As evening starts to fall, democratic jackdaw flocks rise up as one from their daytime roosts, bidden to action by the reaching of a precise cumulative noise level,[11] much like members of parliament, only cheaper and rather bolder. If it weren't bad taste to do so, you could throw road-kill badger into that leitmotif list, as well.*

* 50,000 killed each year, out of a population of 450,000, according to a 1995 study. (Badger Trust)

Salisbury Plain and I go back more than 40 years together, to when my soft, privately-educated hands wielded military pickaxes and shovels deep into 'the largest known expanse of unimproved chalk grassland in north-west Europe',[12] digging trenches in the hard chalk and then living for a few uncomfortable days within their damp walls. Like all old soldiers, I am inclined to reinvent history from time to time and pretend to myself that these cold exercises were a highlight of my life. They weren't; they were largely wretchedly uncomfortable and full of opportunities to miss out on food and sleep, and to be shouted at by people who had nothing better to do. The best a junior officer could hope for on one of these exercises was not to have been noticed by someone more senior by the end of it.

As a young soldier, I would enthusiastically see a little wooded valley in the distance as a place from which enfilade machine gun fire could be raked against invading baddies, whereas these days I have changed eyes that simply see a chance to find more firecrests, or perhaps a lurking goshawk. In the right place, I might even be lucky enough to see one of the hundred great bustards who now, after reintroduction in 2004, just about have a sustainable population on the plain. Back then, I was utterly oblivious to the scientific significance of the place as I trudged endlessly across it, and certainly ignorant of how much less damage I was causing as I thundered over it in Land Rovers and armoured cars than modern intensive agriculture would have done, had it been given the chance. Then, over the years, it slowly dawned on me that squadrons of 60-ton main battle tanks racing by, or the occasional white phosphorous smoke grenade, were far easier absorbed by the ecosystem than the steady drip, drip, drip of chemical fertiliser, broad-spectrum pesticides or endless doses of cattle wormer.

Some conservationists, in my experience, can be temperamentally uncomfortable with the notion that boots, bayonets and bombs turn out to be rather better for wildlife than the tools of modern food production, even than the regular disturbance of dog walkers. Somehow, it just doesn't seem right. But, species by species, it proves so, from the tuberous thistle to the Adonis blue butterfly, and from dyer's greenweed to the stone curlew; and, providing you don't mind your birdsong being punctuated by the distant rattle of small arms fire or the odd 120mm main armament explosion, it is as good a walk through nature as the south can offer. Just as I am celebrating this idea, I am suddenly brought up short by a chain-link fence and a red 'live firing' flag at Porton Down, and have to make a costly diversion. It is an avoidable mistake (my old army colleague would have referred to it as a failure of the 'seven Ps'*) so I can only be cross with myself.

Troop-carrying helicopters fly low across the valley as I start to make the deviation across Figsbury

* 'Prior preparation and planning prevents piss-poor performance.' © C/Sjt Tony Bohan, 1st Battalion, Royal Green Jackets, January 1984; lost, wet and cold, somewhere on Salisbury Plain.

Ring that is needed to go round the blocked training area. Two fighter jets roar overhead in lockstep. Later on, an armoured personnel carrier wheezes its way down through the automatic gearing as it makes its way up a steep chalky hill to the north. These are indirect yet uncomfortable reminders to me that the total war we were preparing for in those damp trenches all those years ago, the one that never came in the end during our time, has just revisited our continent. Tanks rumble across midnight borders, missiles slap into the sides of buildings full of sleeping people, and a killer in a dark suit stares us down through our television screens and dares us on a daily basis to do anything about it. He is mad, they say, he is ill; maybe someone will kill him. But he will be a part of my journey whether I like it or not, and remain so long after I have finished.

Indirectly, the presence of that nearby war makes me feel closer to my fellow countrymen whose communities I am walking through, and whose routine normality I have subconsciously been avoiding. These days, I need them, so I take deliberate diversions through villages just to reconnect with humans there. Each village seems to have its comforting primary school, its part-time pub and its full-time defibrillator tucked away in the old red telephone kiosk; there are always eggs for sale somewhere on the side of the road (£1.50 for a half dozen) and normally comforting notices on the board about some up-coming lecture in the Memorial Hall on Elizabethan Tapestries, or Bridge for Beginners. I lose count of the number of 'lost cat' posters that urge people to check outbuildings for any sign of Tiddles, who is out there somewhere in the shadows, probably terrorising the biodiversity.

In Farley, I get out of the cold wind at lunchtime in an exquisitely comfortable bus shelter, lined with shelves of books, DVDs and jigsaw puzzles. I rootle idly through the boxes of books next to me as I eat my sandwich and, to my astonishment, find right at the bottom of the second box a suspiciously mint copy of the first book I ever wrote, the happiness of finding it cruelly balanced by the knowledge of someone else not having even wanted to start reading it; a dutiful gift, maybe, from a godfather to a boy who then wrote an equally dutiful thank-you letter for it, without meaning a word. Not exactly remaindered in the sense of being sold for a pound or two in a tourist shop, but still unwanted enough to have been consigned to the box of books whose fate is not to remain on a household shelf, the victim of a clear-out during which it didn't quite make the cut. Looking up to make sure that no one is watching, I sign it extravagantly with today's date, add a line about the nature of my journey, and put it back again. It is the last of my books that I will see until Inverness, when I stay with friends who rather sweetly put one of them on my bedside table, like a child's drawing exhibited purely for the child's own benefit on the front of the fridge.

I find myself having short conversations, little puffs of social oxygen to store away for the quiet times: a window cleaner in Porton who is dealing with an unfeasibly high round window, the 'highest on my round'; a carpenter in East Grimstead who has just created a wooden deer sculpture in a front garden asks if I like it; two walkers high up on Figsbury Ring check their route with me.

'Where are you off to, then?' one of them asks, as we gaze comfortably westwards towards Stonehenge.

'Cape Wrath,' I say. And then, after a pause: 'In Scotland.' Obviously, I am showing off. They know it, and I know it, but I want to see what the reaction is. I am secretly delighted that she asked the question, as no one else has yet done so.

'Scotland?' says the lady. 'That's where my godson has just moved to for his job.' For a second, I think that she is going to introduce us.

'No,' says her husband. 'That was Sunderland.'

'We're finishing at Newton Tony,' she says cheerfully, after we have chatted a little longer. 'So let's hope we all get in before the rain.' A few hours later, I see from my emails that they have quietly donated £100 to the charity I am walking for,* and suddenly I love them, with their elderly, arthritic dog and their understated generosity.

And all the time I walk, I start to notice the things I never see when I hurry, which in normal life I generally do. On the tarmac roads, it is the magnificent

* www.curlewaction.org

robustness of cat's eyes; in the verges, the endless discarded face masks; in the gardens, it is the birds, and in the woods, the echo of their spring song; on the farms, it is the almost total absence of human beings, but on the field-edge tracks, it is the moving sigh of the breeze as it advances up a hedgerow behind me.

4. PASTURES AND PLAGUES

Pewsey to Fairford: 42 miles; two days
(PRINCIPAL HABITAT: IMPROVED GRASSLAND)

'Despite all our accomplishments, we owe our existence to a six-inch layer of topsoil, and the fact that it rains.'
PAUL HARVEY, AMERICAN BROADCASTER

'Food has to be cheap enough to feed people in poverty, yet expensive enough to support those who grow it. It needs to be grown at low cost, but without the corner-cutting that destroys the living world.'
GEORGE MONBIOT, *REGENESIS*

Someone was here almost 5,000 years before me, and they have been here ever since.

In a list of places that appear supremely at ease with their historical context, the Ridgeway would come high.

By and large, I will come to dislike place names that convey a sense of height, like 'ridge' or 'top' or 'hill', which indicate a requirement to go energetically uphill to get there, preferring instead ones like 'bottom', 'marsh' and 'water'. But for the Ridgeway, an 85-mile trail that cuts south-west to north-east on the higher ground between Avebury and Buckinghamshire, I am happy to make an exception.

Four days into the journey, I have left Salisbury Plain and the Vale of Pewsey behind, and am now slowly approaching the upper reaches of the Thames. Roads are the rivers I cross, ticking them off as markers of familiarity on my pioneering progress northwards: the M27, A36, A30, A303 and, somewhere just over the horizon, the M4. At West Kennett, I add my lone footprints to the five millennia of feet that trod the Ridgeway before me, the farmers, preachers, minstrels, soldiers, pedlars and drovers who were striding, marching or shuffling along it 3,000 years before the Romans, not to mention the animals that accompanied them. It is the oldest road in Britain, and all alone among its sparse hawthorns and lark song, I am its newest traveller. It is a place where grand-scale landscape and history merge, and within which the little vanities of my life seem trivial, pathetic even. It is also startlingly divorced from the high-pressure, high-density world a few hundred feet below: in the right mindset, a traveller can be both in a different age and a different land.

Maybe for the first time since I left Lymington, my body has come to accept the inevitability of constant movement as its lot, and for the most part its various muscles and bones are doing exactly what they are supposed to do. On schedule, and getting fitter by the day, I successfully disconnect myself from the temptations of the expensive phone in my pocket, and instead watch mixed flocks of linnets and yellowhammers exploding like tiny fireworks out of the scrub, red kites riding the breeze all around me, and the first legal muck of the year being dispensed onto a nearby field. Satish Kumar would be proud of me, I think. Then again, the Ridgeway is an official pilgrimage route, so he may well have come by this way himself.

It has taken a few days, but I am a traveller now, and the pilgrimage is on.

*

'Mallards don't really get it.'

For a moment, lost in a dream of watching the M4 motorway snake its broad way below us, I completely forget what we are talking about. It strikes me as rather a broad-brush indictment of our most popular duck's intellect.

'Or, if they do, they don't get it badly.' Now I remember that we were discussing the latest outbreak of avian flu, likely to be the worst in history. Even the free-range chickens are locked indoors now.

I spot her at Barbury Castle, sitting down on an old bank on this north-facing slope, and after we have exchanged greetings, she gestures towards the ground alongside her by way of a wordless invitation to enjoy the view with her. She thinks that I look tired.

'This isn't a day for rushing,' she says.

As it turns out, she also wants to talk about her chickens, who she reels off by name. Mabel, Daisy,

Grumpy, Sarah and Spot. 'They are rescue chickens,' she says, 'and they mean the world to us.' She is an academic from a west country university, teaching one of the sciences, and she is confident and articulate; but the chickens are also a substitute for some sadness from a few years ago that she alludes to but doesn't specify, and she cannot bear to think that this new incarnation of a disease that has been around since the dawn of time might carry them away. While I may see the progress of avian flu through the prism of occasional headlines and the occasional early morning edition of *Farming Today*, she sees it as a dark cloud sweeping across the bleak landscape towards Mabel and the gang, and it fills her with dread.

'It's the way we live,' she offers neutrally, by way of a reason. 'That's why these things happen.'

But, in this instance, she might only be half-right. These things are not always directly our fault, or at least not entirely our fault, in that we start them and then nature takes over. While it is more than likely that the virus started in a Chinese commercial goose farm around a quarter of a century ago and that it often gets moved around in truckloads of exported chicken and turkeys, it also gets brought westwards annually by migrating wildfowl, and will pose a terrible risk to wild birds in their coming breeding season. Just how terrible, I will only find out much further north and much closer to the sea, but 16,000 dead barnacle geese on the Solway Firth in the winter just gone (2021–22) gives an idea of the scale and ferocity. By the time the summer comes again, there will even be talk of possible extinctions for the great skua and the northern gannet, and any amount of carnage for fragile populations like the little colony of roseate terns on Coquet Island. No bird, not even the golden eagle, is immune, but there is just too much going on in our unsettled world for the story to make it into the front pages of our attention. 'The scale of mortality is unprecedented,' says a Natural England statement, 'with significant losses of adult birds and even larger mortality of chicks being reported.' Everyone talks about the effect on farmed chickens, but all over our cliffs and coastal islands, researchers and scientists are packing their bags and heading home, so that they do not inadvertently act as a conduit of infection. Two springs ago, they were doing this to protect themselves; now, it is to protect the very birds they are studying.

It strikes me again that, for a nation of alleged animal lovers, we have managed to squeeze out of our everyday lives just about every single one of them except those we take for walks, shoot from the air, or get food from. When each of these virus strains starts off with zoonotic potential, meaning that some of them will skip over to humans and make us ill, this seems like a major oversight.

These days, we might like to invite nature in from time to time, but it is strictly on our own terms, and never if it is inconvenient.

We mutter some understated farewells and I stride down the hill towards the as yet unseen glories of Swindon. There, under the watchful gaze of a faded poster in a shop window that reassures me that Jesus is watching over me, I put him to the test by trying to walk in one piece across the entirety of that town's Magic Roundabout. A friend has told me that he and his mates do it non-stop as a dare, when high on beer from the neighbouring Swindon FC ground. For some reason, I think that this is a good challenge for me in the middle of a busy day, at the age of 62 and carrying a 16-kilo backpack.

Stone cold sober, I am saved, whether by Jesus or not I couldn't say, but only at the price of an extended view of the middle finger of the driver of a national tyre-fitting van, and a fleetingly shouted word that may or may not have rhymed with 'anchor'.

I will learn this lesson often: as a walker on these roads, I am generally only here under sufferance of the hurried motorist. But I am heading for farmland, so I find I don't much care.

*

And in that farmland, some time around dawn on February 24th, 2022, just before my walk, British farming changed dramatically, and possibly for ever.

For the advance guard of T-72B3 Russian tanks and supporting armour that thundered over the Ukrainian border were not just invading someone else's country, they were shoving a gigantic stick into the spokes of two of the world's most important agricultural suppliers, Ukraine and Russia itself, who between them provide 20% of its high-grade wheat, 75% of its sunflower oil, and a high proportion of its fertiliser. This has caused a food price shock around the world – which many say was Vladimir Putin's clear intention – most particularly in its poorest parts. It has also come as a stark reminder that farming always has been, and always will be, subservient to the changing events that surround it. You can do all the micro-planning in the world to increase the number of yellowhammers in your hedges and headlands, but if some dictator starts firing off missiles into someone else's country, you must expect the rules to change. Anyone thinking that Russia's invasion of Ukraine won't directly impact British wildlife in the short-term, and probably long afterwards, is probably clinging to delusions.

Within British agriculture, the effects of the invasion have produced, and will continue to produce, a series of immediate pressures. Input costs (basically, anything that has to be bought in from off the farm with real money) have soared, especially with imported nitrogen fertiliser going from £284 per tonne in May 2021 to £731 a tonne a year later;[1] at the same time, wheat prices have risen by around 70%,[2] a figure which may well make a farmer who is struggling to break even look with a jaundiced eye at land they have previously set aside for nature. It has brought into sharp focus a nation's prime duty to feed its people and, after years of not really having to think about food, it is now front and centre in the national debate again. It has also made us ask what exactly we mean by 'cheap food', and how sustainable it can be in a country where 5 million of us are already in food poverty,[3] to throw a third of that food into landfill.[4]

Finally, with fertiliser prices at an all-time high, it has highlighted the question of what we have done to our soil and watercourses through the application of decades of chemicals, and the opportunity we may now have to undo some of that damage. After all, the majority of all British land is used for agriculture, 70% of it, so it makes sense that the majority of British wildlife is trying to eke out a living there, and that it is there, principally, where our biodiversity cataclysm has taken place.

Other than to lovers of fairytales, returning it all to nature is not an option, either: one of the National Food Strategy's four main recommendations was that we create a food system that will be 'resilient enough to withstand global shocks',* and you don't achieve that by relentlessly increasing imports, which then run the parallel risk that we trash someone else's wildlife in order to feed ourselves. We need wheat for our bread, grazing for our livestock, and barley and vines for our beer and wine. Perhaps nothing signals better the Kafkaesque nature of the current system than the fact that we are now using thousands of acres of farmland to produce seed to artificially feed wild birds that can no longer find it naturally on those same farmlands for themselves.

Ironically, a glimmer of opportunity has been unearthed by all this tragedy, and it will take me the next

* National Food Strategy. 2021. (The other three headline aims were to make us well not sick, to help restore nature and halt climate change, and to meet expected standards on health, environment and welfare.)

seven weeks to understand that our entire farming system will need to change in order to realise it. But I also start to trip over a central part of the solution here and now, in a little meadow somewhere in the Cotswolds, a day or two north of Swindon.

*

The first thing I notice about Conygree Farm is its small, horned cows. You don't get too many small, horned cows these days, so these traditional Herefords catch the eye.

Ever since Robert Bakewell started the process of selective breeding of livestock back in the eighteenth century, Britain's cattle have been on a one-way journey of rapid growth, so much so that milk yields of dairy cows, for example, have quadrupled since the Second World War, just as their life expectancy has halved. Our gift, it seems, to what may well soon be one of the largest animals on earth, has been to genetically engineer it into being just another stage in a vast national just-in-time supply chain.

'These are my little biodiversity engineers,' says farmer Jonty Brunyee when we look at them. 'Traditional breeds tend to be much smaller than the modern hybrid ones.' They are also powerfully well adapted to improving the land, through the way they graze, the massaging of the ground with their hooves, and the manure they share. They are hardy beasts, and thrive on grass and natural forage while turning sunlight into Sunday dinner.

Jonty's journey to the tenancy has been an unusual one. Raised on a Nottingham family farm that, when faced with the realities of modern farming, chose the intensive way out, he spent a childhood quietly watching its depletive effects, and deciding that he didn't want any part of it.

'Hedgerows were removed,' he explains at his kitchen table, over an album of black and white photographs of his father, heavy horses and farm hands. 'In the 1970s and 80s, the grassland was ploughed out, traditional buildings knocked down and we had a labour force that went from twenty to zero, nearly overnight. Dad was producing food in the way that the government had told him to, but sadly any sense of community had gone, let alone the biodiversity. We even rented in helicopters to do the spraying! Intensive farming was not for me.'

Long before it was fashionable, and having had his journey kick-started by reading Jonathan Porritt's ecological manual *Seeing Green*, he started to interest himself in concepts such as natural capital, public goods, soil health, water quality and the culture of the landscape and its people. He studied rural resource management at Seal Hayne Agricultural College in Devon, and then made an early career in advising farmers how to sustain what little wildlife they had left, including the countryside stewardship schemes.

'It was ironic,' he smiles. 'This descendant of Dutch engineers who had themselves come to England a few centuries before to help drain the fens, now wandering round Lincolnshire advising farmers how to re-wet them. I have ancestors turning in their damp graves.'

I find myself thinking about all the contractors I had watched over the last two or three years, planting hedges that their grandfathers had once been paid to grub out under government instructions. Recent British farming policy, if you can really call it that, has often been circular, contradictory and short-sighted, and there is precious little evidence that the many lessons of the past have been absorbed.

'Rome was burning,' as he puts it, but each successive year he became more aware of the potential solutions and opportunities, and was determined to get back to his roots. 'Sometimes it was as simple as just getting someone to cut their hedges after Christmas once the song birds had stripped the berries; other times it could be explaining how well-produced artisan food could be sold for more, or how to link the environment to entrepreneurism. It was simply making the point that you could farm for nature alongside farming for food.'

It was while he was working as a farm and countryside adviser that he and his young family took on the 73-hectare tenancy of Conygree. Unusually, or at least ahead of its time, one of the conditions that the National Trust owners set down for the tender process was that the potential farmer had to demonstrate another income source, so that it could be farmed part-time, and for nature, rather than intensively, and just for the financial return.

Initially, the farm was not in good heart, as previous times had taken from the soil without putting back; but, for a year, he did nothing, choosing instead to watch what the seasons threw up. In nature, doing nothing is surprisingly often the best course of action. Any farm that has run livestock intensively, for example, has probably used a wormer to protect the cattle against the effects of not being allowed to roam; the wormer has then worked its way through the system, killing off the dung beetles that feed on the dung, which are then not available to the hedgehogs and starlings whose numbers, we already know, then plummet. And, while much of what the seasons threw up was a carpet of invasive weeds, he also uncovered banks full of orchids, and fields still full of corn buntings and lapwings. Barn owls hunted every acre, and brown hares boxed in the biggest fields. All the time, Jonty studied the prevailing agri-environment schemes on offer, and used them to build the farm in the image he had chosen – mainly new hedges and species-rich margins full of wildflowers.

Over the next few years, he and his partner Mel (a grazing specialist whose expertise has allowed him to spend time away teaching and researching) worked with those schemes to deliver their ecological vision. Barley and silage production was replaced with native wildflower grassland (some sown and some left to natural regeneration), hay-making, diverse herbal leys, field margins full of wild carrot and other plants for insects, and plots of fallow and unharvested cereals to help feed farmland birds. Out went the worst of the weeds and in came proper livestock fencing and hay-making, followed first by Cotswold sheep (as rare and nearly as tall as the cows), the wonderful Herefords themselves, and a pig or two. Walls were repaired, hedges were gapped up and laid, and 1,000 trees were planted. The farm gained organic status and moved to a no input/low fossil fuel pasture-fed system, feeding no grains or imported soya to their animals. All the meat they produced was sold from the farm gate.

Jonty left the world of farm conservation advice and threw himself at academia, teaching farm business management and sustainability at the Royal Agricultural University in Cirencester. 'I love inspiring young farmers and land managers – I always try and link food production to ecology and entrepreneurship, looking for the win-wins and ways of doing things differently.' These days, he is head of sustainable farming at Farm Ed, a not-for-profit agro-ecological teaching farm a few miles up the road.

The award of a Nuffield scholarship allowed him to travel the world and see for himself the burgeoning regenerative farming movement, a new approach (in fact as old as the hills) in which all efforts were directed at *improving* soil quality, biodiversity and water quality, not just maintaining it. Terms like holistic management, mob grazing and enterprise stacking* came to him for

* Holistic management: a management system that 'builds healthy soil, sequesters carbon and supports rural communities'. (www.savory.global.com) Mob grazing: a high-intensity, short-duration system of grazing, where the grass thrives through having adequate time to recover. Enterprise stacking: exploiting the possibilities of adding new businesses to an existing farming operation with minimum cost implications. Adding laying hens to a cattle business, for example, where the hens follow the livestock in a natural rotation.

the first time, and he started to explore ways of making them relevant to Conygree, and to include them in his teachings for tomorrow's farmers.

'I had my light-bulb moment on Joel Salatin's farm in the Shenandoah Valley,' he remembers (a farm in Virginia that is referred to these days in hushed tones of respect by the regenerative community). 'Everything I had done up to that point had been directed by where the money was. From now on, it was about improvement.'

The consequent work that he and Mel have done has seen a further 8,000 trees planted, a 2-hectare organic market garden partnership established,[5] farm walks organised and a summer-long glamping operation rise out of nowhere. A small farm shop opens once or twice a week to sell beef harvested from the Herefords, and surplus vegetables from the box schemes.

'We offer the opportunity to get married in a flower meadow,' he says. 'It sounds strange in a world where farmers are expected to want to exclude people from their land wherever possible, but the teaching and sharing aspect of regenerative farming is as important as the rest. We are actually pressing for more footpaths through the farm, rather than less. Apart from anything, people walking through and seeing what we do are an opportunity for future income, such as a farm shop, or bike rentals.' When, in 2017, they won the Farming with Nature Award from the National Trust, it was a relief to know that what they had achieved had been measured, reviewed and approved by their peers.

The improvements, other than to the eye of experts, are often unnoticed by passers-by. After all, the steady degradation of our national soil capital by chemicals and erosion is an invisible process to all but a handful of scientists; worms and dung beetles generally go about their business unseen, and you can't see soil structure from six feet up, or tell whether subterranean watercourses are full of nitrates; mostly the mammals pass by secretively at night, and the corn buntings are just another little brown bird. Even the delicate colours in a wildflower meadow are fleeting in mid-summer, so it took the visit of a consultant entomologist, Jonty says, to lay out for him the full extent of what their work had done to Conygree's biodiversity.

'He came quietly up to me after a farm walk,' he recalls, 'and showed me what he had caught in his sweep net, and said that it was probably a hundred years since there was this variety of insect life here. It was one of those moments.'

A greater variety of more insects means more for everyone, all the way up the food chain, from the foraging hedgehog all the way to the swooping little owl and beyond. Aside from little enclaves of variety like this, it is a landscape that you would need to go to eastern Europe to find these days, and even then to very specific spots.

We lean over a gate and watch a red kite circling above the Herefords, and I ask him, in his capacity as a teacher, if he thinks that the message is getting though.

'Yes,' he says after a moment. 'It is starting to seem like the norm now. Ten years ago, I would have told you that about one in a hundred farmers got this; now I'd say half of them do.'

A great deal now depends on the schemes that eventually replace the European Union ones, not least in the opportunity they present to create a clear directive on soil health, one of our key assets of natural capital, and something that the EU consistently avoided tackling. It probably won't happen, but at least in this one small punctuation mark on my long walk north, and in a country where nearly three-quarters of the land is given over to farming, I take what I have seen as a sign of huge progress. It may only be 72 hectares of the 22 million in the country, but it is one of many such projects, and they are a start.

At the same time, the visit makes me painfully aware of how much we rely on small farms like Jonty and Mel's to roll back the tide of agricultural biodiversity loss, and how vital it is that, in the race to deal with one problem (climate change), we don't produce an operational and financial environment within which only the big can survive in the long term. It's not for nothing that larger farms (those above 200 hectares) have been remorselessly growing in both size and number since the turn of the millennium, or that the number of farms overall has consistently reduced by around 1% a year since 1950.[6]

Reluctantly, for this is a good place to stop for longer and to breathe a little, I pick up my pack and get back on the road.

*

A few miles to the north, my eye is caught by a bright green plastic bag hanging like an oversized fruit off a thorn bush overhanging the Monarch's Way.

It has been left by some dog walker in full expectation, presumably, that the dog poo fairy will come and waft it away during the quiet night watches. I stop and stare at it a while, trying without success to understand the thought processes in the brain that made the original decision to leave it there. Maybe they intended to return this way and collect it, but just forgot. Maybe they never gave a damn anyway. Although they clearly did, as they bothered to scoop up the poo and put it in the bag in the first place. This is *Homo sapiens* at his most mystifying, and it is not entirely clear how a species that routinely does something as stupid as this managed to become top animal in the first place.

I wish that I could say that the sight of a discarded bag like this will be a rare occurrence, but it won't. Abandoned poo bags are the way-markers of my walk, inelegant signatures left behind by modern dog owners, and they are very widespread indeed; weeks later, for example, I count twelve similar bags discarded within half a mile of the car park of a popular Scottish beauty spot, Schiehallion, the last of them within twenty metres of a bin. Holkham Beach, a popular attraction on the north Norfolk coast, reckon that they collect over a tonne of dog poo in its various forms each *week* during the high summer.[7] But then we allow our pets to inflict other damage as well; our dogs kill around 18,500 head of livestock each year,[8] just as our cats dispatch somewhere between 27 and 100 million songbirds over the same timescale,* so we have form in this game. One eighth of all cattle abortions in Britain are caused by cows eating grass that has been infected by the *Neospora canium* parasite, commonly available from dog faeces.[9] And eventually, I will give up counting the number of dog walkers who are gaily allowing Rover to bounce through the heather during the ground-nesting bird season. 'He just loves playing with the birds,' one of them says to me, by way of explanation, when I suggest that she puts him on the lead. 'Well, he's not doing any harm, is he?'† Actually, yes he is, and lots of it. And, by the way, it's not about your dog running free; it's about you being lazy.

It is not so much that we have too many pets‡ (although we almost certainly do), as much as the fact that so many of us don't really have a clue how

* The lower of these figures comes from the RSPB who, conscious perhaps that many of their subscription-paying members are also cat owners, assert that there is no evidence that this affects the overall bird population. Experience in my locality suggests otherwise.

† Full disclosure. I own an old Jack Russell/fox terrier cross, and he has caught just the one thing in his thirteen years on the planet, a cock pheasant who bizarrely turned round and ran at him while he was half-heartedly chasing it. It would have taken skill that he simply didn't possess to avoid catching it and, anyway, when he did, he didn't remotely know what to do with it. So much for evolution. We recycled the protein with a redcurrant sauce, and some rosti potatoes.

‡ Statista says that there are 13 million dogs and 12 million cats in the United Kingdom.

to look after and responsibly control them, and this matters for our biodiversity. Having killed off all our natural apex predators centuries ago, we now have 25 million not very good replacements knocking around, whose sheer numbers and enthusiasm make up for their lack of subtlety in driving wildlife ever deeper into the background. Apart from anything, creating regular disturbance, which is in every dog's skill set, will eventually drive even the most patient ground-nesting bird away from its nest. Given that a wolf's natural territory is around 5,000 hectares in extent,[10] their modern descendants are theoretically dispersed at 10,000 times that density. The resulting challenge is self-evident.

To my surprise, thoughtless pet owners (to whose numbers millions more were added during the Covid lockdowns*) will be one of the most consistently frustrating themes of the first half of my journey, but then I suppose I've already spent 50 years watching the decline of British bird life.

A mile down the footpath, I sit on a fallen tree, get out my notebook and write the first entry into what will become my personal post-walk manifesto. 'Become the best pet owner you can be.'†

*

* About 3.2 million, according to the Pet Food Manufacturers' Association.

† Available in full at Appendix 3.

We can't stop smiling.

If Jonty's regenerative Cotswold farm lays the first brick in the wall of future resurgence for me, it is as soon as the following day that I am celebrating the second.

I am walking with Mary Colwell, friend, co-worker and film-maker turned tireless campaigner for natural history education, but at first, it is generational memory that is very much on our minds.

'We're in danger of forgetting past abundance,' she says, a cautionary note as I wax lyrical about the plant and insect life that I have seen at Conygree. 'We need to seek out generational memory while it is still available, so that we never lose sight of the all the moths, birds and wildflowers that were once here, and which we have replaced with houses, silage and Amazon warehouses. That's where we need to aim to get back to, not some pale imitation of it.'

We agree that the critical and urgent challenge is to halt the de-naturing of our lives, and that starts with education.

'Think about it: 40% of all the plant species on the planet are endangered,' she says, 'but the thing that is actually going extinct is the botanist.[11] Botany used to be a common degree in its own right, while nowadays it's just an occasional adjunct to biology. Lose them, and you lose the ability to identify plants and give them the best chance of survival.'

Bit by bit, a child's grounding in natural history has fallen victim to a virtual world, to 'time-poor' parents, and to school programmes obsessed only with what is provably useful to a modern CV. These days, it is a rare parent indeed who leads a family safari down a local hedgerow or gazes with their children into a pool of frogspawn, just as it is a rare teacher who has the time to explain the simple ecology of a tree to a fascinated child. Arguably, nowhere, apart maybe from intensive cereal farming, has nature been evicted from the surrounding air more than at our schools. And it matters, not just because today's fascinated children are tomorrow's ecologists, botanists and ornithologists, but because children who don't understand the importance of the place of nature in our lives can't possibly be expected to be good stewards of it when their time comes. How can they, when we never told them? If we only ever teach them for the dreaded syllabus, for what is immediately impressive on the 'list of attainments' section of an early CV, where does a sense of respect and awe for the nature that sustains us fit in?

But despite all this, we are still smiling as we walk, and we will smile all our way to the pub. We are smiling because we have actually won a battle.

In another life, Mary has spent a decade campaigning for a Natural History GCSE, a fight that I have also been a very small part of in its latter stages. And Mary has specially come out to meet me on my walk to let me know that she has heard, informally, that after years of delay, of Covid, of ministerial changes and general inertia, the Secretary of State for Education has finally agreed that it is to go ahead. Children embarking on their GCSEs from September 2025 will be able to study for a qualification in Natural History.

'You can't tell anyone yet!' she tells me. 'But we did it! We bloody did it! There actually *is* a god out there somewhere.'

So we go to the pub and investigate the deeper mysteries of that god at the bottom of a pint pot, albeit, in my case, one of alcohol-free lager.

*

Once Mary has headed back home, I hear a text arrive on my phone and try to ignore it. I have taken to walking with the phone in my back pocket and on silent mode, precisely so that I don't have to be too mindful of the outside world beyond the immediate path that I am walking on.

It arrives again, so I take the phone out of my pocket and see that it is from my next-door neighbour.

'Just tested positive for Covid. Saw you on Sunday. Suggest you test, too.'

I mull her suggestion over for a moment. On the one hand, I feel fine, and I could probably justify not doing so; on the other, my ignoring her might eventually kill someone I have never even met. After all, I am staying with different people every night along the way, and for all I know, they may have vulnerable people in their house, and elderly parents they care for. With deep reluctance, I take from my pack one of the two test kits I brought with me and, two minutes later, watch the unmistakable shade of a second line getting bolder.

As that second line strengthens, my imaginary pathway to the north recedes before my very eyes.

After two years of evading the virus, and three weeks of being almost comically careful to avoid it, I now have no option but to break route and go home till I test negative again, however long that is. I think of what Satish said about expecting hardship, having so recently thought about his advice on distractions.

Five hours later I am back in Sussex, coughing like a lifelong smoker, and staring at a television that I had hoped to have seen the last of for a few months.

It wasn't supposed to be like this.

5. GOD'S ACRE AND GOD'S GARDEN

Stratford-upon-Avon to Tissington: 111 miles; five days

(PRINCIPAL HABITAT: HUMAN SETTLEMENT/URBAN)

'We all have dreams. But in order to make dreams come into reality, it takes an awful lot of determination, dedication, self-discipline and effort.'

JESSE OWENS

Six days later, I re-join the trail.*

The virus has leaked quickly away from my body, as it has started to do, in more pedestrian fashion, from the news.

A GP friend calls me when he hears that I am on the train north and heading straight back out, and cautions

* To avoid a mass of reorganisation, I rejoined the route at the point where I was scheduled to be that particular day, rather than the one where I left it. Those missing 'Covid miles' are covered in Chapter 13.

me against over-exertion. 'You should be fine,' he says, 'but just don't push it too hard and get a load of long Covid.' He suggests that I limit myself to a dozen miles a day for a while, and build up from there. I promise him with all my fingers and toes crossed that I will be careful, but with each of the next four days each requiring twenty-plus miles to keep up with the schedule, I don't mean a word of it. None of my clever plans allowed for illness, let alone subliminal ones that make me feel more annoyed than ill. Now that the plague within me has receded and it is only my body that will suffer, I just need to get on with it.

And it is pure delight to be back on those byways again, back in the groove of a life of more or less perpetual motion. Back under the weight of a comforting pack. Back strolling past the empty golf courses, white delivery vans and conference hotels of north Warwickshire; back among the manicured hedgerows, pretty streams and greening fields of a spring whose progress those few days of absence seems to have unleashed and re-energised.

And, above all, back under a sky full of birds.

*

Birds define my walk.

They soar over it, dive through it, chatter from thickets alongside it, and run away from it across fields. They bob around on its waters, and swoop through the edges of its forests and gardens. As spring develops, they scream after insects in tracer lines across the skies above it, and sing out their evolutionary love for each other from every fencepost beside it. Often, they are all that bring it colour on colourless days, and noise when there is silence. But above all, they start to tell me how things are within the habitat that we are sharing. The answer, sadly, is not good. Across our continent, we have lost around 600 million (or one in six) of our breeding birds in the last 40 years, of which about 50 million are from our island alone.[1] While the rate of decline seems to be slowing a little, the root causes remain clear to see on either side of my pathway: chemical farming that is also obsessively tidy, a shift to autumn-sown cereals (which make it harder for birds to build nests in taller crops come the spring), over-drainage and a general loss of habitat and diversity. You might also add the effect that some 60 million pheasants and red-legged partridges that are imported each year for game shooting has on the local bird population, a figure that each August makes up no less than 50% of our national avian biomass.[2] And it is all still definitely going in the wrong direction.

As it happens, the only bird that I consciously notice every single day of my walk is a mallard. Somehow, I thought it would be a sparrow or wren but, no, it is a mallard. Buzzards and chaffinches will eventually run them a close second. And pigeons. Obviously pigeons. And corvids.

From the neat village ponds of Hampshire, via the peaks of Derbyshire and the industrial foreshore of Edinburgh, all the way to the tiny lochans behind Cape Wrath, the mallard is virtually always in evidence, always unconsciously maintaining and extending little corridors of wetlands as she goes, by spreading seeds across our landscape in her waste.

Like pigeons and rats, mallards have learned how to adapt and thrive in our modern world. Long-lived,* fast-flying, unfussy and busy with 'extra-pair copulations' (which is why you so often see two males chasing the same female), they are the ancestor of virtually all domestic duck breeds on earth. And unlike, say, the secretive goldeneye, far from avoiding us, the mallard appears actively to seek us out. Watch over any busy village pond, and you will gradually understand why this might have been a good evolutionary move for them.

Throughout the early Midlands, I put myself in mallard heartland by following the canal network. I haven't planned to, but a man loading his van with gardening equipment up in the village of Hopwas patiently redirects me from my proposed walk up the River Tame and onto the adjacent Birmingham and Fazeley canal. And he is right; like any mid-term government, my route has started to stray from its original 'manifesto' according to many factors – the weather, local advice, my body or the proximity of a flat white. Sometimes, I just change the route because I *can*, a happy novelty in our prescriptive world. For two whole days, I lose myself in the Staffordshire canal system, describing vast 'S' shapes through the countryside just so that I can walk on flat

* The oldest one on record was shot in Arkansas in 2008, 27½ years after he was ringed.

towpaths and see the world from below, rather than six feet up. Even though this is all only a few feet below the surrounding fields and roads, it has nonetheless a brand-new feeling, full of unexpected delights. This is a new-minted world of carp fishermen, of tiny bridges, of moorhens sounding like tiny cycle horns, of bankside badger runs and barges that have seen better days, and of a single coffee shared from a rusty bargeware mug.

This is the beating heart of slow Britain.

'Where are you off to?' calls the owner of that mug out of the early mist, as I lope past. He is sitting by the rudder of his barge in the morning chill, carefully adjusting the badge on his sailor's cap.

'You look knackered already,' he continues after I tell him, peering over the top of the dirtiest spectacles I have ever seen. 'My advice is get the train. Here, come and share this.' He motions me onto the barge and, in joyful contravention of two years of Covid distancing, we pass the mug back and forth between us, sipping its bitter contents from either side of the rim as we tell each other the stories that took us here. His is a journey, too, but a slow, slow one out from the shadows of a recent bereavement towards the uplands of he knows not yet where, his grief at once tangible and adventurous. His fixed point turns out to be the changing view that each day brings, the new world that opens up round every bend of the canal. We talk of waste, and how the sheer amount of concrete needed to build just one motorway bridge only reveals itself to the slow traveller passing below. We talk of nature, and of the wreckage of mangled fields and woods that we have both seen, where an unneeded railway line is bludgeoning its unwanted way through irreplaceable history and beauty, 'affecting or destroying 693 Local Wildlife Sites' as it does so.[3]

'It's the sunk cost fallacy,' he explains, lighting a tiny cheroot and watching the smoke curl up into the thin air, until it is lost in the mist. 'A bunch of corrupt, incompetent politicians who are in the thing far too far to get out and not look like idiots.' He looks delighted with the abrupt certainty of his commentary.

We talk of love and of loneliness, of stillness and silence. I think we even talk about cows at one point. It amazes me now to think of just how much ground we covered in those short moments, and yet how unhurried we were.

'Go well, you daft bugger,' he says eventually through a thick, bearded hug, when we part. His eyes are very slightly moist, but that might just be the cold morning air.

'You too,' I reply, hitching my pack onto my back, and returning to my trios of mallards and half-hidden boat yards.

'Let me know if you ever get there,' he shouts after me through the echoing mist, before I disappear under a bridge and round a corner. I want to shout the same thing back, but I know that his journey is more complicated than mine, and I resist. To say it would be to assume that his journey had to have a destination, rather than just be a healing process.

'Will do,' I call back, although to do this will require extrasensory perception, as we never even got round to swapping contact details. Our friendship has lasted precisely fifteen minutes and, if he ever mentioned his name, I have forgotten it already. It might have been Jim. Whatever it was, it was the same name as his late partner. Just as Satish had implied, a life on the road is allowing me to live in the moment, and to treasure the good ones simply for the pleasure they give.

And on I go, ever northwards. I notice strange things, like how few windows are open on this mild spring day, and how many houses are empty, even boarded-up empty. I see the percentage of spotless four-wheel-drive SUVs in the driveways of the dreamy villages, and the distances hard-working people will go to fly-tip electrical appliances in beauty spots.* By now, I am getting fully into my new way of life. 'My habitat has become the journey itself, and my new habit is to walk', was the way Simon Armitage, the current Poet Laureate, put it as he trundled in the wrong direction† down the Pennine Way. I have developed little routines around my backpack, unpacking in full on the floor each evening to ensure I actually use what I have brought along, and then repacking it the following morning in reverse order of likely need. Later, the pack will become my friend, but for now we are still in the phase of sizing each other

* There are about 1.16 million recorded incidents of fly-tipping in the UK each year, the vast majority of which is household waste, meaning we probably shouldn't kid ourselves that it is a minority activity. (House of Commons Library, May 23rd, 2022)

† North to south, apparently.

up. In my plans, I had thought to read a chapter of a novel each lunchtime, and write up notes from the morning; in reality, I normally wolf my sandwiches in a couple of minutes and press on towards tomorrow. Having thought that I would cover the ground at an average speed of 2½ miles an hour, including stops, I am actually going at rather more than 3. One day of snow, I walk 23 miles in just under seven hours. 'It is cold and uncomfortable here,' my body tells me, 'so let's just get the job done, eh?' The restless traveller moves quicker, and the surprise of my short attention span turns out to be the gift of just getting on with it.

When I leave my last canal, or at least the last one until North Yorkshire, I join the Staffordshire Way. In the event, this seems to be a purely conceptual notion whose authors appear to have forgotten to tell the landowners, or ramblers, or both, that it had ever been designated. A give-away feature of a footpath that is going nowhere, I come to discover, are signposts that point almost apologetically at the ground, as if to conceal the vulgarity of actually wanting the walker to reach somewhere. Lurching from faintness to invisibility through the middle of fields, through yards full of slurry and over stiles that have known better centuries,* let alone

* For some rather bizarre reason, I counted the cumulative number of stiles that I clambered over, until I lost interest after a day of about 70 of them on the Staffordshire Way. With 62-year-old bones, a 16kg backpack, and the benefit of hindsight, I am now able to confirm that any day not involving a stile is a good one.

days, it eventually runs out of steam altogether in an enormous field full of curious cows and swans near the A50 at Uttoxeter. Mind you, it competes on level terms with the National Forest Way which, without a shred of irony, leads me through five admittedly delightful miles of mainly treeless fields and villages, and then the Limestone Way, whose disappearing route was almost certainly inspired by the way that its own watercourses appear and disappear within the geology of its limestone country. It doesn't matter: any footpath is better than the rock-hard, crowded asphalt strips which make up the alternative, and the wonderful thing about walking is just how easy it is to put things right when they go astray. There are no one-way systems, no dead ends, and anyway, Staffordshire folk are very kind and patient with their directions. I guess that they have had to learn to be.

Those mallards, on the other hand, are leading me inexorably back towards settlements, and right now I am thinking that, while only 4% of our land is made up of the urban habitat, the vast majority of us happen to live there.

*

Anyway, suddenly I find I love towns.

Having spent half a lifetime trying to avoid anything urban, I start to develop a new fascination with them, as ecosystems of plenty in their own right that can help keep my little show on the road. Besides, it turns out that I miss the fun of spending small amounts of money on things I don't really need.

So, far from deliberately bypassing them as I aimed to in the planning stages of my trip, I am now doing sizeable deviations just to be in their centres, to make available the shops full of stuff I would never normally find useful, let alone buy, and to sit for a short while in their cafés, absorbing the fat of the land. Being still dry, pubs remain off my agenda for the time being, but, everywhere else, I buy things simply because I can. After all, I have never spent so little money in my life.

At the southern outskirts of Uttoxeter on a day that happens to coincide with the town's horse races, a formidable lady is standing guard at her driveway, sweeping up last year's brown leaves from her beech hedge. She is equipped with a mad spaniel and a rake that is missing half its tines, and tells me when I ask her for directions that I should avoid the centre at all costs, as I would only find it 'full of spivs in loud checked jackets'. Variety is the spice of life, I think, so I head for there only to discover that all her 'spivs' have departed for the racecourse, and the place is consumed instead by a gentle Saturday afternoon torpor. But it still has everything I want.

I pick up a new USB cable, knowing for a fact that this will merely prompt the missing one to reveal itself almost immediately. It does. In the optician, where they kindly unbend the contorted arms of my glasses for free, after I had sat on them, they are discussing the eye test that one of their children had the previous week, as if eye tests really are the only item of small talk that colleagues might share in an optician's practice.

'Not quite at the glasses stage yet,' she says. 'But next time for sure.'

'It's all that screen time they have nowadays,' says the other. 'And all that not being outdoors.'*

At Tesco, I buy six cereal bars, not because I particularly want them, but because someone who should know about these things told me in Tamworth that I would need them for the harder miles ahead, and that they would make my life easier. I start to eat one that afternoon, hate it, shove half of it in the bin, and then eventually leave the other five in someone's store cupboard in Bakewell when they are not looking. I have become a silent mover of food, a human leaf-cutter ant dragging things from home to home. Sometime in the middle future, a man will head out to his job among the art collections of Chatsworth House, with a packed lunch that has been supplemented by a cereal bar from someone else's misguided and out-of-date purchase decision, and the circle will be complete.

But all of that is just the prelude to the main event, the coffee and the Swiss cheese and red onion toastie. It matters not the least that I have already had my lunch out on the hill a couple of hours before; I am now eating at every opportunity, as hunter-gatherers have done through the centuries. I have transcended mealtimes.

* She has a point. By the end of my journey, and with seven or eight hours each day in natural light, my eyes really did seem to work better.

Besides, I adore Swiss cheese and red onion toasties, even if I always end up leaving the salad garnish and tiny unripe cherry tomatoes on the side of the plate.

'Don't you want your salad?' asks the lad clearing the plate way. He smiles patiently with the air of a man who finds a lot of salad left on the plates he clears, and who won't be helping himself to any of it, either.

For my own part, I am cheerfully refuelled, and on my way to Derbyshire.

*

'The key was to start small and stay credible. I mean, you don't really need a PhD in biosciences to kick off a village nature restoration project.'

It is three days later, and Phillip Neal is pointing out an unmown square of grass in the churchyard of Hartington, a small and rather beautiful settlement in the Derbyshire dales.

'This is one of seven little areas dotted around the village which have been given over to wildflowers. It began as an idea in the village primary school after the first lockdown in 2020, and we took it from there. Each plot is someone's specific responsibility, and each one tries to offer something a little different from the others.'

In our urban world, small and beautiful villages tend to be fragile ecosystems themselves, often buffeted and held back by competing interests that might involve high house prices, absentee owners and a fundamental difficulty in reaching a critical mass for just about anything, whether it is the shop, the school, the cricket team or the village pub. Hartington is lucky, with its extensive hinterland of farms and smaller hamlets to boost its numbers, and it has managed to sustain two shops, a post office, a garage, two cafés and even a surgery with its own dispensary. Critically, it also hosts around 30 active interest groups. For a population of just over 300 people, this is little short of extraordinary.

'Up until recently, we just had a few flower boxes around the place, but to be honest that was more about a splash of colour for the visitors than nature for its own sake. So, when the children came up with this idea, we seized on it, and agreed on three general aims: increases in biodiversity, in promoting physical and mental well-being and in community engagement.' It is another of the countless examples I will find of biophilia, and of the pivotal role that nature should play in our mental health.

'What we have done sounds small,' says Janet Bray, who also works on the project. She describes herself as a 'newbie' round here, having only been in the village for nineteen years. 'But it's like an iceberg, with most of the activity going on unseen elsewhere, and the whole thing amounting to more than the sum of its parts.' She ticks the things off on her fingers. 'A Facebook page for the project, an email address for advice, so that gardeners can wild a little bit of their own patch, an art competition. We're even making plans for a wildlife trail. That then leads to other things, like an IT support network and wildlife lessons for the children, where they take, for example, their wildflower knowledge back from school and pester their parents into planting some of their own.' Even the parish magazine has a regular wildflower feature.

When we walk around the different areas, I can start to see the understated genius of what they are doing here: a few yards of roadside verge opposite a housing development, an overgrown bit of scrub by the youth hostel, an unmown patch on the edge of a field in the middle of the village. When I ask them what have been the specific biodiversity gains, Phillip tells me that they did a wildflower count after the first year and found twenty 'new' types, most of which had not been in the original planting scheme. 'That brings the new invertebrates,' he adds, 'and they bring the increased bird count. And all of that brings people back outside, especially the children.'

A strange thought comes to me. Sometimes, undertakings like these seem to mimic nature themselves, with thousands of mycorrhizal strands of mostly unnoticed episodes of human inspiration, activity and communication under the surface bringing in the nutrients that enable, for example, these little patches of wildflowers to happen. In a world where corporations obsess over the productivity of their staff's time down to the nearest minute, it is an irony indeed just how much of the nature we have left in this country depends on talented people giving uncounted hours of their time for free. Beyond some small financial seeding from a supportive parish council, this has never been about money, or needed much of it. This has simply been a modest exercise in reopening the doors to nature, and welcoming her back in. One of the abiding themes of my journey is just how very simple the reversal of species loss can be when it is not too late. A sparrowhawk moves into a fresh territory to hunt a newly arrived songbird who is foraging for a long-forgotten insect that is pollinating a flower that has risen up out of a seed bank in which it may have lain dormant for centuries, simply because someone has stopped mowing the grass. That's roughly how it goes, the bountiful outcome of an ultra-local trophic cascade.*

Liz Broomhead, who says she had only come along to make us all a cup of tea, but stays to chat for two hours, adds: 'This kind of thing is all about communication. That's how it happens.' I sense that Liz is the mother tree round here, a lifer in the village, parish councillor and that all-important bridge between the old and the new. When someone needs to know who to speak to about something these days, you can probably rely on Liz to know who it is.

Like so many good ideas, the Hartington Wildflower Project is scalable and has synergies. Scalable, because other villages in the area, Bradwell, Wirksworth, Hathersage, for example, are already doing their own

* A trophic cascade is a set of indirect actions that end up influencing what goes on two or more levels down the food chain. In this case, the sparrowhawk may well be influencing upwards the number of insects, which are now no longer being eaten by the songbirds that the sparrowhawk itself is eating.

versions and are sharing information with each other, while other local villages, such as Newton and Taddington, are being helped to set up their own. Similarly, other district councils are seeing what Derbyshire Dales are up to, and asking for advice and examples themselves. (Indeed, you only need to look at cities like Newcastle, where 18 hectares have recently been dedicated to 45 public sites that aim to plant 2,500 trees and 25,000 bulbs in the urban grassland, to understand that the idea is limitless.[4]) Synergies, because it dovetails neatly on the ground with the council's commitment to leaving road verges to nature, rather than the regular blade of a contractor's mower, save where road safety demands a cut. Emma Mortimer, Community Development Officer for the council, is regarded as an enabler, not an obstacle.

'In the early days, people thought we were just cutting costs with our verge programme. Then they started to see the cow parsley, vetch and mallow and something clicked for them. Now it is a policy that is overwhelmingly supported.' It would help, we all agreed, if rate-payers across the land demanded their councils did the same.

Those seven little wildflower patches amount to no more than a few hundred square metres, not even a pinprick in the quarter of a million square kilometres that make up our island home. But, as I pick up my pack and head on northwards again up the Tissington Trail, that annoying old truth about long journeys starting with single steps re-echoes in my brain,[5] and I first start to wonder what a thousand Hartingtons could be like, in clusters that are linked by the unmown verges and vibrant hedges that run along the roads that link them.

*

As I move north through the unusually warm spring, I develop a strange but subconscious habit of arranging my meet-ups in churchyards, at least those of them that take place in settlements, which feels a bit like a throwback to some Thomas Hardy novel.

This is not entirely from a deep gothic obsession, but more because graveyards belong to churches which generally have tall spires, and are therefore instantly recognisable both on the map and on the ground, for me and for the person that I am meeting. Also, ever since I was a soldier, I have made a point of visiting the inhabitant of each Commonwealth war grave in every churchyard I happen to be in, to pay my brief respects; it is a habit I continue all the way north. When you have known even a small amount of violence yourself, one of Lutyens' immaculate white Portland stone graves reinforces, as if it needed reinforcing, just how little has been achieved by our own species' propensity for killing each other. Only in one churchyard in my entire journey, Upper Slaughter in the Cotswolds, do I find none; Upper Slaughter, despite its name, is one of only 56 'thankful' villages in the UK that lost no one at all in the Great War. In fact, it is one of only sixteen 'doubly thankful' villages that lost none in either world war.

Above all, I found that churchyards are places where travellers can rest. Thus, on warm afternoons, I might find myself lying against 'Jeremiah, dearly beloved', or 'Gracie, now with God', as I wait for a new companion, or my evening's host. I find that you can learn a lot about a community from its old graveyards, all the way from its local geology to the sense of civic pride in its upkeep; tragedies, shipwrecks and plagues rub shoulders with long lives lived well, and villages well served. But, as I lie beneath an umbrella of yew and rooks, I also sometimes find myself wondering how many acres of churchyard there are around Britain's 40,000 churches. The Church of England famously and secretively owns 105,000 acres of other land, but it interests me more how many of their acres contain the remains of older versions of you and me, and how they promote biodiversity.

The answer, or at least a part of it, lies in an auction yard in Shropshire, where an organisation called Caring for God's Acre has its headquarters, and from where it strives to protect these spaces for communities, their heritage and for local wildlife. In terms of biodiversity, their volunteers have already collected 75,000 records of sightings, all of which have been fed into the National Biodiversity Network Atlas; they also promote chemical-free maintenance and avoid inappropriate mowing. And, while you may not personally be ready for a 'Love Your Burial Ground Week', you should draw comfort from the fact that thousands of volunteers are out there making sure that, when you finally come to rest your own weary bones below the turf yourself one day, if that's the destination you choose, it will likely be under a sward full of insects and a sky full of birds.[6] Other public spaces apply equally. Golf courses take up between 0.5 and 2.5% of our total land area* (depending on which county you are in), and can easily be a haven for wildlife if their members insist on an organic approach being taken, rather than the extravagant use of scarce water, herbicides and pesticides as they so often do; but only if their members insist. Add to this the area taken up by cricket grounds, football pitches and even our own gardens, as owners and volunteers, we can all influence the health of nature in our country effectively and immediately.

But then our country, for all its many imperfections, is rammed full of community-based volunteers.

*

Eighteen miles to the north-east, more of those strands of community emerge again in a Sheffield suburb, in Jo Dobson's Hangingwater allotment. This time, it is all about food, which will always be the bedrock of our relationship with nature.

'When I'm here,' she once wrote in her blog, 'I'm really aware of being a person with a body. I sweat, I ache, I get dirt under my nails, and my fingertips get so abraded by the work that for a little while afterwards, my phone no longer recognises me.'

* It's a little-known fact that golf courses also take up twice as much space as housing, in the UK. (*Huffington Post*)

Interest in allotments, of which there are around a third of a million in Britain, rises and falls over the decades like the tide, but it is hard to overstate their bounty and their biodiversity contribution to urban ecosystems. Right now, in the wake of lockdowns, rising food prices and mental health challenges, their star is high in the firmament. Because most plot-holders compost their allotment waste, these patches of ground carry a third more carbon and nitrogen than surrounding fields,[7] and are a great deal more fertile. What began as a scheme to allow poor families the space to grow fresh produce for themselves* has now branched out across all other economic groups in our topsy-turvy world of idiotically priced food, and it now also plays a vital role in local food systems and countless people's mental health. In a country where bad health outcomes are increasingly seen as being in direct proportion to the degree of deprivation experienced, and where, by most metrics such as mortality and time spent ill, things are getting worse, sustainable food initiatives are priceless.[8]

'I'm not sure I could have got through the various lockdowns the way I did without mine,' says Sarah Deakin, Jo's friend and fellow activist. 'You don't all need to be friends, or know each other's phone numbers, but just to be there and work alongside each other creates the strongest sort of community I know.' We

* Back in 2008, department store Harrods offered a bespoke gardening service for people too busy to tend and dig their allotments themselves. Make of that what you will.

are standing in Jo's steeply sloping allotment, admiring her pollinator bed of lavender and poached egg plants, and chatting animatedly about the benefits we all get from nature.

'Worms get me most excited,' says Sarah, 'followed by robins.' For a while, we stand in silence and just listen to the symphony of spring going on in the trees and hedgerows all around us. The song of chiffchaffs and great tits echoes loudly out of the sloping wood.

Rather fittingly, they met in activism. In 2012, as part of a private finance initiative (PFI) between Sheffield City Council (SCC), Amey PLC and the Department of Transport, a plan had been quietly drawn up to fell 17,500 of the city's mature trees, for highway, pavement and streetlight renewal,* and, for a few years, the project went largely unnoticed. Then, on what Sarah describes as 'that infamous night on 17th November 2016', Amey, supported by a large contingent of police, felled all but one of the healthy lime trees on Rustlings Road, arresting pyjama-clad residents who were refusing to move their cars. If no sadder example exists of wanton and planned natural vandalism, then there is also probably no finer example of effective and prolonged protest than that which followed. Politicians, nature writers, musicians, poets and broadcasters all lent their voices and creativity in support of the umbrella organisation,

* SCC assured the world at the time that they 'only' planned to fell 10,000 trees, a far lower figure than the 17,500 that were actually set down in the minutes of an earlier cabinet meeting.

Sheffield Tree Action Groups (STAG), whose members regularly linked arms around targeted trees, the better to create a public outcry that would eventually silence the chainsaws. By the time the council backed down in March 2018, two-thirds of the trees had been saved, and a new strategic partnership established to provide a sustainable template for the future.

'Then I helped to set up a community art group,' says Sarah, 'in response to the grief people were feeling at the loss of their trees. We'd encourage residents to come out and draw or paint pictures of their favourite trees before they lost them. You might not think that art can change much, but it quickly developed into active silent protests at live felling sites, complete with camping chairs, drawing boards and paints. People couldn't help noticing. And when they noticed, they joined in.'

'Even the wretched pigeons helped!' Jo says, looking gloomily down at the shredded leaves of her kale. 'Pigeons nest all year, which meant that we could use the need to protect them in the winter as part of our evidence.'

Both Jo and Sarah became heavily involved in a project they called Lost Words for Sheffield, where they raised enough money to provide one copy of Robert Macfarlane and Jackie Morris's book *Lost Words* for each primary school in Sheffield, so that children could have a chance to know and understand the words of nature that our relentless, time-poor world was busy tearing away from them. Indeed, Robert Macfarlane's attention, having been attracted by the fact that the campaign was nominally being run by a tree and not a human, led him to write his protest poem 'Heartwood'. Illustrated by Nick Hayes, the poem imagines a conversation between a tree and the feller sent to cut it down, and is now freely available in poster form for any individual or group trying to save a tree.

Campaigners remain campaigners, though, and there are strong connections that lead away from their allotments, and those of others, into education, sustainability, hyper-local food security and food poverty alleviation. Cutting through the technical terminology, these people speak the language of food, and food that is handled in the right way, in turn, enables all sorts of benefits. Sarah volunteers at Sheffield's Food Works, a well-established social enterprise that 'builds fair and sustainable food for Sheffield', and which saves 500 tonnes of landfill food waste each year by upcycling surplus local ingredients into meals, sharing surplus ingredients at their market, and by developing local food production on their farm. In 2021, two coordinated anti-food-waste schemes ('Repurpose your Surplus' and 'Grow a Row') provided 2.5 tonnes of food from allotments, organic growers, market gardens and vegetable box schemes, which was then turned into 5,108 meals, all from produce that would otherwise probably have just been composted. Lately, a piece of unused agricultural ground has been made available and is now run as the Food Works Farm, bringing in volunteers on a regular basis to work the land.

'Food Works,' she tells me, making sure that I am concentrating, 'is very much *not* a food bank. It is about redistributing surplus food across the city.'

Jo's interest in food and growing was sparked by the 'Incredible Edible' scheme that started in Todmorden, West Yorkshire, and which has quite literally created edible, and freely available, landscapes all around the town, from cemeteries to towpaths to sidewalks to the edge of the brand-new doctor's surgery. If this sounds like a gimmick, it is not. It is now being used as a model for scores of other towns and villages, from Ilfracombe to Inverness, and it has the education of children in healthy food at its very heart. In some of these schemes, in Bristol for example, a level of sophistication is emerging as to the distribution of the food produced by the scheme, to the people who need it and at the price they can afford. In a country where 90% of food is controlled by just eight boardrooms, this is a tiny demonstration of food democracy fighting back, and it happens also to be great for biodiversity.

Jo ended up co-authoring a book on the story with one of Incredible Edible's founders, Pam Warhurst, under the auspices of a supportive writing agency called Urban Pollinators, which helps people 'work through complex and challenging issues about place and society'.

'What we both do is about everyone eating well,' says Sarah. 'The idea that access to good food should be a middle-class thing is a terrible British misconception.' I remember a past conversation I had with a food poverty campaigner about how it would always be this way until we stopped accepting the inevitability of an underclass who ate less well, lived less healthily and died earlier than the rest of us. An uncomfortable lesson of my journey is that there seems to be a direct link between how we treat ourselves, and how we treat our wildlife.

It seems hard to believe that these are just two of Sheffield's three-quarters of a million people, or that they have time to do anything else with their lives. But they are, and they do. And happily, so do many like them, all over Sheffield and all over the rest of the country. And they prove three new truths to me in this journey of newness through a land I had previously thought that I understood: that cities are almost as key to nature as the countryside; that how we deal with food is at the heart of our future biodiversity; and without vibrant communities, that concept whose very existence Margaret Thatcher famously questioned, we might as well give up.

*

On occasion, I walk with other people all day. People like Sally, with whom I hiked on the Limestone Way, and whose retirement present to herself a couple of years before was to spend £40,000 on buying 13 acres of degraded peat bog on Clough Moor, just south of the Pennines, and make it her remaining life's work to resurrect it.

'I go up there at least twice a week,' she tells me as I struggle to keep up with her comfortable runner's lope. She is a decade older than me, but almost embarrassingly fit.

'I might be mending walls, building little dams, transplanting sphagnum and reprofiling the peat hags. It beats going on cruises. I'm mainly on my own, but I've also got friends who will come and help from time to time. Eventually, you get to know every twist and turn of the place. I've also signed my bog up into a wader survey, so I can tell in real time what effect my work is having, with golden plover, wheatear, short-eared owls and curlews all in evidence. I'll get there in the end.' Peat restoration projects both large and small will be a recurring feature for me, and although I will be walking through that type of habitat almost every day from now on, it will be a few hundred miles before I get up close and personal with it.

A few days north, outside Hebden Bridge, I walk with Ed, whose idea of a great team-building day out for the staff at his local clothing company is to head for a bit of depleted peat bog with a picnic and plugs of sphagnum moss to plant, and just improve the world around him a couple of square centimetres at a time.

'Why would I want to go paintballing,' he asks, 'when we've got all this out here?'

Then, at twelve minutes to two on the afternoon of the fourteenth day, I hear the unmistakeable bubbling call of my own first curlew of the walk, a gorgeous, siren sound that rises and falls on the breeze in the middle distance. First, I make a mental note that this place is called Pomeroy. Then, for a moment I stop, holding my breath so that I can pick up the notes all the better. Ears hear better sideways on, so I turn away to try to discern where it is. I'm not an overly emotional wildlife watcher, but I have spent so much of the last three years working with these birds in another compartment of my life* that it doesn't surprise me at all to feel my eyes stinging. The point about this particular bird is not so much that it is here, although that is reason enough to be joyful, but that its location and the nature of its call means that it is a breeder, or at least a hopeful one. This is a start but, with so much ranged against it, there is a vast chasm to cross before it fledges chicks in a few months' time.

I am on a disused railway line† a day or two south of the start of the Pennine Way, and the signs of spring are in evidence everywhere. A lapwing rises up and down in a neighbouring field, calling as it goes; a red-tailed bumblebee queen hurtles down the breeze in search of a nest along the line of a dry-stone wall. Tiny buds of green break out on the hawthorn, while the blackthorn – that latecomer to the party – is still swathed in white blossom.

It has been a dry, warm spring so far, with rivers running gently and reservoirs half-empty. It is so warm that I have taken to breaking trail at lunchtime and finding a wood edge to hide in, or a hedgerow to slink behind, and giving myself ten minutes of half-sleep among the

* The charity Curlew Action, established to do more than mere words to give these birds a fighting chance.

† The Tissington Trail, a thirteen-mile cycle track on a disused railway line that manages to deliver the holy trinity of the end-to-end walker's needs: flat, pretty and just about due north.

nettles and ground elder. On the curlew day, I dream through the red brightness of the sun shadows in my closed eyes that I am being stared at from close at hand by a roe buck, but when I slowly open my eyes and turn my head, there is nothing.

When I turn on the radio that evening, there is a rumour of snow and sleet coming in from the north. To my surprise, this rather excites me.

Sometimes, adventures need snow.

6. A HUMAN SUNDIAL

Tissington to Middleton-in-Teesdale:
124 miles; eight days
(PRINCIPAL HABITAT: MILLSTONE GRIT AND LIMESTONE PAVEMENT)

'Never fear to deliberately walk through dark places, for that is how you reach the light on the other side.'
VERNON HOWARD,
AMERICAN SPIRITUAL TEACHER

I have been here before.

One of the features of my journey is the series of tiny memory pulses that come into play when my route crosses over a road, or through a town, where I have passed through in a previous life. Most often I only sense them in retrospect, and I have to look at the map to check whether I am right. But I have been here before for sure, and last time round it was not good.

Two days after that first curlew outside Pomeroy, I am on Jacob's Ladder, the long haul up from Edale onto Kinder Scout at the start of the Pennine Way. It is here that the unsubtle change from the white limestone of the last few days into the black millstone grit of the High Peak serves as some sort of metaphor for the general toughening up of the whole trip. From here on, my road is generally closer to the sky and further from a flat white than it was in the honeyed villages further south. Sweat is pouring off me in the sunshine under the weight of my pack, as it had been 46 years earlier, during that drought summer of 1976 when I set out to walk the Pennine Way with two school friends.

Back then, I only made it through the first few days, diplomatically twisting my ankle somewhere near Hebden Bridge. In reality, I suspect I was simply not up to it. Under a vast, metal-framed pack, cursing my way up Kinder in useless boots that contained fragile feet, back then I probably wouldn't have noticed the little dipper in the stream, the drumming of the woodpecker in a nearby tree, the first 'go-back' calls of the red grouse or the mountain hare in half winter livery. I liked nature, but not if the act of finding it required any effort. The long-distance path's guidebook warns how hard the first day is, and in consequence how many walkers give up by the time they get to the A57 only a handful of miles in. These days, a combination of the lower expectations I have of myself and rather more inner toughness will keep me going, although it is a sobering thought that I am still only ever one slip, one turned ankle away from a repeat of that one-way train journey home. From now on, the background fear of failure will serve as a useful line manager in my head across every mile I walk.

Up on the hill, spring is quickening her pace and making her presence felt. There is frogspawn in the peat ponds, skylarks screaming out their floating, aerial territories above, and grouse, golden plover and oystercatchers pairing up all over the middle distance. If you came in from a distant country, you could immediately tell it was spring by the sheer level of noise and by the fact that everything alive seems to be going two-by-two. We see this progression every year and yet every year it seems to catch us unawares, like a British train that is actually on time, or a recipe that looks on the plate like it did in the book. 'It is spring again; the earth is like a child that knows poems by heart.'*

The going is good up high, far better than it had been all those years before. What had then been an untrustworthy path that zig-zagged anonymously through the damp base of the peat bogs and brackish ponds, has evolved into what is in effect a walker's motorway. How often, in the next 150 miles, will I have cause to bless those lifters of slabs, layers of planks and builders of boardwalks, as I move easily across open bog with dry feet and maintained morale?

'Takes all the challenge out of it,' grumbles one grizzled local walker in a bobble hat somewhere up by the Kinder trig point, fuelled by an apparent resentment against all things that make life a tiny bit less daunting. 'Makes it too bloody easy for people, who then come up here in their droves.' I think of asking him where the problem lies with that, but reckon I know already what his reply will be.

---

* Austrian poet Rainer Maria Rilke (1875–1926).

And there are more people around me now (50% of the English population live within two hours of here), and I often find that I want to chat with the 'end-to-enders' when I come across them. You can usually tell the long-distance Pennine walkers from the trig point-baggers and day trippers at a glance, by their unfeasibly big packs and their unreasonably clean kit. Decanted by train into Edale the previous day, they are still bubbling with the childlike enthusiasm that comes from the discovery that the shackles of routine have been broken, while still being unaware of what it may all do to their bodies. We all have our stories. Stories of sabbaticals and searches, books and bereavement, divorce and discovery; of new romance or old chemotherapy survival, or maybe just gifting ourselves that one last adventure before old age closes off the opportunity for ever. It is surprising just how many of them are walking requiems for a lost parent.

'It might have got him,' says one woman to me, gently patting the left side of her chest. 'But it's not bloody well going to get me.'

Up in these parts, the accepted wording as we pass each other is 'You alright?', muttered quietly with a brief eye contact, at once a greeting, a question and a civic duty. Even if only subconsciously, we are actually checking to see if other solo walkers are OK, and in control.

On Wessenden Head, an elderly couple I fall into conversation with ask me what I do for a living.

'Oh, how exciting!' laughs the woman, when I say that I am a nature writer. 'Have I heard of you?'

Unlikely, but it's nice to have it at least laid out as a remote possibility.

'Are you Robert Macfarlane?' asks the man, and I tell him 'No.'

'Then she won't have,' he says, in flat Huddersfield tones, and with an almost apologetic expression on his face.

I half wait for her to ask me my name just in case, but she has established that it is not Macfarlane, and has already mentally moved on. My not being him was all that mattered.

In the background, the smaller of her dogs is trying to hump the larger one, a feat of gymnastic endeavour that both she and the other dog are at great pains to ignore, but which her husband and I steal a quiet wink over.

At times the path acts as an information highway as in medieval times, and I sometimes find that news of my 'end to end' walk has filtered up or down the line. At the bottom of Black Hill, a young fell runner and his high-energy dog easily catch up with me in the noonday silence of the winding valley.

'You the bloke going to Cape Wrath?' he asks, and then says 'Magic' when I confirm it. 'Bloody magic.' How he knew about my journey, I still have no idea.

For a moment, I am almost suspicious when he offers to carry my pack up the long hill for me, as if he will somehow run off into the distance with it, but then I shake it off my back with alacrity and hand it to him before he can change his mind. The absence of its weight from my body feels both glorious and also a tiny bit wrong, as if by mitigating the effort, I am somehow cheating the prescribed hardship of the walk. My sherpa is called Owen, a quantity surveyor from Oldham, and I gladly tell him that there is no finer feeling on a long walk than that of following your own heavy pack up a steep hill. I volunteer a sandwich to him by way of thanks when we get to the trig point at the top, but his own packed lunch is of an altogether higher standard, and he gives me a little bag of peanuts for the road instead.

'Safe trip,' he says, as he starts the long run back to his car at Torside and I head north towards the reservoirs, and Diggle beyond. 'Let me know if you get there.'

When I turn around a minute or so later, he has been reabsorbed into the hidden folds and contours of Black Hill, and I am alone again. We were friendly ships passing in the night.

*

'There are three communities in this bird conservation game,' says Mark Cocker as we bounce towards Bolsover in his car the next morning. 'First, there are the activists and environmentalists; then the birders, who see it all as some instrument of spiritual and psychological fulfilment, and finally the recorders. No one gives a second thought to the recorders; there are no MBEs for them, and yet they are the bedrock of our knowledge, and the work that is then done with it.' I have been enjoying Mark's words for over two decades now, and have a quiet thrill hearing them straight from his mouth.

I have taken a day off walking, and Mark is driving me over to Carr Vale, a 12-hectare nature reserve built on the waste of an old colliery tip outside the town in another glorious example of what can be done with a landscape when humans have extracted all the profit they can from it. We have come to see an old friend of his, Mark Beevers, who has spent the last 22 years, almost to the day, faithfully recording the birds he sees in front of one particular hide at roughly the same time of every day. He has recorded 226 species, of which 70 or so have bred here, and his meticulous 90-page annual reports are most often banged out on a laptop in his car in the middle of the night, while he waits for the out-of-hours doctors for whom it is his paid work to be a driver.

'The best conditions for what I do,' he says, unscrewing the lid of an old and battered flask of tea once we are in the hide, 'is eight-eights cloud, a north-east wind and slight drizzle. If I get that, I know I'm going to have a good day.' Today is sunny, still and dry, but we plough on regardless. He has the robust confidence of the career policeman he once was, and talks quietly of the battles he has faced to get investment for the reserve, to build ponds and scrapes, and generally develop what has now become one of the very best places in Derbyshire to watch birds. Conservation work shouldn't be an uphill struggle against the system, often pitching fieldworkers against academics, but my experience so far indicates that it too often is. He says he doesn't suffer fools gladly, but then, in a world already overflowing with them, who would?

I am in awe of their fieldcraft, honed as teenagers in the 1970s by their maths teacher at Buxton College Grammar School, Jim Lidgate, who had died only the week before. When I check his funeral notices page a few hours later, it is full of expressions of gratitude for the changes that were wrought, and the eyes that were opened, under his gentle guidance, and I remember that most naturalists have a Jim Lidgate somewhere in their past. Mine was my grandmother, and I displayed my thanks by helping myself to her revolting Turkish cigarettes when she wasn't looking. The two Marks call out birds to each other almost casually. 'Willow tit,' says one. 'Reed bunting behind you,' replies the other. 'Chiffchaff at the bottom of that bush.' And on it goes.

'I send it all to the Derbyshire Wildlife Trust,' Mark Beevers says, when I ask him what happens with all the information. 'God knows if they actually read it, but it then becomes part of the vast, national database of what is happening to our birds, whether the news is good or bad.'

Back in my bed-and-breakfast that night, I do the maths. Mark Beevers has spent around 30,000 hours of his life collecting, collating and submitting this information, in every weather and always for free. With colleagues covering when he is away, they have not missed a session, even through lockdowns, for over 8,000 days.

As for me, I will never look at nature population statistics in the same way again. Possibly you shouldn't, either.

*

At the White Holme Reservoir to the north-west of Rochdale, something strange suddenly strikes me.

I have been walking north through the hot, sunny spring for weeks now, and my shadow has become my friend. That in itself is not unusual: shadows have always befriended their lone walkers, but there is something more sophisticated going on.

In the mornings, he slants long and low to the west, my left, as the sun makes its way up from the eastern horizon. Out of the corner of my eye, I watch him raise the binoculars to his eyes when he sees that first twite of his journey, his decade in fact.

By lunchtime, he is low and squat out there in front of me, almost getting in the way of my feet as I walk the dusty, flat trail around the reservoir system. He calls for a stop, and I see him shake the pack off his back and rifle around for a cheese sandwich from the top compartment.

But by late afternoon, he is thrown far out to the east, as the sun starts to set over Blackburn, his long strides looking weary on the ground when he starts to call me in for the evening. Hebden Bridge is still a long two miles away, but Caroline will be meeting us at the railway station, and he hurries me on so that I can get there before she does.

I haven't worn a watch for the best part of 30 years, but suddenly I can tell the time to the nearest half hour simply from the position of my shadow. I know from the map when I am heading due north, and the shadow that gets thrown becomes a timepiece that is perfectly reliable enough for my unfussy purposes.

A little dividend of my aloneness is that I have become a human sundial.

*

A few days later, at the top of the long pull up to Malham Cove, a cow on the path ahead suggests to me that I might have arrived at my next appointment.

The cow is one of a picturesque group under the current watchful gaze of a farmer I correctly guess to be Neil Heseltine. He confirms this is the case when I ask, and then mentions that there were probably easier ways of getting up that hill than on foot and under 15 kilos of baggage, like in his pick-up. For a farmer who is 150 miles from the breed's native home, Neil Heseltine runs one of the largest herds of Galloway cattle in the country. Black, white, belted and even little Riggits,* his cows roam easily over the thin pickings available from the rocky North Yorkshire grazing on offer. They didn't always. They may be picture-postcard pretty, but these cows are also some of the greatest examples of biodiversity engineers that I will meet on my journey. In a country that had already lost just about all of its wild megafauna a millennium before Julius Caesar cast envious eyes on its shores, this is no small thing.

'We've been here for four generations,' he explains, as we stare across the eye-wateringly beautiful limestone upland around us, 'and we've always been sheep

* The Riggit is an 'archaic strain' of the Galloway cow, identifiable by the white stripe running down the spine. (www.riggitgallowaycattle-society.co.uk)

farmers. That's what is in our blood. It's hard to explain the way of life, the lambing, the shows and all, that goes with the sheep. In common with lots of farmers, we started to realise that we had been over-grazing the land, because that was the only way we could see to turn a profit on our main business.'

The defining moment was in 2012.

'Nature was gradually becoming a bigger part of what we did, and with the whole farm in HLS,* it had to. Then one day, I did the maths. My sheep made me most of my money, all right, but that was because I had so many of them; the margins were so bad that I could calculate that it worked out at about 15 pence of pay for me for each of the 70 hours I was working every week. The cattle on the other hand made a decent percentage margin so, theoretically, I just needed more of them, and less sheep.'

'How so?'

'Less work. Less medication. Less problems. There is a natural stocking rate for everything and, if you do things less intensively, you will have less problems.'

Just as you cannot separate biodiversity loss from farming, not least because farming takes up over 70% of our land, so you cannot ignore the cost to biodiversity that has arisen from the fact that Farming UK PLC has been unprofitable for decades, something that Neil is not alone in highlighting to me. That unprofitability

* Higher Level Stewardship scheme, with larger grants awarded for land management that beneficially impacts nature.

has led to half a century of sidelining of nature brought about by over-exploitation, short cuts and a chemical assault on the land and its animals, which is only now beginning to be addressed. After all, the cheap food that we have become used to appears not once but twice on nature's balance sheet, the second time as less wildlife, expensive subsidies, pollution clean-ups, and the very real medical costs of our expanding waistlines.

'I see things quite simply,' Neil goes on. 'Any solution had simply to be good for the area, good for the farm, and good for my family. I could see that beef could be the answer to the four abiding questions: climate change, nature, biodiversity and profitability.'

'Climate change?' I ask.

'Absolutely. They're outside all year, fed only on what grows under their feet. The methane goes back into the carbon dioxide which goes back into the ground and is stored.' All the time, a three-quarter-ton ground-aerating machine with sharp hooves, constantly dispensing two types of organic manure, is wandering across the hillside bringing life to the land. He adds that, in a mild winter, his Galloways can make their thrifty living on the hill all year round, with no extra feed, which has its own upstream benefits in less fossil fuel usage in transporting fodder to them. 'March is the hungry month,' he adds, 'so we always keep enough hay to see us through an emergency.'

Sometimes, he will shut off part of a field in May and leave it undisturbed until August.

'It's sort of agri-wilding,' he offers, when I ask him if what he is doing has a name. In an age when there is so much talk of 'rewilding' and 'regenerative farming', especially by people who do not understand what either mean, I like that. It brings together those two vital elements of a good farmer's work: producing high-quality food, and being a good steward of the land.

I ask him what the effect of the change of all this has been, a decade later.

'My 70 hours a week has become 40,' he laughs, pointing out that the hours saved have been taken up in other things long ago, such as chairing the North York Moors National Park board. 'The farm is profitable. But it is the biodiversity gains that have amazed us the most.' He talks of quick wins, out there on the steep fells, of harebells and yarrow, moths and butterflies. Up on the huge field we are looking at, he has seen a return of skylarks, redshank, lapwing and snipe.

'We get more wheatear than we ever did, more woodcock and more barn owls, as soon as we put some boxes up.'

I ask him about curlews, just as I have asked everyone else about them. 'Loads,' he says. 'Breeding again all over the high ground.' We watch one, seeming to hang off its own high wings on the wind, like a paraglider, and the two of us don't need to say anything to know that she is, and always has been, the currency of our respective journeys. It turns out that Neil and, especially, his wife, Leigh, are driven by the love of the curlew almost as much as anything else.

Then he remembers something else. 'Bluebells,' he says, breaking in to a broad smile. 'We suddenly got bluebells right out on this piece of open bank. Right where they shouldn't have been. No trees, no shade, just a mass of English bluebells that had been lurking in the seed bank, and must been released by the grazing pressure from the new cows.'

I love that, and tell him so. So often, we agree, you can have all the science and planning in the world, and then just end up with the surprise and delight of one of nature's conjuring tricks.

He looks at a group of walkers struggling up the hill towards us.

'It might surprise you that I feel honoured to have visitors on my land. I get support for running it, and it is my privilege and pride to share it with the people who want to pass through.'

I am reminded that one of those people is me, and I have fifteen miles to cover if I am to make it to Horton-in-Ribblesdale by nightfall. After shaking hands and moving on for about a quarter of a mile, I stop to turn around and look back, wondering for an instant what the support schemes that follow Brexit will bring the way of farmers like Neil.

'Britain doesn't need farmers', said one senior treasury advisor[1] in his weird submission to the 2021 National Food Strategy, because the food sector 'isn't critically important to the UK.'

God help us.

*

Four hours later, the threatened snow finally arrives. It starts by leaking in faint geometric shapes out of the suffocating greyness above, down onto the edges of Pen-y-Ghent, slowly at first like a distant memory of Christmas. Then it comes in large flakes that melt on my nose, an elemental feeling that makes me strangely happy.

I am both excited and concerned by this change. By the next morning, when I set out from Horton-in-Ribblesdale, there is a heavy fall, and I conduct a hurried internal debate about the wisdom or otherwise of proceeding on a day like this. Most of the ground that I will cross is high, but I come to the conclusion that I am well equipped and it is never dangerously steep, and I press on towards Hawes. Privately, I am rather pleased that this decision reflects the increasing confidence that I am feeling about the walk, and all that it might throw at me from time to time.* Anyway, I don't exactly have a Plan B if I stay where I am, except to join the sad-looking mongrel down the road, waiting for his owner to come out of the house, and disconsolately lifting his leg against a snowy car tyre. Apart from anything, I am getting quite cold conducting my little internal debate outside the famous but determinedly shut Pen-y-Ghent Café. (The further I head north, the more I come to realise that most of the iconic Pennine Way stop-overs are either closed or disappointing, while the unsung ones on the edges tend to be lovely.)

* The fact that I carried a large, orange survival bag in the depths of my pack throughout the journey was an insurance policy that was always directly influential in any boldness behind my decision-making.

Over the next two days, snow falls on me intermittently, but I am comfortable as I press on over the high ground either side of Hawes. High up one lunchtime, I huddle from the blizzard in the shelter of a dry-stone wall, eating my cheese and chutney sandwich and idly wondering how tricky the next five or six miles are going to be. My health, both mental and physical, is better than it has any right to be, and I have food, water and sufficient kit in my pack to bail me out if things get really bad. People in their sixties tend to lurch between the states of being walking wounded or worried well, but up here I find I am mining an old seam of energy and enthusiasm within myself that has lain untapped for a decade or more.

I am averaging about twenty miles a day, other than over the worst ground, but generally covering it in seven hours, rather than eight, thus giving myself more time to recover each evening. Above all, I am starting to develop an appreciation of the incredible simplicity of what I am doing, which is fundamentally no more than putting one blister-free foot* in front of another a couple of million times in an unfolding landscape. My choices each morning are minimalist: 'Salt or sugar in my porridge?', 'Dirty shirt or very dirty shirt?', or 'Sandwich now or in half an hour?', and I seem to have given up all the elements of overthinking things that mark my normal life. Instead,

* 'Runners Rub' is the trick. The name may be awkward in polite company but, after coating my feet in it each morning before putting socks on, I never so much as developed a single blister the entire trip.

I set up simple little rules, like tick inspections on my lower body every evening, and never looking at the weather forecast more than 24 hours ahead. After all, it's not as if I can do anything about it, or avoid it. Only once, and then by mistake, do I look at a map of Great Britain, and see at a glance how little of the distance I have done, and how much there is left to do.

A layer of snow has built up on my mustard yellow Patagonia jacket when I get the sense that I am being watched, not by just one set of eyes, but from both sides. The eyes to the right of me belong to an old Swaledale ewe with whom I am sharing my wall, and she just looks bored, as if my arrival there is a potential disturbance to her otherwise peaceful afternoon; the eyes to the left of me belong, it turns out, to a local gamekeeper or farmer, and they are full of concern.

'Are you alright there, mate?' he asks, when I look up at him.

'I think so,' I reply cheerfully, understanding that I must look like the hiker's equivalent of a train crash, an old man sitting against a wall in a blizzard.

'It's just that you were looking a bit unresponsive.' This is not remotely surprising. I have been socially unresponsive for most of the last month, but I thank him, and tell him so. He says that when he first saw me, he had a passing feeling that I might actually be dead, another baleful statistic in the list of idiots who went beyond themselves out into the worst of the weather. 'But then I saw the sandwich moving towards your mouth, and I realised you weren't.'

'I've got the jeep just round the corner,' he adds, after we have chatted for a while. 'Hop in. I'll run you down to Hawes.'

I explain that I am walking every inch of the way and that, however tempting the offer of a ride, I can't bring myself to accept it.

'Mad,' he says cheerfully, but in a voice that tells me he understands, approves even, knowing that it takes a lot of effort to break away from what is safe and sensible. And with a quick 'You take care', he disappears, yeti-like and seemingly in slow motion, into the storm.

I have survived the first temptation.

Whenever the snow stops, I take photographs of the beauty around me, taking care to keep my phone dry. For all the harking back to the good old pre-mobile days that my generation continually bangs on about, that phone is little short of a miracle to me on my walk. It is at once communication device, log book, camera, album, diary, recorder, notebook, alarm clock, torch, calculator, navigational aid, plant identifier, card holder, step counter, games console, information kiosk, payment system and provider of music, all in the size of a playing card, and at a shade over 250 grams. I treat it with the same reverence as my merino socks and the Evelyn Waugh trilogy somewhere in my pack, and cannot help but think that the species who had the ingenuity to come up with it might one day also just about manage to learn to look after its wildlife and leave less litter by the roadside.

And rising above all that litter, above the discarded Red Bull cans, plastic cups, grey boxer shorts and fast food boxes, spring's rolling progress is greening up the hedgerows around me, even if the oak trees are still determinedly stuck in winter mode. The soundtrack changes from larks to lambs and back again, depending on whether I am up high or down low. In a field south of Keld, I see rabbits, currently a rarity where I come from, and the first redshanks of the season, noisy medium-sized waders whose numbers have recently plummeted through the draining, seeding and fertilising of their usual breeding habitat. Their plight, and the possible routes out of it, are yet another example of the nuanced ongoing debate that needs to be held between conservationists, policy-makers and farmers; it's all very well for observers like me to talk about the need for clever interventions like varied sward height, late silage cuts and drain blocking, but I have no financial skin in the game. Redshank land is typically hard land, surrendering only a meagre living in return for a lot of back-breaking effort, and the farmer has a right to have his or her voice heard as well. Walking alone gives me a chance to think about these issues beyond mere headlines, and to just start to imagine what our countryside would be like if we routinely allowed efficient food production to sit alongside vibrant corridors of nature, instead of little islands of both.

*

The onrush of spring is accelerating every day.

A couple of days later, I see from my phone messages that the first BTO-tagged cuckoo of the year, Ellis, has finally made it across the Sahara Desert and is bearing down on a country that will obsess, as it always does, over the precise timing of his arrival.* Nothing, not even the bubbling curlew, says the word 'spring' to us more enticingly than that bird, not least because it is a staggering and hazardous journey that Ellis is undertaking each year. It seems incredible that most of the males will be away again to the south within 60 days of their arrival on these shores, but then that is the benefit of letting someone else bring up your children.

Around me, the snow abates and vanishes from the hills like an eiderdown sliding off a bed, and almost overnight I am in the heart of grouse country. On Gunnerside Moor, known in shooting circles as the holy grail of grouse moors, there is enough warmth back in the air for me to sit on the grass eating my morning Mars Bar, and for the first time fully take in the orchestra of birdsong around me. It starts with a plaintive, wavering note from a lone curlew, until that is joined in turn by the short, almost questioning, intervention of a golden plover. From there, layer upon layer of musicians come in: the flute of the oystercatchers, the urgent bicker of the redshank, the invisible trill of the skylarks somewhere above me and, punctuating it all, the honking bass of the descending greylags. I am old enough for

* The British Trust for Ornithology (BTO) has been ringing and tagging cuckoos since 2011, to try to better understand why the UK population has declined so far and so fast. Enthusiasts can and should follow their progress on www.bto.org

this probably to have been a standard concerto from my childhood, often heard and little noticed; but now, apart from managed uplands like this, it is one that the last three generations have been quietly wrenching away from the ears of their children.

Not far off a million acres of Britain's national parks* are given over to grouse moors like this one, and, until I reach Scotland at any rate, it will be the most divisive of all conservation issues that I meet. On the one hand, the owners will point to the rich populations of waders benefiting from the habitat management, wildfire prevention benefits, the ongoing peatland restoration projects, the tree planting on the moorland fringes, and the jobs created within these fragile communities.† Ranged against them are criticisms of the emissions resulting from routine heather burning, damage to the peat, flooding down below and a general sense of natural succession being interfered with, and other species thus ignored. Nowhere is the argument more emotional, however, than in the issue of predator control, both legal (e.g. foxes, stoats and crows) and illegal (in the always unacceptable form of persecution of inconvenient raptors).

For my own part, I cannot conveniently un-see and un-hear the natural bounty I have seen and heard on Gunnerside Moor, but I am also far from being a

---

* 852,000 acres of our national parks are managed as grouse moors. (*Guardian* article, August 5th, 2021)

† 2,500 jobs, according to the British Association of Shooting and Conservation.

good enough botanist to understand the true costs of single-species management. Nor can I possibly downplay the reality of the killing of birds of prey, particularly the hen harrier, that takes place on more than a small minority of moors. From maybe 30 conversations that I will eventually have with people on all sides of the debate, I suspect that driven grouse shooting,* at least in its current form, has a limited future and that, whatever your views may be on the conservation, ethics and privilege of it all, it will have been lost to those who treasure it, and depend on it, largely by the continuous and illegal actions of a small group of their own people, and the people who direct them. The people who will be damaged are generally the lower-paid ones whose living, and culture, depends on it. Equally, if someone were to suggest tomorrow that we suddenly changed our upland land management system to simply deliver large numbers of one species for the exclusive enjoyment of a tiny number of wealthy landowners, there would not be a cat in hell's chance that we would adopt it.

It would need a book in itself to do full justice to this debate, but again, the saddest thing is that the noise on the extremes of the fight drowns out the fact that most people involved on both sides are genuinely seeking to promote biodiversity, even if in very different ways, and for rather different reasons.

---

* As opposed to shooting grouse over dogs, which involves far lower bags of game and therefore rather less intensive habitat management.

'Anyone who has a grievance against someone like me,' sighed an old keeper I spent an evening with a little further north, 'just goes round the place quietly making assertions and spreading rumours. We should all be on the same side. We might not agree on everything, but anyone interested in getting nature back in this country should be pulling the boat in the same direction.'

I ask him about the other side of the coin, the small but well documented group of 'ultra' keepers who shoot raptors, disrupt activists' meetings, interrupt forums, burn cars and daub threatening messages on the gates of key campaigners. He recognises and acknowledges it as the unacceptable outlier of a threatened community, but how and why some parts of British conservation have reached this situation of eternal conflict is beyond both of us.

In the half light of daybreak, he takes me on his rounds.

'Half my burning now needs to be licensed each year by Natural England. Their local man told me that he had never seen greater biodiversity on his patch than we have here, but that it's more than his boss's life is worth to take the professional risk of letting me burn more. They bang on about burning restricting successional regeneration,' he says. 'But what else is supposed to grow up here apart from heather and sphagnum moss?' ('Trees of all sorts, along with juniper bushes and native wildflowers', said a distinguished professor when I asked him the same question a few days later.)

A lone black grouse, the first of my walk, flies away from us into the low cloud. Somewhere below us, a curlew bubbles out its morning song.

'Each morning, those curlews tell me what is going on on my moor. From the different calls, I will know who or what is about, and what has been happening over the last few hours.'

When we get back to his house for breakfast, he brings out an old box of newspaper clippings that he has cut out over the years, every one of them about wildfires, and hands me an article about a fire on Saddleworth Moor from the previous week's *Manchester Evening News*.

'Whatever your position on shooting or heather burning,' he says, 'there will be more wildfires on our land when we are gone. And the harder and longer they burn, the more they will really damage the peat below.'

A golden lizard scuttles across the path ahead of me as I continue on my way, and the great forests of the north country beckon.

7. A SITKA SILENCE

Horton-in-Ribblesdale to the Scottish border:
98 miles; six days
(PRINCIPAL HABITAT: FORESTRY)

'If you judge a fish by its ability to climb a tree,
it will spend its whole life thinking it is stupid'
ALBERT EINSTEIN

'In many ways,' said Simon Armitage, as he made his way south down its route, 'the Pennine Way is a pointless exercise, leading from nowhere in particular to nowhere in particular, via no particular route, and for no particular reason.'

With similar sentiments, and bit by bit, the Pennine Way and I start to fall out of love.

Mirroring my first serious teenage relationship, there has initially been sufficient novelty and enough highs to keep us both interested, but then it slowly grows into an atmosphere of minor disagreements and harsh words. It all begins well enough down in the Peak District with bold landscapes and a strong northerly pull, but then, in Middleton-in-Teesdale, it turns a right-angle lurch to the west, with the sole apparent intention of making itself both longer and hillier. Further north, it suddenly develops a morbid fascination with bogs and marshes, together with another strange turn in the opposite direction, as if it can't quite decide how to stretch something that should be 200 miles into something 75 miles longer. It has possibly achieved the status of national treasure, I find myself thinking, more by reputation than experience.

Having said that, the people I meet on the Way and around it remain largely delightful. We give each other the time of day as we stare up at red kites, or down at rock patterns; we help each other take stuff out of awkward pockets in the back of our rucksacks as we pass and, in one instance, we laugh together at a lone left-foot size 11 hiking boot stuck high on the top of a footpath sign.

'We were wondering how on earth he got home,' giggles one of a pair of high-energy elderly ladies near High Force waterfall. 'So what we're going to do this afternoon is look out for a single right-footed boot print all the way home. That should keep us out of mischief.' And chuckling, they stride off towards Middleton.

It is with the hospitality trade that I still occasionally struggle.

'We're not doing coffee today,' says the man in a small-town coffee shop towards the border, clearly vying for the hotly contested title of worst hospitality venue in Europe. And then, as if it explains everything: 'We're cleaning the deep fat fryer.' The silent tables behind him stand testament to the years of effort he must have put into being unwelcoming and useless. Even the calendar on the wall is open at a page that became irrelevant over a year ago.

'But the sign on your door says that you are open. And I've made a two-mile detour to be here. And I don't need my coffee made in a deep fat fryer. So please can I have one?' I keep it jovial, as I foolishly think that I can win him over.

'No,' he says with a tiny hint of menace. 'You can have a banana, if you want.' He looks down at the little cabinet, where a middle-aged banana sits on a glass shelf in miserable solitude, chaperoned only by the crumbs of yesterday's baking.

On Hadrian's Wall, and having met just a handful of solitary walkers coming the other way in the last six days, the Pennine Way and I finally agree to a mutual separation; me towards the 'debatable lands'* to the west of Kielder Forest, and it to Kirk Yetholm. After all, I am an end-to-ender of the entire island, and the Pennine Way was only ever a lazy excuse not to have to think about navigation for a couple of weeks, and I can use it exactly as I wish. I never dreamed that at some point in my life I would use a 270-mile footpath as no more than a small navigational aid.

My final act on the Pennine Way is to fail to find the miniature bottle of whisky that my sister had hidden for me in a dry-stone wall where her Coast to Coast path

* Land to the north of Carlisle that has wound up the English and Scots since time immemorial.

crossed my own route at Greenhead. She texts me the What Three Words location of the bottle when she knows that I will be approaching the junction, but some lucky passer-by has got there first, and pocketed the Lagavulin.

I may already be at the top end of England, but slightly over half the miles on my journey will be Scottish ones, so there is much left to do. But any concerns I had about the wisdom of walking through the early part of a British spring have evaporated in the reality of a relatively dry and warm season, with the added benefits of a lack of biting insects, even if it often seems that no one has tapped the tourist trade on the shoulder and reminded it to throw open its doors to travellers like me. In the brave new world that tiptoes uneasily out of the shadows of Brexit and two years of Covid, hospitality businesses that are either temporarily closed or visibly understaffed vastly outweigh those that aren't. Anyway, by the end of my journey, I will only have used my full-on waterproof kit on two occasions, which amortises out at around £180 a time.*
Back home, they think I'm probably bravely struggling through the hardship, but inside my body and head, I am having the time of my life.

Also, as a southerner, I am properly in the north by now, and heading for the trees.

*

* Unlike my promotional £19 hiking trousers, which I wore just about every day, at around £0.30 a day.

The last time I was in Kielder Forest, I broke my nose walking into one of those trees while I was fast asleep.

Admittedly, this was all a very long time ago. Snow, sleeplessness and Jona Lewie's Christmas hit 'Stop the Cavalry' are the only remaining pillars of memory from that previous visit to England's largest forest, as a young platoon commander on a winter exercise in 1980. At one point, we marched heavy-laden throughout the wintry night to make contact with the 'Russian' enemy, and my accident managed at least to create huge amusement for my soldiers in the depths of the snowy darkness.

'Most dangerous thing on earth?' quipped one of them. 'An officer with a map.'

This time, I am here with John Miles, a Carlisle-based wildlife consultant and author, who wants to show me some trees. Lots of trees. In fact, the thick end of 150 million trees in 250 square miles of the largest man-made forest in the country. But he really wants to show me what he feels is the king-sized muddle that is the current British relationship with trees, and why it matters.

These days, 13% of our land area is wooded,[1] a very significant decline from perhaps five times that figure before Bronze Age man started clearing it with a lot more effective enthusiasm than we might give him credit for, but an increase from a low of around 5% by the end of the nineteenth century. The Forestry Commission was brought into being under the 1919 Forestry Act, with a remit to increase Britain's timber security by restoring its woods and forests. When successive post-war governments reacted to the continuing shortage by giving out those famous, or infamous, tax breaks to encourage planting, slow-growing native trees such as oak and ash were ignored in favour of a quick-growing, easily managed dark green shroud of Sitka spruce, wherein lies the muddle. Out of place, of limited outdoor construction use and biodiversity value, and half as effective at carbon sequestering as native deciduous trees, the Sitka is nonetheless the bedrock of a vital industry that now employs 40,000 people.*

A new phase of mass-planting has been instigated by our national effort to reduce our carbon emissions, or at least to make ourselves feel better about them. By being able to buy credits that make us, or our businesses, relax about a fossil fuel habit that we may have little actual intention of changing we have, in effect, reinvented the old system of papal indulgences, where our guilt is monetised for us by someone else. Companies with fleets of diesel trucks tell us in glossy brochures how good we can feel about buying from a business that is carbon neutral. You see, trees are simple and easy to count, which is why politicians love them. In the UK's 2019 election, the different political parties indulged in an arms race of eye-catching tree promises, 30 million from the Tories, 60 million from the Liberal Democrats and just the 2 billion from Labour,[2] none of whom, of course, had any detailed plans for actually making them

* Sitka is the UK's main conifer, and is used for construction timber, pallets, fencing and packaging.

happen, let alone doing them sensibly. Because politicians don't like to tell us inconvenient truths such as that we actually need to make do with less of everything, including less fossil fuel, they find it much easier to sugar-coat the problem in a haze of countable trees. One direct effect of this is to enable the rich, who already have the money available, to get even richer by using the grants and tax breaks available to buy up blocks of land that may already be doing useful things like mixed farming, and then swathe them and their communities in a green cloak.

And there is the muddle that John is trying to explain to me. With our quick-fix, quick-buck mentality to the fore, 40% of our new woodland is now non-native, and 51% coniferous, a figure out of all proportion to the rest of Europe, and terrible for biodiversity: 'Most of our birds do not need more trees. They need trees that they can understand.'[3] Unlike most other life forms, much of the tree's contribution to nature actually happens long after it has died, through providing accommodation for waves of invertebrates, food from the fungus that grows on it, and early protection for other trees that grow up through it. But the trees in forestry blocks never stay in the area for long enough to get the chance to rot and provide this service; once cut, they are almost immediately carted off to storage, or the sawmill. And, maybe because our distance from nature is now so wide that we shy away from culling and from eating wild food, we have four times the viable quantity of the wrong sort of animal (deer) preventing regeneration in our native woods, while depriving the beneficial grazers like our old biodiversity friend, the cow, of what a native wood could provide. What people like John think we should be planting is copses and corridors of native species, loads of them, randomly, and all over the place, but it will take me another 300 miles to find any evidence of this actually happening. Another approach that is slowly gaining traction is agroforestry, in which agricultural crops and livestock combine directly with trees and shrubs. This is clever on multiple levels, not least in that it uses the land both horizontally and vertically, helps biological protection of plants, works to regenerate the ground below, and tends to ease the way for quicker and healthier growth all round.

Meanwhile, the Forestry Commission pilot paper promoting the new scheme of Forestry Investment Zones (FIZ)[4] is long on 'strategic pre-scoping', 'up-front mapping' and 'updated datasets', but less so on how the overall local biodiversity will actually benefit. By its own admission, it is clear that 'productive forestry is the core driver', but a sceptic reading between the lines might easily reach the conclusion that it is no more than a scheme to replace thousands of hectares of marginal farmland with financially attractive Sitka plantations. Meanwhile, the many incremental new blocks of forestry likely under the FIZ scheme will be even worse for waders than first thought, worse even than the existing big blocks; it turns out that each forest (meaning not just the huge ones) throws out an additional 200- to 300-metre cordon of surrounding ground where waders still avoid nesting, which removes even more of their appropriate ground.[5]

'Someone needs to think this all through again,' says John. We agree that this is not what John Fowles had in mind when he wrote: 'Slinking into trees was always slinking into heaven.' There is nothing heavenly about slinking into a dark Sitka monocrop.

For three days on and off, I will walk through this tall green darkness of tangled roots and stumps, a monochrome world where huge timber trucks trundle down the forest trails, and £250,000 harvester machines take trees from standing to stripped and logged in 40 seconds. There is other wildlife here than just the ever-present corvids, of course there is (famously, there are now about eight pairs of Kielder ospreys, and I thrill once to the sinister flash of a goshawk on the forest edge), but it is wildlife that seems utterly divorced from its nature, and there has been a vanishing of much of it, especially the songbirds and waders. (By the way, it could also be one of the favoured introduction sites for that great ecosystem engineer, the lynx, if we ever became bold enough to take that step, who would then go on to help control both deer and fox numbers, with all the consequent downstream benefits of that.) When I mention the forest's lack of natural variety on social media, I instigate a Twitter-storm of indignation from the forestry community who tell me that I must be blind, stupid or both, and that I don't know what I am talking about.

They may be partly right, but I cannot make myself see or hear what is not there, or does not reveal itself.

Compared to where I have been, and where I will go, this is like a sterile world. John thinks that there needs to be a strategic approach to tree-planting, one that is driven by ecological realities and takes everything into account, and not just the knee-jerk, numbers-at-all-costs, financially incentivised one that is centre-stage right now.

As I will find out later on with the beaver, and with other things besides, the right tree in the right place, planted in the right configurations and maintained in the right way is an almost unbridled good; the wrong tree is the wrong place just isn't.

*

As I approach the border, I have become obsessed with food, a modern-day hunter-gatherer plundering the fridges and larders of where I stay, then heading for the privacy of the hills to eat it.

In sharp contrast to the research I put into the matter of kit, the research I have done into specialist food turns out to be next to meaningless in the day-to-day realities of the walk: slow-release food at breakfast, nibbles at lunch and anything I can lay my hands on at dinner. Fundamentally, I eat what I want to, and lots of it, in an unusual battle to try to prevent the loss of any more than the 10 kilos that have gone already. Cereal bars and protein shakes, like walking poles, are just things that happen to other people, and are consigned to history.

The fulcrum of it all is porridge, my slow-release breakfast of choice. In consequence, I find I eat porridge in just about every house I stay in, and in a bewildering array of presentations: with cream, milk, water, salt or sugar; porridge with Highland honey or lowland strawberries, with marmalade, compote or bananas; porridge with raw ginger or cooked rhubarb, pistachio nuts or raisins; vegan porridge with coconut nectar sugar or carnivore porridge with crispy bacon festooned all around the saucer below it. I even once have porridge with a dram of whisky, and another time with a little splash of Drambuie. If an army marches on its stomach, I am personally marching on last season's oat crop. If I never see another bowl of porridge in my life, it will be far too soon.

Porridge aside, breakfast is the high point of my day. Adventure beckons, and there is an urgency to conversations, driven by a tiny uncertainty as to whether we will ever meet again, or at least any time soon. From the hazards of setting a Tully rodent trap to the skills of tuning a violin for a specific concert, and from the tally of live lambs delivered overnight to a tutorial on how to use a tennis ball to unstiffen my back, conversations rove to the limits of my imagination. One morning in Hawes, I am challenged at seven in the morning by the resident ten-year-old to a series of viciously competitive games of bagatelle on the basis that my victory the previous night had neither been fair nor final; a few days later, I am helping another child write deeply improper words on the fridge of a bed-and-breakfast, with magnetic letters.

'You don't spell it like that,' she says. 'It's got an "H" in it. Surely you know that at your age.'

Then there is lunch, which I have frequently been advised needs to be substantial and processed so as to power me through the waning of my strength in the late afternoons. This, it turns out, is wrong, or at least it is wrong for me. Lunch actually evolves into no more than a couple of small cheese and pickle sandwiches, a banana and a Mars Bar,* spread over a couple of pleasurable hours. One host goes so far as to give me a whole cucumber, saying that it would keep me amused, fed and hydrated for ages; in the event, it is all a bit embarrassing, and I dispose of it responsibly by the side of a canal. Another enigmatically hands me a grapefruit, on the off-chance that I would find it useful, which I don't, and I quietly leave it in the following night's fruit bowl while no one is looking. Grapefruits, in my experience, are rarely useful, especially if you are not carrying a knife. They are, as Oscar Wilde pointed out, simply lemons that 'saw an opportunity and took advantage of it.'

Dinner, which normally follows a snack at teatime, always consists of huge quantities of whatever my host has prepared, or the local pub is offering, invariably followed by seconds and occasionally thirds.

Nonetheless, with all this food I continue to put in fewer calories than the 2,000 or so that I am using up on my twenty-mile stages, but I feel fit and well as I manage

* 97 Mars Bars, 116 bananas, 72 apples and eight packets of digestive biscuits went into the making of this book, not to mention those 68 flat whites.

to shed in two months the weight it took me 30 years to gain. Caroline is at once impressed and amazed.

'Bloody hell,' she exclaims, as she climbs out of a car at the roadside a couple of weeks later in Tayside, having not seen me for a month. 'Where's the rest of you gone?'

*

It is an explosion of red grouse from almost underneath my feet that alerts me to the fact of my arrival at the summit of Peel Fell, a border hill on the edge of England's largest forest. Before that, I have just been staring at the ground through the sweat streaming down my face, the echo of my heartbeat pulsing through my ears.

By and large, I have been trying to avoid anything with a name that suggests high altitude on my journey, especially something where the route to the top consists of clambering steeply upwards over the stumps of clear-felled forestry, but I have an appointment to keep, so I need to go on.

Rachel Coyle, the Peatland ACTION project officer for the Tweed Forum,* is 34 and looks rather more relaxed than anyone has a right to, having scrambled up that 600-metre bank. A graduate of Animal Biology from Edinburgh, she leads on the Forum's peat restoration work.

* Founded in 1991, the Tweed Forum works to 'promote the sustainable use of the whole Tweed catchment through holistic and integrated management and planning.' They have now become a leader in the field of integrated land and water management, and are extremely helpful to wandering writers.

'So why does it need restoring?' I ask after we have introduced ourselves, hoping to have given her a good, meaty subject to dwell on while I get my breath back. I have walked well over a hundred miles on peat recently, so I am familiar with the landscape, if not the breadth of issues.

'It's basically to do with drying out peat that needs to remain wet. That's the thing about peat, its natural state is to be saturated.'

We stare in silence at the flat landscape of quietness and mystery, stretching away into the mist.

'Years of over-burning the heather for regeneration when this was a grouse moor, followed by decades of over-grazing by sheep, led to the disappearance of the keystone vegetation, sphagnum moss, and then the consequent not-so gradual erosion by wind and rain of the flat peat surface into hags* and eventually gulleys. Those gulleys allow the water to pour off the fell before its time, and basically, the water that should be stored in the peat runs off down the hill, and the lack of it dries the peat out. In good weather, that means brown bath water in the houses down below and carbon released back into the atmosphere up above; but after heavy rain, it also means bad flooding in Newcastleton. It doesn't look a very fragile habitat up here, but it absolutely is.' I know what she means: the bed-and-breakfast I stayed

* A peat hag is a bare face of vertical peat, often overhanging, caused by water and livestock erosion, and a sure sign that it is in trouble.

in the night before had recently been flooded again for the first time in 50 years. When the owner talked about the memory of it, it was towards these cloudy hills that he was looking.

The obvious corollary to the damaged peat is the loss of the biodiversity that, in better times at least, makes a habitat out of it. Declines are consistent across the classification groups, whether it is toads, skylarks or mountain hares, but no species has declined more than the beleaguered curlew. The presence of nearby large-scale commercial forestry, which has removed breeding and foraging habitat, coupled with the loss of invertebrates through the drying out process, has been a disaster for them, and the hope, as it sadly has to be across much of the country, is that this kind of 're-wetting' work is enough to bring them back.

In 2016, Rachel's predecessor had written a report assessing the depth and health of the peat on the fell, and the conclusion was to get funding in place to restore a small part of it, just 10 hectares, by intervening with machinery to flatten it out, re-profile the slopes, and then spread cut heather, or brash, from elsewhere on the moor, like a skin graft, to start the process of restoring the original vegetation. Ten hectares is a drop in the ocean, but it is a start, and is a means of proving the concept.

'Funding never seems to be the main issue,' she says, when I ask her how much it had cost. She looks up the figure on her phone. '£36,436.60,' she says. 'It took seven weeks of work, which would have been four had it not been for the Beast from the East,* and involved three low-pressure ground diggers and a Softrak load carrier to cart the brash over from the donor site.' One of the abiding surprises of my journey is the revelation of how rarely funding appears to be the principal obstacle in mending what we have broken. Though not in this case, a mix of wilful ignorance and fierce protection of vested interests are normally the stumbling blocks.

There are slightly under 3 million hectares of peat habitat in the United Kingdom (about a tenth of our land area), of which just over 100,000 have been subject to some form of restoration activity, and around a million are within some form of agri-evironment scheme. It is sobering to think that only 7% of these are assessed as 'near natural', with a further 2% 're-wetted'; the other 91% falls into a mix of eroded, modified, cropland and grassland, with no less than 18% being surrendered to forestry.[6] It is sometimes hard to escape the conclusion that peatlands, whose attractions may be less immediately obvious than other areas, may always end up being the Cinderella habitat, fated to be overlooked. And yet, as we will see, it is the one most important not to lose. Those 3 million hectares put the 10 hectares at Peel Fell into some sort of stark context, in the cost of the work, the human activity involved, and the scale of the job to be done. Rachel is undaunted.

---

* The Beast from the East was an anticyclone storm that brought an unexpected wave of extreme cold to the UK at the end of February 2018.

'We've got a number of these going now,'* she says. 'The idea is to leave each one for five years and then do an assessment to work out what to do next.' I ask her if it depresses her that garden centres can still go on selling peat until 2024.†

'I suppose so,' she admits, after a pause for thought. 'But all these decisions affect people's way of life and livelihoods, so I guess you have to give those people and their companies time to adjust.'

She is right, of course, but the conversation also uncovers the elephant in the room that has been trotting urgently around behind the sofa, trumpeting the words 'carbon storage'. Dr Rebecca Artz, an expert in peatland ecosystems at the James Hutton Institute, explains: 'Only 3% of our land area on the planet is covered in peatlands but they are the largest carbon store that we have. They have grown very slowly since the last Ice Age, and only accumulate about a millimetre every decade. It's a very slow-growing resource and it's very easy to lose it.' According to the Office for National Statistics, the theoretical £8–£22 billion cost of restoring 100% of our peatland would be dwarfed by the potential benefit to climate change objectives of some £45–£51 billion by

---

* 2,000 hectares, in all.

† Garden centres must stop selling peat by 2024, contractors by 2028. Depressingly, peat sales rose by 9% during 2020, to around 3 million cubic metres. (*Times* article, May 18th, 2021) The delay between now and then will cost an extra 1.5 million tons of CO_2 being released. (Wildlife Trusts report, February 2022)

restoring just half of it,[7] but until that is a national ambition, we will continue to rely on individuals like Rachel.

It is starting to become a trope within my journey that just about everything that is good for biodiversity is also helpful in mitigating climate change. Just about everything, but not quite. The absence of breeding waders up here explains eloquently that the nearby forestry doesn't work for everyone. As was patiently explained to me during a walk along the River Tweed a little later on my journey, 'the needs of biodiversity restoration and the drivers behind its loss are not the same as those for climate change action.'*

The gold standard on this type of restoration project is to conduct a baseline survey of the biodiversity before it starts, and then at regular intervals after it has been completed. In a perfect world, this would be also run alongside an equivalent survey on an unrestored area, which is the only way of confirming that what was done was what produced the results on the ground. Only in that way do you accurately monitor the long-term effects of your actions. The reality is that these are expensive and time-consuming activities generally involving many different areas of expertise (botanist, ornithologist, entomologist, etc.), and they are rarely feasible. Peel Fell is no exception but, as so often in nature, delight comes in the precious moment rather than the scientific list. I ask Rachel about any survey plans.

* Professor Chris Spray.

'No survey. At least not yet,' she says. And then, with a half-smile, 'but I saw teal using the pools created by the bunds we have installed in the gullied areas last time I was up here. That made me pretty happy.'

And simple delight like hers, as much as anything, is what it is all about.

*

When I finally reach it, the border between England and Scotland is anonymous and unmarked, just the theoretical middle point of a little stream outside Kershopefoot. I take a picture of my feet astride where the line might theoretically cross the bridge, and send it to my family as a token of progress, 480 miles or so in. Later, from the sunlit bridge I spot what at first sight seems to be a bright blue crisp packet stranded on an overhanging branch that quickly turns out to be a kingfisher, and a red clown's nose stuck in some hawthorn that, on closer inspection, belongs to a cock bullfinch.

Beyond the accents, and the fact that they are still wearing face masks in public spaces up here a couple of months after we have discarded them down south, there is one visible difference between the countries that affects me straight away. In England, I have had constant use of a vast array of public footpaths, long and short and to all points of the compass, not to mention canal towpaths, that have given me options on the ground when I arrive at each new place. In Scotland, where there is precious legally-enshrined open access across any land that isn't garden, farmyard or covered in livestock, the actual footpath network seems to diminish slightly, and even where it does exist, such as the Pentland Hills, it often isn't marked on the map. For the long-distance walker, the reality of open access is sometimes rather different when faced with climbing over a long line of fences and walls under the weight of a 15 kg pack, but nonetheless welcome for all that.

Instead, what I find in its place is a delightful network of drove roads at my disposal, traditional routes over which the cattle were once driven from their highland farms to fatten up in the lowlands, from where they would head down towards London or one of the other big market towns to be sold. As I work my way northwards, I will supplement these from time to time by hopping on and off one or more of General Wade's Military Roads, laid down at a cost of £90 per mile 300 years ago so as to be able to move troops quickly around the place to react to Jacobite insurrections, and still largely in excellent condition. But the longest path of all that I will follow in Scotland isn't a path at all, as it happens, but the controversial 137-mile-long service road for the Beauly–Denny power transmission line, but that is still well out there in the future. Sometimes, I walk on small roads, but only when there are no comparable alternatives.

If part of the joy of my journey is the sudden discovery of an unfolding route, then another lies in the myriad of unplanned conversations, both engaged with and simply overheard. In Hawick, which has the inescapable air of having been slapped sharply in the face by recent circumstance,* I go into the First Light Café for a coffee. It is a charity concern that supports men and women with PTSD who come from the armed forces and emergency services, but I also go in because it looks light, airy and welcoming, with conversation flowing freely between staff and the individual tables. As it turns out, the coffee is excellent. The man on the neighbouring table to mine tells the waitress that he has just been released after a short stretch in prison. He has a disorder which manifests itself as a strong tic and the occasional colourful burst of language. Having engaged almost everyone else, mainly the staff, he turns his attention to me.

'Where have you come from, buddy boy?' he asks, holding my gaze with an unblinking eye. A month ago, this engagement might have made me uncomfortable, and I would have ended it as quickly as I politely could; now, I just feel rather flattered that he has included me in the list of people he wants to talk to. I tell him where I had started the day, not the journey, and he considers this for a moment.

'How old are you?' he asks, and I tell him that, too.

'Too old,' he says.

'Too old for what?' I am genuinely interested, and slightly offended. I'm actually feeling quite young at the moment.

---

* Or, to be more specific, by the disappearance offshore of the fine wool trade that had sustained it for centuries.

'All this fucking around.' He doesn't specify which fucking around, but I think I know what he means. I suggest to him that we are all too old for the fucking around the last couple of years have dealt us, and he nods in agreement. He takes ten years off my age when I ask him to guess it, but it makes no difference – he still thinks I am too old. Fucked, I think is the word he uses, but he says it with concern for my wellbeing.

'So where are you going to?' he eventually asks. And, in for a penny, in for a pound, I explain that I am going all the way to Cape Wrath. Subconsciously, I want to demonstrate to him that I am a man of steel, and not just some soft southern lounge lizard. The prospect of this long journey intrigues a man who, until two days ago, was behind prison bars. For one moment, it occurs to me that he is going to insist on coming along, and I can see how this might liven things up a bit for me during the quiet times. Some of me even thinks that we would be a good double act.

'Aye,' he says after a thoughtful pause. And then, without a shred of malice: 'Well, you'd better be fucking off now, I reckon.'

He may be yet another ship passing by in another night, but he is right. I have 450 miles to go, so I buy myself an extra cheese scone for the road, pay my bill, and do as he says.

PART 3

Scottish Miles

MAP 2. SCOTTISH MILES

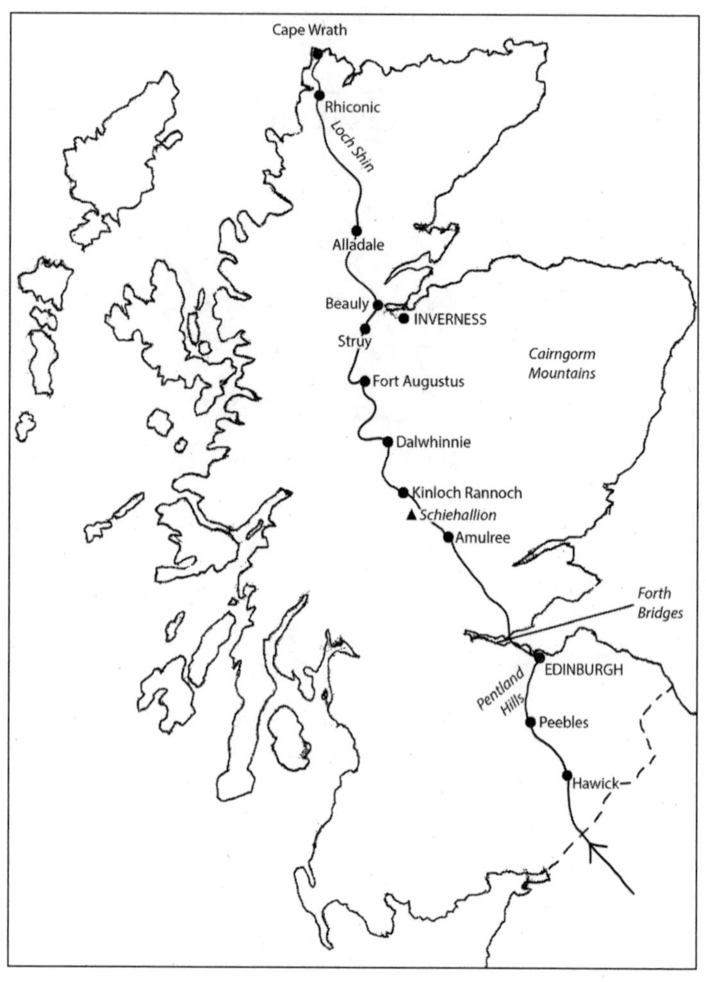

8. QUIETLY FLOWS THE TWEED

The Scottish border to Edinburgh, via the Pentland Hills: 111 miles; five days

(PRINCIPAL HABITAT: RIVER SYSTEMS)

'It is better to light a candle than to curse the darkness.'

CHINESE PROVERB

The greening oaks have not yet reached the border, but cherry blossom has. Cherry blossom, frogspawn and a foreign flag.

If the hidden chant of my walk has been the bubbling of the curlew, then its attendant prayer flags have often been the yellow and blue colours of Ukraine. Although I haven't really watched, read or listened to the news for a month, and won't for another, I find that I still absorb what is going on by a process of osmosis from passing travellers, headlines on news-stands, and evening conversations. And still those flags fly defiantly in nearly every settlement I pass through. There are posters and pennants, collecting tins and calls to action, not to mention bumper stickers and graffiti along the way. Outside Hawick, I am moved almost to tears by a collection of roughly painted pebbles for sale in a washing up bowl on a kitchen chair in the driveway, and a mis-spelled paper message from a child urging people to buy one so that they could support their brothers and sisters in Ukraine.

Recently, though, this has also become a journey of river crossings.

It shouldn't surprise me, but it does. To a large extent, days are now tending to start and finish around river systems, and then to lose themselves in the higher ground between times. It's entirely logical, given that settlements, which are where I generally spend the nights, are most often found by watercourses. Up in the morning, down at night: that is how my days are structured, sometimes once, sometimes more. Rivers such as the Trent, the Aire, the Tees, the Tyne, the Teviot and now the Tweed, all of them provoking little pulses of memory from old geography classes, and all hinting at an industrial life downstream. Each bridge I cross, be it at Alrewas, Gargrave, Middleton, Alston, Hawick or Innerleithen, comes as a moment of enhanced significance, another brick in the wall of my journey. I am returning, as a companion from earlier in the walk pointed out, to what my medieval self might have been, a follower of the old natural ways. After decades on tarmac, I have become a slow-moving creature of paths, rivers, hedges or green roads.

And, just like those medieval travellers, I start to find that useful parcels of news come up and down the trail if I let them: not so much the grim news of atrocities in eastern Ukraine, or of parties in Downing Street, but of nearby paths that are blocked by Storm Arwen's fallen trees, of cafés worth visiting, or a bull worth avoiding in a field near Selkirk. In the absence of guidebooks, which would be far too heavy to carry anyway, I find myself instead exchanging the information I need with the people I meet along the way, which turns out to be a fine substitute. A walker coming southwards near Philiphaugh tells me for the first time of the devastation that avian flu is wreaking among the barnacle geese in Galloway, the plague of choice now that I have moved north of ash die-back. It joins a little list of other natural diseases that I have noticed along the way: a juniper killer on the Upper Tees,[1] for example, or a parasitic worm[2] that is threatening to affect fish on rivers like the Tweed, all signs of the inherent vulnerability that our interconnected lives bestow on the natural world around us. A month later, a couple of gannet corpses near Cape Wrath show me physically what I have been picking up on social media, that the same avian flu is working its way through north-west Britain's packed seabird colonies, another crisis in a world that already has too much to think about.

Then just before Innerleithen, a settlement that marks my arrival in the Tweed Valley, one particular conversation brings me up a little short.

I have been on the road for about a month when I overtake a solo hiker under an enormous pack, high up on the Southern Uplands Way. I slow my pace, and we fall into conversation.

She is walking the entire 214 miles of the path from Cockburnspath to Portpatrick, and it suddenly dawns on me that, apart from the occasional local dog walker, she is the first woman out on her own that I have met in about a fortnight, maybe more.

'It's boring, and you really don't want to know,' she says with a weary expression, when I ask her why she is doing it. 'But let's just say that I need the break, and leave it at that.' For a second, I think about offering to carry her pack up the long hill in front of us, as Owen had lugged mine up Black Hill all those weeks ago. Then I realise simultaneously that she is probably stronger than me, certainly younger, and her pack looks at least 10 kg heavier than mine. Handing it back to her halfway up the hill because it was too much for me would not be a good look. Besides, who says that she needs help from me anyway, just because I am a man?

Instead, some time after we fall into an easy lockstep on the path, I tell her that I have seen only solo men on my trip, not solo women, and eventually ask her if she feels safe up on tracks that are miles from help. The irony is not lost on me that I am making a giant assumption that she doesn't find me threatening, let alone anyone else.

'Yes, and no. When I started off I felt vulnerable every time I walked past someone, or caught up with them. The worst was being overtaken. That and my own imagination.' I think of my own arrival in her life, and how my cheery greeting from behind might have been misconstrued. 'Now I'm fine. I've developed an inner confidence that I'm capable of most things on my walk, but also an understanding that just about everyone out here is OK. Better than OK, in fact.'

Until now, as a man, and probably in common with many other men, I haven't ever really considered that I may be just as threatening a prospect to some people high on a beautiful hillside as I would be on a dark, inner-city street; or that this likelihood self-evidently creates more male hillsides which, in turn, perpetuates the problem. When I tell her that I want to include her story in my book, she looks delighted, but asks me not to identify her. 'Give me an alias,' she giggles. 'Call me Doris.'

We part company as I accelerate away at the top of the hill, and she stops to check messages on her phone. 'Cheerio, Doris!' I shout from where a corner in the woods is about to hide me from her view, but she seems not to hear; her shoulders are once again hunched, and her face is buried in her phone.

Later on, it also dawns on me that the majority of solo walkers I have met have been like me, white, middle-aged men or, as the expression goes, pale, male and stale. 14% of our population may well be black, Asian and minority ethnic (BAME),[3] but you find less than 1% of them out in the national parks.[4] I had started to notice this absence earlier on in the Peak District, and had made contact with Maxwell Ayamba, a Ghana-born Sheffield academic who has made it his life's work to understand and reverse this.* While he says that there is no holistic picture of the problem, he points to some obvious issues (e.g. transport availability, cost, traditions) but then hints at some more surprising ones.

'Here,' he says, 'you have to pay for nature. Boots, jacket, trousers, pack. Back home, no. In Britain, rich people tend to live in the country, and poor people live in the towns, as a rule; where most of us originate from, the opposite may well apply. Also, I think there has to be a conscious reaching out to minority people by marketing in order to ram home the idea that this is positive inclusion. Just little things, like having more black instructors in the outdoor sector.'

This all matters for biodiversity, I suspect, as much as it does for fairness and accessibility, as it is only when all parts of the population are invested in the outdoors, and in nature, that the scene is truly set for all of us wanting to do our bit to protect and enhance it. Why would I care for the fate of a curlew if I have never even seen the fields it calls over? What do I care for a forest if I have never left the inner city?

*

Our warming planet is not exactly a new theme, and nor are suspicions about its human origins. Even back in 1896, Swedish chemist and physicist, Svante Arrhenius,

---

* A subject dealt with in detail in a paper called 'Black People in a White Landscape', which carries a disturbing allusion to 'native', 'alien' and 'invasive' species.

was suggesting to a sceptical world that 'humanity's consumption of coal, petroleum etc. were indeed capable of changing the climate, not just locally, but for the entire planet.'[5] (Actually, being Swedish and therefore often cold, Arrhenius saw this warming process as more of a benefit than a problem. His fellow countryman, Anders Celsius, even originally made the hotter end of his temperature scale the minus one, and the bottom end the plus one, on the basis that it made more sense to allot the 'plus' to the conditions you were used to.[6]) Humans, however, have an extraordinary capacity for simultaneously understanding and ignoring dire threats, and so it became a can that just got kicked down many roads for the next century.

Climate change is but one of a whole range of pressures on biodiversity, but it is the one that inexorably pushes species northwards, and further uphill, in search of cooler conditions, until there is nowhere left to go. With science's gift for memorable simplifications, this process has become known as the 'escalator to extinction'. In practical terms, this means that birders like me can now routinely find spoonbills and bee-eaters on the north Norfolk coast, while our equivalents in Inverness see fewer and fewer snow buntings every year, which is obviously bad news for the bunting. It also means that I am probably seeing different things at each level of my journey north than, say, my grandfather would have seen at the same time of year.

Perhaps no single project highlights this more clearly than Oxford University's 75-year study of great tit populations at Witham Woods, a few miles north-west of the city. Back in 1947 when the project, now one of the world's longest continuously running studies of a single species, was getting going, the first great tit egg was hatched on April 27th; 75 years later, it was March 28th, just about a full month earlier.[7] The average acceleration of date is now over three weeks, and is already producing profound changes for the bird itself (as is, coincidentally, the lengthening of British great tit beaks thought to be caused by the increasing importance of bird feeders in their nutrition[8]).

While the bunting and the spoonbill are highly visible examples of the direct effects of our warmer and wetter climate – as are, for example, the 800-plus vineyards (and rising) that we are now able to have in the UK[9] – it is to the invisible ones that we should perhaps be paying more heed: ash die-back, for example, a disease that was brought to Britain by our insatiable habit of moving plants from one place to another for profit and delight, is now accelerating through the country not least because of our milder climate and higher rainfall, and is on course to kill 80% of the entirety of our second most abundant native tree.[10] More frequent and ferocious storms bring down more trees than can be quickly replaced – over 800,000 were knocked over just in National Trust Scotland's properties during Storm Arwen[11] – which, in turn, removes vital habitat for woodpeckers, pine martens and wild cats. (Ironically, because conservation is never simple, the fallen trees that are left where they lie will also provide wonderful habitat for other wildlife.) Also, as we saw in Chapter 1, the acceleration of spring has a nasty habit of taking incoming migrants by surprise, a factor that may be behind the rapid decline of a species like the cuckoo, timing being everything when you are a brood parasite reliant on an active meadow pipit nest being ready and available when you arrive. It doesn't help if the moths that you prey on have declined four times faster than the local ones that don't interest you.[12]

There are winners in this process, too, albeit fewer in number than the losers, and it has to be said that most of nature is adapting to climate change rather quicker and more effectively than the humans that caused it. It is our misfortune that a proportion of the winners will be parasites and other agents of destruction who will rip through a new habitat that has not had time to build up defences or immunity.

But here in the Upper Tweed Valley, I am in a field, looking at a large photograph of a silver estate car jammed backwards under a footbridge by the flood waters that are trying to bear it away.

'This is Peebles in 2008,' says Hamish Robertson, the project officer leading the riparian tree-planting programme for the Tweed Forum. He has come armed with a presenter full of images, maps and plans. 'It used to flood regularly and often, like this, devastatingly.'

I ask him why.

'There are four burns which feed into the Tweed at Peebles,' he explains, 'of which this one, the Eddleston Water, is key, with a catchment twice the size of the other three put together. Back in the 1810s, when they were building the road to Edinburgh, they straightened the burn in order to economise on building bridges. Straightened it, and then dredged it from time to time, and then in 1855 added a railway line to reinforce the new alignment. I suppose they didn't realise at the time that this would speed up the water flow, and knock out the ground's ability to hold water for long enough, and release it slow enough, to avoid catastrophic flood events downstream.'

As it happens, the road was a money-earning turnpike, and the gentlemen involved were early venture capitalists, in a neat foreshadowing of nature's needs being subordinated to those of commerce. An old local rumour suggests it all started when a cart full of beer barrels fell into the burn while turning the corner to cross the bridge, thus creating the demand for the whole road to be straightened.

A recurring theme to my journey seems to be the consequences of our human habit of speeding up water flows, and the dawning realisation that it is normally less effective to spend money on flood defences where the problem happens than on flood mitigation projects upstream. After all, straightening river courses is what we have spent half a millennium doing. Sometimes, all that flood defences achieve is to make it look as if the politicians are doing something, when they are under pressure after it's all gone wrong. Towns such as Hull,*

* Hull leads the way, with more than 7.5% of its homes flooding during 2018, over double the number in Carlisle, in second place. (MoneySuperMarket)

Carlisle, Lancaster, Gloucester and Worcester all suffer from regular flooding for the same reasons, so it is in no way a phenomenon unique to settlements like Peebles.

'Add to this a few badly sited weirs and bridges, a few shopping trolleys in culverts, and the increase of rainfall brought about by global warming, and you almost have a guarantee of regular future flooding.' Hamish lists the subsequent flood years after 2008 on his fingers, accepting that it might have been quicker to list the years that weren't.

The United Kingdom has around 1,500 discrete river systems, covering around 200,000 kilometres of watercourses.[13] In a global context, our rivers are tiny: short, shallow and subject to considerable man-made disturbance, they are now especially sensitive to climate change, not to mention abstraction and land use alteration. With regard to Eddleston Water, we get a hint on how land use had changed from an article written in 1834, which confirms that 'almost every spot capable of irrigation has been irrigated, and wet land has been made dry.'[14] Over the centuries, we have channelled and straightened many of our rivers, creating one-speed rapid flows through the catchment and then building heavily on flood plains, until we get theatrically surprised that half the new houses are uninsurable. Corners that slow the current have been cut away, and the new speed of the river has washed the gravelly fish beds out to sea. We talk a lot about how we have degraded farming land and lost our wildflower meadows, but surprisingly little about the dire state of many of our rivers. As I will find out with the sea grass habitats in the Forth estuary in a few days' time, presumably this is because we can't see beyond their surfaces and into them.

Thus, in conjunction with University of Dundee, and funded by the Scottish government,* the Eddleston Water Project was drawn up by the Tweed Forum, to 'investigate the effectiveness of natural flood management techniques, and habitat restoration measures at catchment scale',[15] official words that complicate the rather simple idea of forcing a bit of the burn to go back to how it was before that road and that railway line, or at least to a more natural configuration. One element of the project, completed in the summer of 2013, lies in the three kilometres of re-meandered channel, which has increased the length of the river, reduced the slope and speed of the water flow and, as a by-product, recreated old habitats for wildlife. Using felled tree trunks, large flow restrictors were also installed deep into the banks of the upstream tributaries, and have already been proven to slow the peak flow in a flood event.

'It's all about delaying the surge during heavy rain,' says Hamish. He's only 24, and one of a new breed of bright-eyed conservationists in a world where the job opportunities for graduates have exploded over the last decade. 'Four to six hours is all it needs in most cases,

* The total cost of the Eddleston project was £2,549,570, of which the re-meandering was only £243,137. By far the biggest cost has come from the various monitoring programmes.

both to give residents downstream time to prepare, and to reduce the peak flows. Longer would be better, and we are hoping that we will achieve this as the trees begin to mature.'

We walk down to the first of the re-meandering projects, and I am immediately struck by its simple beauty, where the burn has been nudged 30 or so degrees to the right, before snaking back round to the left again and rejoining the old watercourse a couple of hundred metres downstream. For a second, it feels to me like an artist has simply reinvented the scene. There is a large holding pond at the far end, and four distinct channel ponds where the recent line of the burn went. The land between the old and new watercourses has been planted up with a mixture of Scots pine, birch, willow and alder, with hawthorn and blackthorn in between, so that water can flood over locally appropriate trees, and be slowed. If you didn't know the recent history, you could persuade yourself that this area of wetland had been untouched for centuries. I ask Hamish if it has all worked.

'Early days,' he says. 'But yes, I think it is showing good signs. There was huge rainfall in the autumn of 2021, and then a new delay of four to six hours to the surge, and much reduced flooding in consequence. Obviously, it's not just our re-meandering involved,* but it seems to be really helpful.' As well as re-meandering

* Other factors include watercourse maintenance, direct defences at vulnerable points, structure modification and an effective flood warning regime.

rivers, the Eddleston project showcases other natural flood management measures such as leaky barriers, tree-planting and pond creation, which all play their part in 'slowing the flow'.

A Senior Research Fellow at Dundee University, Chris Spray has been overseeing the scientific aspects of the project, and he cautions me a few days later not to overstate the contribution of re-meandering alone to flood mitigation. 'If that was all you did,' he says, 'and without removing the flood banks and reconnecting the river with its floodplain, it wouldn't have that much effect. Much better to stop building houses in stupid places. But the great thing about re-meandering is that it creates more river habitat and greater diversity in the structure of the river, which in turn has a hugely positive effect on biodiversity.' He may well be an academic by career, but he is a bird man by passion, and he starts to wax lyrical about the gains that he has seen since the work was done.

'Dippers,' he almost purrs. 'Kingfishers, little grebes; I even saw a jack snipe down there recently. There are now around 39 new ponds on the whole system, which has created the same number of opportunities for river birds, amphibians, dragonflies and other wildlife to come back.' This chimes with much of what I have seen on my walk, where biodiversity gains have often been the unintended consequences of some physical change.

But Hamish is a farmer by birth, a natural enthusiast, and his first love is cows, not birds. Back on the river, as we talk about the resulting biodiversity gains from re-meandering, he battles manfully to talk about invertebrates rather than belted Galloways, or mob grazing.

'One way or another, this is probably one of the most monitored stretches of river in Britain,' he says. 'River levels, water flow speeds, precipitation levels, temperature, ground water ... they measure it all. They've got evidence of huge gains in aquatic invertebrates, and the gravel bars will hopefully be enough to bring good quantities of spawning salmon back.'* The little birchwood surrounded, as it is, by water on three sides, is alive with spring birdsong. I ask him about beavers; after all, everyone in Scotland either asks about beavers or has a strong opinion on them.

'Not yet, or not as far as I know,' he smiles. Beavers, as I will discover more than once in the coming weeks, are a great deal more complicated than a cheerful three-minute section on popular TV nature programmes.

A humped, dark shape moves quickly across the ground behind him as he is speaking. It is an otter, and it runs to the river and then pours itself silently into the water without so much as a ripple, insinuating itself into the current like a memory. By the time I point it out to Hamish, all trace of it has gone, bar a few bubbles from its pelt that are borne quickly away on the stream.

*

* Salmon success is sorely needed. A 2022 Environment Agency report has established that 37 of Britain's 42 salmon rivers are 'at risk' or 'probably at risk', meaning that stocks have fallen below sustainable levels.

Sadly, and for the sake of balance, every good river story these days must be evened out by a bad one, and we won't be heading in remotely the right direction until we push back against the wreckers.

News filters through that evening on my email alerts, for example, of the state of the River Wye, theoretically one of the most protected river systems in Europe. By giving planning permission for a giant, million-chicken-a-week processing factory, and all the supporting chicken farms that this entails, Herefordshire and Powys County Councils have ignored any cumulative impact consideration, and set in train a vast manure lake that the neighbouring fields simply can't contain. And where do uncontained lakes go? Down into the nearest available river, of course, where the accumulated phosphates poison everything in their path, not least the water crowfoot (an aquatic member of the buttercup family) which 'like mangroves in the tropical seas, anchors the entire ecosystem',[16] and whose numbers have been decimated by 90%. Through this, and through the algal blooms brought about by warmer weather, the lightless stream is being choked to death. A few months later in the heat of the summer, and I read that the same issue is imperilling the north end of Windermere, England's biggest lake: again, this is caused by algal blooms which 'feed off the nutrients from phosphate, nearly half of which comes from sewage from waste treatment sites owned by United Utilities'.[17] The remainder derives from septic tanks and agricultural run-off of one sort or another, which, in my book, doesn't make it any better.

It gets worse when you consider the work of the water companies who, between them, managed to discharge raw sewage into our rivers for more than 3 million hours and on over 400,000 occasions in 2020 alone.* In exceptional circumstances, such as heavy rain, these discharges are permissible, but this is now happening routinely on a truly astonishing scale. If you happen to live alongside the pretty River Mole in Surrey, downstream from Thames Water's Dorking treatment works, for example, untreated sewage has been sent your way on no fewer than 223 days out of the last four years, which should give you pause for thought before plunging in for a cooling dip on a hot July day.†

It's going to take a lot of Eddlestons to make up for that. And a lot of boldness.

*

Ah! Boldness. If ever there is a common human theme on my journey, it is that the larger the organisation, NGO, government department or charity, the less boldness it is often inclined to exhibit.

A surprising percentage of the fieldworkers and naturalists I spend time with on my walk (and there are a fair few of them) think that the organisations they work

* House of Commons Environmental Audit Committee report, 2021.

† Thames Water denies that Dorking is the worst offender in the country. It is comforting to know, however, that with a package amounting to £1.23 million in 2021, their CEO probably won't need to take her summer holiday swimming in the filthy River Mole.

with or are employed by, particularly the larger ones, have become too 'top-down', too politically sensitive, too theoretical, too cautious and too led by academics and bureaucrats who don't spend enough time on the ground. This may be harsh, but my limited experience suggests that they might have a point. For all the important contributions that these organisations have made over time, which they have, and for all the egg-shell-walking that they have to do so as not to offend any one wing of their stakeholders, progress often seems pitifully slow. At the very least, there can sometimes be a worrying disconnect between the political wing of conservation and the activists in the field, where the latter are often seeing things on the ground that they do not then have the spreadsheets of data to prove, or the time or skills to gather it themselves.

'Our reaction to something that needs to be done,' offers one worker, 'is never just to get on and do it, but instead to commission first some research, then some "further research" and finally, for good measure, a bit of computer modelling, almost in the hope that people will get bored waiting, and the problem will go away. Everyone knows that we need good research, but we also need to get on with it. It is all so frustrating.'

'When an organisation like ours keeps changing its logo,' agrees another, a bird charity worker, 'the whole world knows that we have too much money, and the wrong priorities. I sometimes think our real aim is simply to keep persuading old ladies to give us their cash, instead of giving it to the Cat's Protection League. We've become just another business, not a force for change.'

Even at 80 years old, that lifelong naturalist and pioneer of modern reintroductions, Roy Dennis, is scathing about the sense of caution embedded deep in modern environmental NGOs. 'The most difficult opposition has usually been our colleagues,' he says. 'NGOs are terrified of failure, and they won't admit it. A young person in an organisation being bold and trying something that doesn't work would get their knuckles rapped. But we should be looking for people bold enough to try.'[18] But then, with the UK's pitifully vague national 'ambition' to 'halt and reverse biodiversity loss by 2030', and 'increasing species abundance by 10%' from its low point twelve years later,[19] possibly he shouldn't be that surprised.

A couple of weeks later another prominent veteran of conservation, John Lister-Kaye, echoes this concern when I call in at his Aigas Field Centre, near Inverness. 'Endless bureaucracy, political correctness and scientific prevaricating blocks common sense every time,' he says. 'And you can quote me on that.' It's a strange thing when two campaigners, 80 and 76 years old respectively, despair of the timidity of those who followed them. 'It has taken 30 years,' Lister-Kaye goes on, 'and one Green MSP to get approval for beaver translocation.' But then both he and Roy Dennis still carry the scars of the endless campaign to persuade Scottish Natural Heritage and the then Scottish Office to allow beavers back in the landscape in the first place. Fresh evidence to support rapid introductions was available from about a dozen European countries, right there and then, but to have acted swiftly on it would have required a boldness that simply wasn't there, and quite often still isn't.

For all the good news with which my walk has been abundantly filled, I am learning that it represents only a tiny proportion of the whole problem, and we are still in the eye of a maelstrom of a truly shocking loss of nature, a dire situation that calls for great courage and a sense of urgency, and probably not yet more protocols and methodologies. The best is often the enemy of the good, and the risk of potential failure needs to be balanced all the time against the risk of going too slowly, or doing nothing at all.

Every step I take on this walk convinces me more that we need to be activists. Every one of us, unless we really don't care.

*

One day south of Edinburgh, I take to the hills again, this time to avoid the traffic and litter alongside the busy A703.

The Pentland Hills might have been specially designed for an adventure like mine; high enough at around 1,900 feet to be claimed as a discrete adventure, but short and manageable enough not to be a particular challenge. By now I am probably fitter than I have ever been, or at least fitter than at any point since the taxpayer trained me to dodge bullets fired by people who didn't like me or my country. I haven't yet started to detect any weariness deep down in my bones, as if they can't quite understand the point of all this. Tiredness is incremental, so I am careful to follow any arduous day with a shorter one, knowing that Cape Wrath will not be reached by any single act of heroism, but by a thousand pieces of boring caution and moderation, all designed to lure my old body northwards. I don't normally do boring moderation, so this is an achievement in itself. Light showers alternate with watery sun all morning to create almost ideal walking conditions, and I don't even bother to put a waterproof on when it rains. Skin is waterproof, and clothes, given time, will dry.

'Keep hydrated and look after your feet,' says an old stalker to me, when I tell him where I'm going. 'And your body will probably get you there.'

And, for now, it seems to be a lucky body. Forty-five years ago, it gave up early on the Pennine Way; 30 years ago, it had to inch itself sideways down Offa's Dyke one Sunday afternoon, knees too painful to walk forwards. But this time, the biggest risk it faces is a turned ankle when I clamber over the stumps and roots of some clear-fell forestry, or a gash as I slide off a rock that I shouldn't be jumping on to anyway. In many ways, this is an easier undertaking for a 62-year-old than his 22-year-old counterpart, as his modern body has lost any of its residual optimism and logic, and seems to be content to be directed to do painful and illogical things against the later promise of a good meal.

At the thought of a meal, and at the sight of an unenthusiastic girl having fishing lessons on the Glencorse reservoir, a sudden and food-related thought occurs to me. I haven't looked at a diary for ages now, and have only the vaguest notion of what day of the week or month it is. I check the phone and find it is April 10th, which, when I add that to the 31 days each of March and January, and the 28 days of February, tells me that my hundred days is up.

Tonight in Edinburgh will be a whisky night.

And tomorrow will be a day of pies.

9. TO THE MOUNTAIN THAT WEIGHED THE EARTH

Edinburgh to Kinloch Rannoch:
104 miles; five days
(PRINCIPAL HABITATS: URBAN, COASTAL AND MOUNTAIN)

'There is a field beyond right and wrong; meet me there'
RUMI, THIRTEENTH-CENTURY PERSIAN POET

For a second or two, I stand open-mouthed on the corner of Princes Street Gardens and take in the gaudy theatre of it all.

After nearly 600 miles on the road, Edinburgh is my second city, after Sheffield. In fact, excluding Hawick, it is the first town of any consequence on my route since Hebden Bridge back at the start of the Pennine Way, or even Swindon. I ease myself into it through the leafy southern suburbs of Colinton and Morningside (and suburbs don't come much leafier than those), and then make my intruder's way into the city centre up the banks and under the graffiti-daubed bridges of the old Union Canal.

I am glad to be too early for the pressing throng of summer visitors but also struck by how unused I have become to everyday activities such as crossing busy roads and avoiding oncoming people on crowded pavements. If you can get bad at being among crowds, then that is what has happened to me, my workplace having simply become those lonely paths of Britain. A tiny bit of me has become resentful of now having to plunge back into it at all.

My unshaven face and oversized pack are not necessarily out of place among the milling backpackers of the city, but its boutiques and general faded elegance make me uncomfortable, as if to be there is somehow to risk the accumulated nature leaching back out of my soul. Only a couple of hours ago, I was listening to wild grouse calling out in the Pentland foothills and I miss it. A month of walking alone, and of living simply in the lonely high places of his homeland, makes a man strangely unsuited to seeing a £4,000 coat in a shop window, or a fast food outlet selling taxpayer-subsidised £2 burgers in polystyrene boxes to a waiting line of people, even if he ends up in the queue to buy one himself. When the loudest sound you have heard for weeks is the scolding of a pair of oystercatchers, or the bass thrum of a keeper's quad bike patrolling in the valley far below, the siren of a police car or the nearby hiss of a coach's airbrakes come as a bit of shock to the system.

The truth is that I have now become inseparable from my journey, almost entirely divorced from the world I was so recently part of, and will soon enough be part of again. Right now, I live for walking and the covering of distance, so much so that daytime hours spent not walking seem to me wasted hours, so that I have come almost to dread the days off I have planned. The hardship of the journey turns out to lie in the bits where I am stationary.

And that journey is simplicity itself. My home-from-home is a 15-kilo backpack with everything I need in it, and the few choices I have to make each day are not even hard ones, especially given that I have the means to make them, unlike many. My version of street life is the bustling activity of the natural world that surrounds me. I normally break each day into four parts, stopping for no more than five minutes after each hour and a half, to ingest some calories, check the map and enjoy the view, and then perhaps a little longer at lunchtime. In contrast to the notion I once had that I will have time to think great and creative thoughts, I often actually find that a whole hour has gone past, maybe even two, and I have no conscious recollection of thinking about anything at all. Not even cricket. Whoever else Nietzsche's idea that our best thoughts are those that arrive while we are walking might apply to, it is not me. For someone whose own mental health sometimes struggles through the dark indoors of a British winter, this bright outdoor spring is making space for something else, something very uncomplicated. Joy, even.

And spring is starting to be everywhere, from the greening hawthorn outside Cramond, to the grey wagtails bobbing up and down on the pebbles of a stream, to the first screaming swallow of my year in a farmyard at Balgowan a couple of days later, 'the surest sign that the earth is alive.'[1] Ironically, for the first time on my walk and in a city of half a million people, my eyes are itching with hay fever from the local pollen. Even more ironically, it is within the city limits that my body picks up the first tick of its travels.

Apart from that, my time in Edinburgh is punctuated by pies, whisky and some old friends, one of whom takes me rather pointedly to the Scottish National Portrait Gallery to top up on human culture, much like a car gets topped up with oil from time to time.

'It'll do you good to remember that this is also about humans,' he says. And he is probably right.

*

Although a third of the size of Glasgow, Edinburgh is growing at nearly three times the rate and, while there are plenty of green spaces within the city, many local people are naturally drawn northwards to the Forth shoreline to exercise themselves and their dogs. One of the most popular areas for this is Cramond Beach on the north-western edge of the city, which is where I meet Research Associate at the Botanical Gardens, Leonie Alexander.

'It's still quite early in the day,' she explains, 'so we haven't even got the professional dog walkers here yet. But you can already clearly see a creative tension between people's right to get some fresh air in a beautiful place and a fragile ecosystem's need for minimal disturbance.'

We both marvel for a moment at a world in which people buy dogs, one of whose primary functions is to persuade them to take regular exercise, and who then pay someone else to do it. I stare along the coast for confirmation, and it is alive with dogs, their owners and, sadly, their waste. Leonie is part of a project that is trying to rid Cramond Beach of the invasive beach rose (*Rosa rugosa*), a spiny shrub that plant hunters brought back from Japan some time in the nineteenth century. In the century and a half since it came to one of the gardens above, it has suckered its way down the hill and out onto the sand, bullying other plants away, until it is by far the dominant occupant of the beach.

When we think about local species loss, it is sometimes easy to forget that one of its major causes is the arrival of alien species that shouldn't be there, or at least don't naturally belong there, in the first place: rats leaving a ship onto a seabird colony, for instance, or signal crayfish destined for catering establishments escaping into river systems. These invaders have, for a time at least, one unassailable advantage: they start with no natural predators. So, if everything else works for them, they are free to colonise all around them. It is not an argument that can or should be conducted in black and white, partly because no one has yet agreed where to set the timing bar for what is a native species and what isn't (the end of the last Ice Age is a common start point), and partly because, in our de-natured land, every bit of nature is still a bit of nature; the hare came in with the Romans, after all, and no one minds them these days. And the worst invaders are sometimes the most difficult to hate: on my slow way south a month later, I listen to someone behind me on a bus between Fort William and Oban say that the purple-flowered *Rhododendron ponticum* crowding out every inch of the hill on our left is 'the most beautiful thing she has ever seen', rather than the sterile bully of the roadsides that I am seeing myself. Unfortunately, some, such as the mink, grey squirrel, muntjac or ring-necked parakeet come at a steep price for one specific breed of local competition, or the local vegetation.

Ironically, our own species has form here: the 3% of your DNA that is Neanderthal stands in feeble testament to the 97% that belongs to the Cro-Magnon man who once barged invasively in on him. When we play God at these moments, we are well advised to do it only after a great deal of rigorous academic research, and in the knowledge that we ourselves are something of an invasive species.

'The issue with *Rosa rugosa*,' continues Leonie, 'is that it smothers the local dune plants, and is extraordinarily tricky to remove.' She hales from the irrepressibly cheerful and optimistic wing of conservation, which is a good place to come from, given the scale of the problem. 'So we get volunteers in, hundreds of them over the years, to work on the little patches bit by painful bit, until we have got somewhere.' She shows me four small, fenced exclosures, one a control, one seeded with a coastal wildflower mix, one planted with wildflower plugs, and one a mixture of the previous two. We can see at a glance how different the structure, the colour and the biodiversity would be if *Rosa rugosa* was excluded.

There is knapweed here, thrift, wild carrot, kidney vetch and sedums, none of which would have had a chance under the high-energy incomer.

'We try very, very hard not to,' she says when I ask her if they use chemicals. 'But sometimes, the only thing that is going to get down to the last tiny bit of root that will spring up again if it possibly can, is a precision application of glyphosate.' In conservation, as I will find out all along the way, the purists at the top can sometimes over-complicate things for the foot soldiers. After extracting every last strand of *Rosa rugosa*, they burn what they have harvested, because even a trace left lying on the beach will take root again; and then they do it all over again the following year. Plant collectors have a great deal to answer for, we agree, but we raise an imaginary glass to the quiet army of volunteers who work on solving the problems they created.

Britain has over 12,000 kilometres of coastline, if you exclude the islands, but it remains a habitat relatively little understood, outside science and our imaginations. This matters. In the early years of the twentieth century, much of our coastal land was despoiled by uncontrolled development,* while, a century later, great swathes of the seabed went on to be raked free of all life by the 'progress' of fishing technology. 'The marine environment has always been ignored', was how one ecologist put it

* We have much to thank the National Trust for, with their role in reversing this despoliation. They now own no less than 1,250 km (or 10%) of our coast.

to me, and, standing on Cramond pier with Leonie, looking out towards the famous Forth railway bridge, I can remind myself why this is. At least half of it is completely invisible, so most of us never give it a second thought.

*

Into this invisibility, especially a hundred miles or so to the north-west and over the last 50 years, have slipped a vast network of more than 200 salmon farms that perhaps highlight the unseen issues best of all. On the one hand, it is an industry that employs around 2,300 people in fragile local economies,[2] brings £2 billion into the Scottish economy and creates a food of worldwide importance that the Scots can be proud of; on the other, it is wreaking havoc on marine ecosystems through pollution, parasites and high mortality rates, and is indirectly causing declines in species like the puffin through the extraction of industrial quantities of their food source of sand eels to pulp and feed back to the salmon. One of the larger operators, Mowi, states in its own figures that it pumps 87,376 tonnes of mainly North Atlantic fishmeal into its own salmon farms each year;[3] one of the main providers, BioMar, states that 9.2% of the fishmeal it provides to fish farmers comprises sand eels.[4] You can sort of work out for yourself whether this might make an important dent in the sand eel population and, via, them, puffins. (Worldwide, nearly a quarter of deep-sea fish that are caught are fed by humans to farmed fish.[5])

Sea lice from farmed salmon are among a number of issues thought to be grievously affecting their wild

A journey of 1,000 miles begins with a single step. Here is that step.

With Russell Wynn in the New Forest.

Left: Canal towpaths and disused railway lines turned out to be great travelling companions.

Below: Volunteers are the bedrock of so many projects: the Hartington village wildflower team.

Above: About 10% of Britain's land area is peat, much of it damaged. This bit has been mended.

Below: Aloneness not loneliness: first day in the snow.

Above: The driest spring in decades: Keld.

Left: Walking into a Sitka silence: Kielder Forest.

Above: Aerial view of the Eddleston re-meandering, showing flood water being held, and the A703 on left.

Below: Not everything is down to climate change; this probably was. Storm Arwen damage.

A tiny Scots pine, and a tiny miracle. Natural succession, Dundreggan.

The morning after the whisky night before. A cold dawn at Melgarve bothy.

Above: By some accounts, the remotest house in Britain: Deanich, Alladale.

Right: Getting the curlew message across whenever possible: BBC Scotland post-journey interview, Inverey.

The author at Cape Wrath, 11 kilos lighter.

Members of the Save Danes Moss Action Group, Macclesfield, Cheshire.

cousins. While this is occasionally disputed, the Scottish government's own summary of peer-reviewed scientific papers on the subject seems satisfied that there is a strong case to answer: 'The body of scientific information indicates that there is a risk that sea lice from aquaculture facilities negatively affect populations of salmon and sea trout on the west coast of Scotland.'[6] Official data shows that numbers of wild salmon caught each year on Scottish rivers (they are all put back these days) have reduced from 111,400 in 2010 to 35,653 in 2021,[7] and there is a very real prospect of local extinctions. We may like our farmed salmon, but we might also like to do a bit more research about its effect on other biodiversity such as the puffin and the wild salmon, before we get too enthusiastic.

When I ask John Aitchison, a wildlife film-maker who has campaigned for years to raise awareness of the hidden effects of intensive salmon farming, what change he would most like to see, he is unequivocal.

'We need the government to call a rapid and urgent cumulative impact assessment,' he says. 'With the emphasis on the word "cumulative". Only that way, and led by the science we already know about, can we roll back from the really damaging aspects of this industry.'

*

Back on the foreshore at Cramond, Leonie has something else on her mind. 'What do you know about sea grass?' she asks, waving her hand out to the left up the estuary. Once we have established that the answer is embarrassingly little, she starts to talk about the new 'Restoration Forth' project, happily announced to the public just as the world's leaders were gathering for the UN climate summit, COP26, 50 miles to our west. Her enthusiasm is palpable, and it is infectious.

'Here's the thing,' she says. 'Sea grass meadows are one of the key habitats in terms of producing oxygen, stabilising the sediment, regulating currents, reducing erosion and even trapping micro-plastics. One hectare will support up to 40,000 fish, about half a million invertebrates, and produce 10 million litres of oxygen a day.' She describes how these grasses are true ecosystem engineers in their ability to create structurally complex and robust habitats, and how, through their quick response to environmental change, they are a true indicator species. They are to places like Cramond what the mangrove forests are to a coastal village on the Bay of Bengal. But it is their ability to capture carbon (they represent only 0.1% of the seabed, but capture 12% of the oceanic carbon) that is one of their key current attributes.

'And yet, and yet,' she adds. 'We have lost 35% of them since 1980, all through human activity.' She runs through a litany of the ingredients of decline that, were it not so important, would be verging on the repetitive. 'Climate change, pollution, disturbance, invasive species and disease. Every hour, the world loses another two football pitches-worth of them.'

The Restoration Forth project aims to jump-start healthy meadows of sea grass on the Forth estuary, by collecting seeds from elsewhere during low tides, and sinking them into the sand in hessian sacks that are filled with a biome from their origin. It is a huge, educational and long-term project that, apart from all the other benefits, pushes Scotland a step further down the carbon capture road. Invisible or not, I find this incredibly exciting. Even more exciting is the fact that the process is quietly going on all over the coast of the British Isles. From the Helford River in Cornwall to the Lleyn Peninsula in North Wales, and from the Isle of Wight to the Forth, wet-suited conservationists are quietly diving down with hessian bags of sea grass seeds, sowing the future of what should be an impressive national revival.

'And alongside the sea grass,' she grins, 'we are going to bring back native oysters, who enjoy a mutually beneficial relationship with the sea grass. Oysters filter water, they remove toxins, they contribute to flood mitigation and ...'

'They are edible?' I interrupt.

'Exactly,' she replies. 'And who knows what that means for local employment a little further down the line, both in the sea and down the supply chain?'

Thus, with the imaginary taste of seafood in my mouth, I heave my pack onto my back and head on westwards, towards the Forth Road Bridge and the Highlands beyond.

The next time I meet an oyster, or the sea for that matter, will only be a few miles from journey's end.

*

Something unsettling happens the following afternoon.

I have crossed over the old Forth Road Bridge, with its unnerving green Samaritan signs and its six lanes of redundant motorway. The Forth bridges are almost a rite of passage for me on my journey, the River Forth being possibly the most tangible east–west line that I will cross on the entire route, and I was almost childishly excited about the prospect long before I actually got there. I have looked east to the iconic 1889 rail bridge with its shades of Richard Hannay and the past, and then down to an Ineos ship passing below, with shale gas for the manufacturing plant at Grangemouth. Ancient and modern.

A couple of hours later I am walking through Crossgates, once a mining village and before that a blacksmith's stop on the drove road south. Somewhere near the centre, a car pulls quietly up alongside me and then hoots. Turning round, I see that it is a taxi, and I assume it to be alerting the next fare of the afternoon that it has arrived. I walk on a hundred yards, and the taxi pulls up alongside me and hoots again, only this time more impatiently, and twice.

'I'm here for you,' the driver says through the open nearside window, when I ask if I can help. 'Get on in.'

I'm still relaxed about it when I tell her that I didn't order a taxi and that, anyway, I am trying to walk every inch of a long journey and so would never have called one. I think that I even hint that I wish I could, as it has been a hard, tarmac-only day.

'Get in,' she says, without humour. 'I've got your description from the control room, so I know it's you. Man on his own. Cap. Backpack. Please don't mess me around. I haven't got all day.'

Thus the asymmetric conversation escalates through the gears until she suddenly says: 'Just get on in,' and then, not quite half under her breath, 'you little fucker.'

For a moment I wonder if I am being set up for something, looking nervously around for someone in the background who might be watching, but then I realise that there is nothing to set me up for: I am just a grubby traveller with a pack in an old mining village. What could I possibly offer, apart from an opportunity for a laundry enthusiast?

'You're unfit to be driving a car, let alone a taxi,' I say. I know that this is very lame almost before the words are out of my mouth, but I can't think of anything stronger without descending to her level. I note down her licence number on my phone, and tell her I am going to report her. She swears again, this time openly, and then, spinning the wheels of her Ford Focus until they squeal jumpily on the afternoon tarmac, she swerves away to the north, and to the unsuspecting folk of Cowdenbeath beyond.

It is only then that I realise that, apart from once being monitored by someone's drone on the Pennine Way, this is the first time in six weeks that I have been anywhere approaching angry.

For me, and in 2022, that is quite a powerful feeling.

If the biophilia is kicking in, the awe is still just out to the north of me in the approaching wilderness miles, but it is coming for me.

*

'No one,' said American ecologist Garrett Harding, 'should be able to enter a wilderness by mechanical means.' In lonely Glen Quaich, below Tayside, I eventually come to know what he means.

It's been a long time coming. The awe creeps up on me slowly, insidiously, almost anonymously, as the morning progresses, initially hidden from my consciousness by the workaday pressure of the northward miles I have to cover. When I am thinking about nothing, which is surprisingly often, my brain kicks into an automatic pace-counting service, with 580 double paces to each kilometre on flat terrain; if I'm not careful, this can smother emotions. It can also disguise the fact that some of this journey is about allowing myself to be utterly aware of the nature around me.

But after an hour or so, when I stop to adjust my pack and look around, I realise that the magic of it all has been bypassing my brain all morning, and is already lodging somewhere deeper, in a part of me whose reactions I seem to have no control over at all. It is hard to say what starts it off: it might be the pair of grey partridge tumbling out of the headland to my right, or a curlew calling above me, so close and so almost stationary in the breeze that I can see the details of its quarter-open bill; maybe it was the first wheatear of the year, bobbing on a strand of livestock fence, or the distant roar of a red stag somewhere on Meall Mòr over my left shoulder. For all I know, it could be the rising and falling of the calling of the greylags on the goose fields that run down to Loch Freuchie, or just the fact that I am here in the middle of it all, a privileged bystander in the movement of a season through a beautiful place. Whatever it is, its effect is to unpick the lock on the self-control that has been such an important part of my adventure, and lay bare the boy I once was, just overawed by nature. I am thrown back 50 years to the side of a mountain on the Isle of Mull, one late afternoon, watching a golden eagle working the ridgeline above me.

Momentarily, a tiny part of me mistakes this feeling for sadness. I stare around, almost searching for something like a house or a car, that can anchor me back to the old reality, but it is too late. Decades ago, when this happened to me, this overwhelming subordination of myself to the nature around me, I would wreck it by going home and writing terrible poetry about the experience. These days, to the relief of a happy country, the poetry is no more.

Instead, I head cheerfully north towards the steep bank that leads me on to Kenmore and the Highlands beyond.

*

Walk for any length of time through those Highlands of rural Scotland, and you will likely as not hear the words 'land ownership'.

A very large amount of Scotland is owned by a very small number of people; or, to be precise, 70% of it is owned by just 1,125 owners.[8] Two of these, the Duke of Buccleuch and Danish retail clothing magnate Anders Holch Povlsen, own over 400,000 acres between them, an area that roughly equates to the size of London. And, while the image of the landed laird still has some accuracy to it, the most significant owners are now more likely to be public bodies,* closely followed by foreign private investors,† many of whom are actually doing ground-breaking conservation work. While community buy-outs now control around a quarter of a million hectares, it is a drop in the ocean among the other 8 million that make up Scotland. And, while it may be tempting to think that low land values will make it possible for a more even distribution, including to community trusts, we shall see in a later chapter that the opposite is actually happening: land values are soaring, and moving ownership out of the grasp of all but the most wealthy. Acknowledging that the key conservation determinant should actually be land *usage* (meaning what is actually done with the land) rather than land *ownership*, you don't need to be a Marxist revolutionary to raise a quizzical eyebrow at this situation, and how it has evolved.

But evolve it did, and the impression I start to get is that, while Scots on the whole seem a lot closer to nature than their neighbours to the south, they are also,

---

* The Forestry Commission owns around half a million acres. Other major landowners include the National Trust for Scotland, the Ministry of Defence, RSPB Scotland and the John Muir Trust.

† By 2019, Anders Povlsen had amassed nearly 100,000 hectares (almost 250,000 acres), making him Scotland's biggest private landowner.

if possible, even more polarised about it. Mention land ownership, beavers, grouse, sheep or salmon, and you will likely find battle lines drawn and as much pure visceral opinion as scientific fact being deployed to push particular views. Mention deer, though, and you will be at a different level altogether.

Deer are everywhere. Around a million of them at the last count,[9] spread across four hungry and highly adaptable species; five, if you count reindeer. In a land that can properly sustain a population of deer at about as low a density as five per square kilometre, depending on the terrain, some areas are running at over 60. In the absence of apex predators, and the general ineffectiveness of stalking as a population-limiting activity, they seem to be on every ridge line, in every little valley and on each mile of road. Deer are biodiversity engineers of the wrong sort: they are death to young trees (themselves a key plank of Scotland's planned reaction to the climate emergency), and ruinous for many biodiversity projects. They graze, browse, bark-strip, trample and fray (rub their antlers against) young trees.[10] Throw in the increasing prevalence of Lyme disease, spread by ticks that feed on deer, and hundreds of road accidents, many serious, and you have the makings of a major national problem. The truth is that Scotland has lost control of deer numbers to an even greater degree than England, a state of affairs made doubly incomprehensible by the fact that our supermarkets still import 1,000 tonnes of venison from New Zealand annually,[11] and our governments still licence new deer farms each year to raise yet more deer, only in captivity. Apparently the wild meat that comes off the hill is a bit rustic for our urban tastes, as if it is beyond most of us to marinade something for a while before cooking it.

And all that is before you consider the indirect effects of deer on the climate: for example, counterintuitively, one report says that a kilo of venison is worth 6 kilos of carbon sequestration, on the basis that the death of the deer will allow an amount of trees to come through that will go on to sequester that level of carbon.*

As a gross generalisation, the watershed between the two conflicting attitudes on deer management (i.e. culling levels) seems to lie in the type of ownership of the land in question. Conservation bodies, such as the John Muir Trust, or National Trust for Scotland, tend to go hard at the deer on their land for the sake of protecting future tree regeneration, which in turn leads to greater biodiversity. Sporting estates, most of which are financially marginal and for whom each deer is virtually a balance sheet item (in terms of its potential value to a paying stalker), are much more reluctant to do so, and often accuse the other side of creating unfair vacuums into which their 'own' deer will wander, and get killed. The argument doesn't stop there, either. Even the subject of the rights and wrongs of deer fencing splits opinion, not least because fences often kill capercaillie.

---

* Don't get too overexcited. The Vegan Society maintains that 1 kilo of wild game meat *causes* 6 kilos of CO_2 emissions, rather than sequesters them. Statistics, as ever, are a minefield.

When I ask two neighbouring landowners of opposing views what can be done to save the capercaillie* from local extinction, the conservation-led one tells me that it requires the killing of more deer (so as to encourage better cover and therefore protection for breeding birds), while the sporting one squarely blames the increasing recent success of pine martens who, he suggests, should now be subject to control themselves. The challenges of the sad old capercaillie demonstrate all too well the tragic difficulties faced by a species confronting extinction in a country with a complex natural history which would probably rather not be asked to make the difficult choices needed to keep it hanging on in there. For a start, it is already a reintroduction itself, which prompts questions as to whether it should still be there in the first place; secondly, no one seems entirely clear about what its habitat actually was when it was plentiful; and, last, the animal that is rapidly herding it back into local extinction, the pine marten, is one that, only recently, was facing extinction itself. Who, then, controls which species in order to achieve precisely what? Should we play God at all? These are genuinely difficult questions.

In Kinloch Rannoch, a local village, I constantly found myself tripping over deer, metaphorically at least.

* A huge woodland grouse, about the size of a turkey, and which can weigh up to 5 kg. Now limited to probably under 1,000 birds, and based in a small area of Scottish native pinewood in the north-east of the country.

'The SNP[*] would love to stick it to the toffs,' said a local in the village that evening when I asked why the government didn't legislate on cull numbers. 'But they know they don't have the resources or commitment to monitor, prosecute, let alone sanction the landowners that fail, so they leave it. They just can't find a good headline that makes it worth their while, so they do nothing. It is the Orkney stoats all over again.'[†]

'Look at the two parts of that hillside over there on each side of the fence,' says Liz Auty, Schiehallion Project Manager for the John Muir Trust, 'and you can simultaneously see the problem and solution.' I am meeting her a few miles south from Kinloch Rannoch to see if I can learn more.

We are sitting on the side of Schiehallion, an isolated conical Munro[‡] in Perthshire, and the mountain on which the Astronomer Royal tried unsuccessfully to estimate

* Scottish National Party, the political party running Scotland since 2008.

† The saga of Orkney stoats has probably not been Scottish conservation's finest hour. The animals arrived mysteriously on the islands in about 2010, and cheerfully set about wiping out ground-nesting birds. While conservationists and rule-makers argued with each other about whether it was stoats or greylag geese that were the bigger local issue, the cost of dealing with the rapidly growing problem rose from around £60,000 to £6 million in the time it took them to get round to finally making a decision, with 6,000 box traps needing to be deployed. Last I heard (March 2022), 2,683 stoats had been killed, but then so had plenty of non-target animals as well, admittedly most of them rats. Meanwhile, the greylag geese continue to devastate the barley.

‡ Any hill in Scotland that tops 3,000 feet (914 metres). There are 282 of them.

the weight of the world in the summer of 1774, instead accidentally inventing contour lines in the process.*

I see her point. The left-hand side, which is open to deer, is almost totally bare, while over the fence, the ground is dark with new-growth heather and emerging saplings. The difference is the 1.8-metre fence that keeps the deer out of the community-owned ground on the right.

Like all honest conservationists, Liz, who has a PhD in Botany (primroses, to be exact) from Newcastle, refuses to oversimplify the problem, believing instead that the answer has to lie in working in partnership, and in a planned way, with neighbouring landowners over decades, based on a shared vision of how it could all be.

'We need to work together to take conservation forwards,' she says while trying to conserve her own sandwich from the attentions of her sheepdog, 'and show how it works as a financially sustainable model. We have to move on from simply looking at our own plot of land, and start to negotiate plans collectively.' She lists the five or six immediate neighbours that they work with in the Heart of Scotland Forest Partnership, and who are a mix of public bodies and private families. 'It's no good working in isolation. We need to plan restoration at a landscape scale, and then involve local

* The idea was to work out which way, and how far, a pendulum would be pulled away from its vertical position by the gravitational attraction of the mountain at various points, and from that to extrapolate what the mountain weighed, and from that the earth. Amazingly, it didn't work.

schools and volunteer groups. Ultimately, the mountain is a community asset, wherever the boundaries lie, and nature doesn't recognise boundaries.'

'Doing things at a landscape scale is an absolutely vital element to restoring our nature,' she says – and dozens of others have said, and will say, the same thing to me as I plough on northwards. 'You cannot just do this work in little pockets.'

I ask her what her main work is on the John Muir patch, and she starts by taking me to an 8-hectare square of protected hillside, where the team has organised for volunteer groups to plant 10,000 trees over the last few years. She lists a number of counterintuitive factors.

'First, we had to fell a Sitka spruce plantation that was suffering windblow in order to clear the ground to plant a native one. Sitka isn't native, so it had to go. Next, having protected the new trees from deer by the fence, we found ourselves having to protect the trees individually from the attention of brown hares. That's more plastic, unfortunately. Then, we had to prevent black grouse from flying into the fence and killing themselves (1.8 metres is a good grouse-flying height), by putting relatively unsightly wooden battens along the length of the top strand. Nothing is easy, but it's all worth it.'

I wonder aloud if culling the deer presents a PR problem for the Trust. 'Surprisingly, no,' she says. She admits that it's a counterintuitive action for a conservationist like her, but knows at the same time that it is absolutely vital. 'There was some recent research[12] done which showed that people both in the towns and out here broadly support effective control, especially if it will reduce the spread of Lyme disease, allow tree growth, and reduce road traffic accidents. Up to three-quarters accepted it.'*

We agree that it is also surprising how little the health of the deer themselves seems to come up in any discussion of the density of their numbers, when it should seem so obvious: too many deer competing for scarce resources will inevitably fail to thrive. The decade-long project at nearby National Trust for Scotland's Mar Lodge, by contrast, where the density of deer is controlled down to about ten per hectare, claims to demonstrate that a lower number of healthier stags is better for the stags, better for the ecosystem, and no worse for the financial income of the estate.[13]

Predator control is another matter, but it will take me another fortnight to the north of here to barge into that particular discussion.

We start walking up the mountain on the path that her volunteers meticulously maintain and improve. A purist might say that the path un-wilded the wilderness in some way, but a purist doesn't have to live with the boring realities of protecting hills from erosion and fragile biodiversity from endless disturbance. I tell her that it looks fantastic, which it does. Then she tells me about

* For a much more detailed look at the complexities of the deer issue, you might want to read the account of how it was dealt with at Mar Lodge under the National Trust for Scotland, in *Regeneration* by Andrew Painting, Birlinn, 2021.

the rural skills courses that the neighbouring community landowner, Dun Coillich, run at Schiehallion, bringing training and work experience to people who often then go on to careers in forestry, farming or conservation, and this opens up opportunities for them that they might not have had otherwise. When you dig down, all these projects are multi-faceted.

Finally, we arrive at a handful of recently planted rowans.

'At the Glasgow Children's Hospital,' she says when I mention them, 'they have an oncology ward that is informally known as the Schiehallion Ward, for children who get diagnosed with cancer. It was named after this mountain to reflect the uphill journey of a child with the disease.' She describes a recent day out for the children at the reserve, and how the trees get planted either to commemorate a child whose journey has come to an end, or to give thanks for one who has made it through to remission, or even cure. 'Sometimes,' she says, 'they are just too ill to get beyond the end of that track by the car park, and they just sit and take it in from there. For us, it's almost unbearably moving, but we forget at our peril that for them, it is a wonderful moment of calm in the storm of a desperately tough life.'

We are both parents, and we just look up at the trees in silence. Eventually, I rub the sting out of my eyes momentarily on the filthy sleeve of my fleece, and we walk on. What goes on here is so much more than a bit of work on a mountain path; what she has just told me both transcends and empowers conservation.

As we walk back towards the wood and the Braes of Foss car park, a pair of black grouse burst out of the heather behind us and set their straight course up towards a ridge leading down from the hill, and the heather and buds in store for them up there.

They, and the ptarmigan, are what I have come here for. Actually, the birds and Schiehallion itself, whose 1,083-metre summit a nod to the purity of my route now obliges me to ascend.

When I get up there, 90 minutes later, the unmistakeable sound of the first ptarmigan of my year filters up to me through the cloud that conceals him. I already know that he is not here by some happy accident. He is here only because the species that for centuries has herded him towards extinction has recently decided to do what it takes to save him. We are like that. Like a field hospital where the enemy soldiers get treated with the same care as our own, humans can sometimes be quite good at trying to fix the wounds of those whom we have only recently been bayonetting.

And, like that red kite in my garden that potato-planting day a decade ago, the ptarmigan proves that nothing is gone until it is gone.

It's obvious, really. The heart keeps beating until it stops.

10. FORESTS AND FARM CLUSTERS

Kinloch Rannoch to Beauly: 101 miles; six days
(PRINCIPAL HABITATS: ANCIENT WOODLAND AND COASTAL FLOODPLAIN)

'The best time to plant a tree is twenty years ago. The second best is now.'
SAYING

Some days I have company.

Back in Tayside, it is Jim, who is celebrating his retirement as Director of Sustainability for Scottish and Southern Energy by spending two days walking with me along his own transmission line, and intermittently explaining the hydro scheme to me. He started life down the East Lothian coal pits 45 years ago, so he has come a long way to be here. Jim's natural pace is the same as mine, which makes conversation easier. He is unnaturally excited by pylons and tells me, correctly as it turns out, that I will be too, by the end of my walk. In fact, so much so that, a week later, I feel a sense of near-bereavement when the line finishes at Beauly, near Inverness.

'If you were a drop of water in Loch Ericht,' he says, by way of explaining the genius of hydro power, 'you would make electricity five times – at each of the dams at Ericht, Rannoch, Tummel, Clunie and Pitlochry – before you got to the sea. You would pass through engineering that is three-quarters of a century old, but still functions almost perfectly. But the combined efforts of you and the billions of other drops that fall on the catchment areas of all the hydro schemes in Scotland, still only contribute 10% of our national power, which itself represents only 10% of British usage. It's a lot of work for not a whole lot of return.'

This difficulty is also one reason why the percentage of electricity generated from renewables has peaked at around 40%. So Jim has spent most of the final part of his career negotiating for and then building onshore and offshore wind turbines.

He talks about the angry voices at public enquiries, and the irritating black and white of public debate.

'I understand the costs,' he says. 'Really I do. No one can pretend that hydro schemes are good for the salmon run, just as no one can claim that wind farms don't create noise pollution and kill the occasional bird. But we are either serious about tackling climate change, or we are not. In the future we all need to learn how to live with less power altogether, but in the here and now, we need to grow up a bit and have a nuanced debate like adults. Nothing is simple, but we can't just live in a museum.'

He raises a really good point, one that I often trip over on my walk and find I have no answer for, that of the 'greater good'. When black guillemots, for example, are regularly sucked into tidal turbines that produce clean power in some Orcadian tidal channel, and killed, what is the right thing to do? If somewhere between 10,000 and 100,000 birds are killed each year in the UK by the blades of wind turbines,[1] how big an issue is it? Where a desperately needed build of a new hospital is indefinitely delayed by the presence of a protected species, who should prevail? These things are giant validations of those infinite connections of John Muir's that we met back in Chapter 1, and there are often no easy answers. So much so that the people I grow to respect the most are often the ones who remain honestly agonised in a world that demands slick, quick answers to everything.

Then, on World Curlew Day,[*] and alongside the litter-strewn A9 south of Dalwhinnie, I walk with Mark Stephen of BBC Scotland's *Out of Doors* programme, who is interviewing me about the trip, and about those curlews. Expertly, he keeps the conversation focused while the microphone is running, but then we run the whole range of our interests when it is off. After so much silence, my river of words and uncultured language will need much editing, although he is too polite to say so.

'This was probably once curlew country,' we agree, as he points the large fluffy microphone westwards but

* April 21st. Invented to draw attention to the plight of the birds by author and campaigner Mary Colwell, with whom, and a few others, I helped to establish and run the conservation charity, Curlew Action.

fruitlessly into the silent valley where we hoped they might be when we planned the conversation, 'but not now.' Ironically, World Curlew Day is the first day for a fortnight that I don't actually hear one.

We share strong views on nature and beyond, and a love of discourse, so we dive into a café once we get to Dalwhinnie, and spend half an hour reinventing the politics of our countries over coffees and bacon butties, because that is arguably what middle-aged men do best. Besides, just being with someone else in a café is a novel experience for me, where it is me being overheard, rather than doing the overhearing, me being observed rather than doing the observing.

A day north again, and it is Trevor, a close friend from home, whose robust sarcasm and biting one-liners I find I have inexplicably missed.

We spend an arctic night in our inadequate sleeping bags by the small fireplace in Melgarve bothy, eating rehydrated Thai green curry from its packet, and drinking whisky from a shared yoghurt pot. To pass the time, we invent a new game of virtual cricket that involves dropping six stones into a chalky circle that we have drawn on the floor for the purpose, and seeing where they land, by the light of a waning head torch.

I beat him in both games, once by dint of a solid partnership between Volodymyr Zelenskiy and William Wallace, and once through an extraordinary display of late six-hitting by John the Baptist.

'Whose stupid idea was this?' he whines, early the next day as we wind our thick-headed way up the hairpins on the track to the Corrieyairack Pass. To escape the cold, we had left the bothy at dawn. 'Yours,' I offer, but then a mountain hare suddenly joins the route in front of us for half a mile, loping along and occasionally looking back as if we are supposed to be following her. Maybe she is leading us away from her leverets; maybe it is something else but, whatever, we are transfixed and, for a moment, Trevor forgets that he is supposed to be miserable.

'What just happened there?' he asks, when the hare finally bolts away across the heather, but neither of us has a clue. Then, for a misguided moment, I tell him about the idea that places like Melgarve are on a map twice: once as a physical location, and once as a story of human culture moving through time, until he tells me to stop being so boring and shut up. So, instead, we turn our attentions to constructing a fraudulent photograph of Trevor ice-climbing on a tiny patch of late spring snow, two days of his company having swiftly unearthed the latent child in me.

Once he heads south at Fort Augustus, I will be on my own for the rest of the journey. From now on, the only person I will bore will be me.

*

But back at Melgarve the night before, something other than the smell of Trevor's socks had surprised me, and I find my thoughts returning to it the following night, before I go to sleep.

Just outside the bothy, a smart dispenser of even smarter leaflets brought to our attention that the bothy was owned by Jahama Highland Estates (JHE) who, on closer inspection, turn out to be an arm of the Gupta Family Group Alliance (GFG), and Britain's fifth-biggest landowner.[2] The land that the bothy is on came into their ownership as part of their purchase of the Lochaber smelting facility at Fort William in 2016, which itself attracted financial support from the Scottish government of a scale and generosity that presumably even their own auditors must eventually notice, and comment on.* While you can't blame GFG for striking what was, for them, a truly excellent deal, you may feel a more nuanced worry about the strong environmental claims being made by a global steel company in that smart brochure, particularly the headline claim that 'JHE works to balance the industrial focus of Alvance [Aluminium Group] and SIMEC [an energy, mining and shipping group], mitigating the wider environmental impact and investing in competent natural resource management and usage (including renewables) to meet our sustainability objectives.' Meaning this place is supposed to make us all feel better about the dirtier ones we don't like to talk about, even though the glen has been

* In a nutshell, the Scottish government underwrote 25 years of receivables (money to be paid) from the GFG Lochaber hydroelectric plant at a hugely inflated price in order to sweeten the deal by which GFG would purchase the smelter, keep it going and create some new jobs that, in the event, never happened. The taxpayer could be in for as much as £575 million.

providing its comprehensive sequestration services for free, and for millennia.

Looking across the idyllic valley to the south of the bothy, and out towards the mountains beyond, it is a strange thought that this land is picking up part of the moral invoice for the carbon-intensive work that the majority of the group carries out worldwide and, of course, what we consumers demand from them. To be fair, the estate looked well managed, and such locals as we talked to seemed content enough with the way it was being run. But it is the notion that the planting of a few trees here and there, and the hosting of a few Downhill Mountain Bike World Cups in a remote Scottish glen can somehow atone for millions of tons of CO_2 being belched out of steel plants elsewhere, that makes me uncomfortable.

This is not some new feature at a late stage of my journey. There have been countless examples of this uncomfortable type of trade-off all the way along, not least the humorous idea that the 'zero-carbon energy new trains'[3] on HS2's railway lines can possibly compensate for the widespread habitat vandalism that it has cost the country to enable it. You might wonder how this practice could affect a lone man walking through his own country, but it can and it does. From the marketing blandishments of the 'world's number one plastic polluter'* comes a thin commitment

* Coca-Cola, according to campaign group Break Free From Plastic (2020 Annual Report).

'to get every bottle back by 2030, so that none of it ends up as litter in the oceans.' This just might have persuaded me to buy a cold fizzy drink one hot afternoon in Staffordshire, because I just might not then have known that Coca-Cola point-blank refused to get rid of plastic bottles in 2020 on the basis that 'their customers like them'.[4] Not this one, who found out in time and was given a glass of delicious water from someone's outside tap instead.

I could go on, but you are busy and would get bored, and these companies probably hope that this will be the case. Bored and busy people don't look too carefully at the small print beyond the soft-focus, feel-good marketing speak. From coffee pod recycling schemes to the mysterious 'zero-waste-to-landfill' schemes, greenwashing at best confuses and at worst misleads the rest of us. But then again, a world that truly believes a Formula 1 motor racing season will in any meaningful way have a net-zero carbon footprint by 2030[5] is probably a world that is easily led and readily pleased. Likewise, an industry that exports 46,000 tons of fish each year in the belly of a jet aircraft out of Heathrow,[6] as is the case with farmed salmon, still gets away with little more than a few soft-focus images of Scottish lochs in persuading us that it, too, is good for the environment. This is in no way to diminish the huge efforts that very many companies – most of them too small to be noticed, let alone to engage some PR agency to shout out about it – make in their everyday business to tread lighter on the planet, and onto my agenda goes a small determination to be better at seeking these out and supporting them.

Some things in conservation are much easier than we give them credit for, and shoving a few extra trees in the ground is never going to be an adequate substitute for increasingly leaving the fossil fuel down there in the first place. The principle of 'polluter pays' is one that, if it is ever really applied, seems all too often to be done with the lightest of touches.

Before turning in for the night, I see a text from Trevor that includes a picture of a pulled pork sandwich with accompanying garnish that he had been served on the train on his way south, having been upgraded.

'Hope you're enjoying your cereal bar,' is the supporting comment.

There, in the slightly blurred background, was the tell-tale red label of a bottle of Coke.

*

A few days later, there is a new soundtrack to my walk.

Descending into Glen Affric from the hills to the south on April 23rd, I hear the unmistakeable sound of my year's first cuckoo. It is a sound that I will hear every day, and sometimes all day, until I am almost on the edge of the northern coast. Much as I love cuckoos, and I do, they have undeniably got monotony down to a fine art, and will soon start to occupy the same position in my guilty affections as porridge does. My determination not to listen to any music during the hours that I am actually walking crumbles for a time under the constant barrage of cuckooing that issues forth from the bonnie banks and braes around me. At times, even Neil Young sounds more cheerful.

Scottish cuckoos, which happen to have fared rather better than their southern cousins recently, tend to migrate on a more easterly track than the English ones, which may possibly be a safer route, and they undeniably arrive in a habitat that is a few degrees cooler than down south, and a few weeks less advanced in the season. Both of those factors may help a bird that is already having to run the gamut of habitat change on the migration route and the odd Maltese hunter.

Then again, migration is another of those activities constantly changing at the behest of our warming world. There is a general trend for our summer birds to spend less and less time each year in Africa (50 to 60 days less, according to research by Durham University[7]), which may have consequences of its own on insect numbers and vegetation south of the Sahara desert, but may also eventually lead to birds like the willow warbler, nightingale and eventually, perhaps, the cuckoo, spending the entire year in Europe. It is yet another example of the connectivity of our natural world. Next time you see swallows on the telegraph lines outside your house in mid-October, you will know that, for good or ill, you helped to enable it.

When I check online that evening, it turns out that my early bird is already two and half full months behind the first credible British sightings of the year. Reports coming from earlier than mid-February have often mistaken the bird for a woodpigeon (for its call) or a sparrowhawk (for its looks), and it is still almost inconceivable that they have over-wintered here. But my Affric bird is undeniably a cuckoo, and a pretty timely one for this part of Scotland.

Once upon a time, where I am standing, and where he is singing, would have been perfect habitat for him.

*

Once upon a time in the early Neolithic, say 10,000 or 15,000 years ago, one of your or my ancestors took a polished stone axe and, maybe for the first time in our island history, chopped down one of our island trees to clear a bit of land for the express purpose of farming.

It is a process that we have been accelerating and improving on ever since. Houses, ships of war, roads, bridges, pit props, coffins, and even protection from wolves – tree-felling is a habit that our forebears tackled with a rare enthusiasm, until they had finally managed to reduce the tree cover from around 65% of our land to a low point of 5% around the time that Queen Victoria died. As I had witnessed in the forest south of Loch Rannoch, what might have taken our Neolithic friend a week and a half of effort can now be done neatly and completely by one man sitting in a timber harvester in about 40 seconds. Spurred by the construction needs of two world wars and their aftermaths, and latterly in reaction to climate change, the tree cover percentage has recently risen slowly back up to around 13%, as we saw earlier, which is still only around a third of the European average, and way off the 70% level maintained and ever increased in Sweden.[8] However, as I have seen at Kielder, instead of natural mixed woodland, we have achieved this increase by planting millions of hectares of non-native, quick-growing, dark softwoods, and we are probably only now understanding the price to be paid.

In theory, I should have been walking through the ancient Caledonian pine forest for eight or nine days now, and I should be in it for another week yet. However, until this morning, I have seen precious little evidence of it. What had once stretched from coast to coast in 1.5 million hectares of magnificent, life-enhancing variety, alive with wolves, lynx, beavers, boar and even wild cattle, has withered away into 30 or so tiny sites covering maybe 1% of its original range. It is the starkest example I have yet seen on my journey of the effect of our Anthropocene wrecking ball.

'What happened next is one of those "one man's dream" stories.' I am with Doug Gilbert, the Operations Manager of the charity Trees for Life, and he is telling me the extraordinary story of how Alan Watson Featherstone spent a quarter of a century bringing to life his vision of restoring the forest and its intricate web of life.

'Back in 1993, he started organising, on a tiny scale, both the conditions for natural regeneration and, because that would never be enough, growing the appropriate trees anyway, and then getting a small army of volunteers to plant them.'

Like the trees that followed, it was an idea that had to take root in some pretty hostile territory, with no land, no people and no money to make it happen. For a long time it was ridiculed, but he went on believing, always gently pushing, always learning. One by one, people started coming on board, and funds started to trickle in to enable some small early projects to get going. A million or so trees later, I am standing with Doug in a nursery at Dundreggan, a 4,000-hectare estate that the charity was able to buy in 2008, a few miles over the hill from Fort Augustus, looking at row upon row of tiny Scots pine, montane willow, rowan, birch, oak, alder, aspen, juniper and hazel.

'Every seed is locally sourced from the appropriate place,' he says, 'from remnant populations of the old forest. That's key. Then, when we start to plant them out as they become ready, we do so randomly, mimicking nature, rather than in straight lines like the new forestry plantations. We have a deer-culling programme that aims to keep a density of five deer per square kilometre or less, and we use fencing only if we absolutely have to, so that people and the wildlife can move around.'

Trees for Life have started by concentrating on Glen Affric, one of the remotest valleys in the Highlands, working their way outwards west and east in the footsteps of ancestor trees, now long gone. As so often in the conservation world, they are enabled to do this by a positive and forward-looking partnership with, in this case, Forest and Land Scotland, the landowner. A few days later, in an illustration of the majestic scale of the ambition, I find myself listening to a farmer fully 30 miles to the north-east, talking excitedly about a cluster of farms he is bringing together to be the easternmost stronghold of this great rewilding. The same distance to the west, near the Atlantic coast, you will find yet more woods being given new life in the same way. This is tree-planting on an epic canvas.

And, at a time when the concept is widely misunderstood and over-claimed, rewilding is exactly what this is. The soil round here is thin and acidic, too poor for all but the barest of food production, and it is time to give the ground back to nature. Such food as comes from the hardscrabble land comes in the form of protein, from the deer, sheep and cattle that have foraged its woods and pastures. In terms of the nation's food security, what is happening here is costing virtually nothing.

Nature discloses herself slowly, like morning mist clearing in a valley. As we walk up the steep wooded bank behind the nursery, and towards the moor, the calling cards of a successful biodiversity appear one by one: long beards of lichen* drooping off the lateral branches of the oaks, pine marten† droppings among the fungi on the grass, a great patch of disturbed ground where a

* Vibrant lichen growth is, among other things, a great indicator of clean air.

† A medium-size predatory mammal that, in terms of agility, comes in almost liquid form, and a symbol of resilience and recovery in a healthy woodland ecosystem.

sounder of wild boar* have moved through. There are feather mosses breaking through in the shady paths. If the deer make this a regular haunt, it seems that everyone else does as well. Generally, the wildlife started seeping back in of its own accord but, where it needed a gentle kick-start, for example with red squirrels, translocation was organised. We are at the wrong time of day for the black grouse to be lekking,† but Doug tells me that they have around 40 males on twelve lek sites around here, which is a very good number.

'No tree is safe from deer until it is two metres high, and has a 10-centimetre girth,' he says. 'After that, the deer lose interest, and the tree has probably made it.' He shows me a rowan that has been shredded by a deer, probably self-medicating, and some brave Scots pine saplings that are starting a new life on the vertical root ball of a fallen giant. After a while, he calls me over.

'Take a look at this.' There is genuine excitement in his voice. 'This is a birch that has arrived through natural regeneration, and has made it intact through to the far end of the winter.' Unaccompanied, I wouldn't have stopped to give the minuscule tree a second glance, because I wouldn't have begun to understand the significance of its survival.

---

* The wild boar was hunted to extinction in Britain 700 years ago, so any you spot now will be escapees, or their feral descendants.

† Leks are spectacular competitive courtship displays by the black grouse, to entice watching females.

'It's a tiny victory,' he says. 'You would never have seen this growth on an unprotected tree a few years ago. Now all we need is about 10 million more of them.'

Unstoppable, he bends down and points out a tiny Scottish asphodel, a rare bog plant with a small green-yellow flower.

'It's not just for trees, all this,' he says. 'Once the habitat is healthy, everything else follows.'

If new trees are one of the key intersecting points between our huge challenges of climate change and species loss, most conversations I have had on the road to this place have insisted that they must be the right trees, in the right place, planted in the right way, and then maintained to the right standards, and that all too often they are not. Additionally, nature will really only benefit in the long term when these activities are all part of landscape-wide solutions, valley to neighbouring valley, rather than just field to neighbouring field. I have found a growing agreement that, all too often, carbon offset through tree-planting is just a lazy excuse for making the rest of us feel better about a carbon habit that we have little or no intention of changing. At a time when we are supposed to be returning to the habit of mimicking nature, a lucrative hedge-fund-owned plantation full of non-native trees that has displaced a human community is the worst kind of 'greenwashing'. I am starting to develop the distinct feeling that this has to change, and quickly.

As I plod my way northwards out of the valley and into another day of wide skies, empty hills and pylons, it strikes me that the genius of what Doug and his colleagues are doing is in giving nature a hand to simply do what it does best itself. Nature is its own best planner, and I am learning all the time that we are usually at our most helpful to it when we remember that fact.

Just as we are likely to be at our least damaging when we allow ourselves to be awed by it.

*

One thing that I am not in any way in awe of is the depletion in the supply of regular flat whites. This is a commodity that has partly become more scarce just because the villages up here are further apart, but partly because there aren't enough people around to make and sell them. The further north I go, the more I find myself stumbling into the effects of the 'Great Resignation'.

We live in a country that has seen any sense of normality shocked out of it over the last six or seven years, and the Scottish tourist industry is merely the latest manifestation of it in my own life. Where, until recently, cafés and coffee shops would be thrown enthusiastically open at the first possible sign of spring, now the lack of staff availability that follows Covid and Brexit has kept many of them locked fast. Shops as well. My generation, or at least those of them who are lucky enough to be sufficiently solvent to do it, apparently quite liked what they saw in the furlough scheme that accompanied the pandemic, voted with their feet, and left the labour market altogether. Even though it is now late April, in village after village, hospitality has yet to migrate its way back in.

This matters, and not just if you are a thirsty traveller on the lookout for a coffee. It's a symptom of more. The same absence of available staff has hit farming and, therefore, food availability and rural income opportunities. For all that we live in nature, and are part of it, its restoration has to take place within the realities of how much we care, what we can afford, and what our lawmakers prioritise, which all needs a coherent plan. The landmark 2010 Lawton review, 'Making Space for Nature', which argued for new Ecological Restoration Zones to connect existing wildlife sites which, themselves, needed to be better protected and managed, has made 'far too little progress', according to its authors. And the money gets less rather than more. Just as one tiny example, the Environment Agency is currently taking 45% fewer water quality samples per year from British rivers than it did a decade ago.[9] Measured against that one otter, those few little grebes, that have appeared since the re-meandering of the Eddleston Water, it is all slightly overpowering. These biodiversity projects that I am visiting, with all the passion and energy that it takes to run them and help them thrive, have to make their way within the wider context of a country that either is, or is not, willing to pay for them, and that feels content to make the little sacrifices needed for wider change. A cynic would say that political policy always follows the weight of votes, anyway, and that the tragedy of our remaining nature is that its future is in the hands of people who produce no more than a handful of them.

If there is a line between reasonable content and prevailing discontent, the Britain I am walking through has slid noiselessly over it. This cannot help but impact negatively on the projects that I am passing through, and the tens of thousands of others that I never even heard about.

*

But Fred Swift is not discontent, even if he has only had two hours' sleep in the last 24, and looks exhausted. However, he also happens to hold the key to one of the previously locked doors of my journey, so I need to keep him awake a little longer.

Two days and 40 or so miles to the north-east of Doug's nursery at Dundreggan, I find Fred in the middle of lambing at his family farm just outside Inverness. Lambing, even though its precise timing is driven by human convenience, is one of those factors that aggregate to make up the visible progress of spring through the land, and I have watched it alongside me for the last five weeks, pulsing northwards through the valleys and fells in a soundscape of high-pitched bleats. But lambing is not why I am here.

For some time now, I have been trying to reconcile how these oases of conservation that I have been visiting can be linked together in some meaningful way within the general desert of our de-natured country. It's all very well for Jo's tiny allotment in Sheffield, Neil's Galloway cattle and Liz's 8-hectare exclosure on Schiehallion to be working to bring back biodiversity, but how about the endless miles in between? Fred reckons he has the answer. Or, at least, one answer.

'Farm clusters,' he says. Hidden behind what looks like just another land management buzzword sits the genuinely exciting prospect of habitat management on a landscape scale.

'It started when my dad got together with a local farming friend over a drink, and the two of them started moaning about the declines in wildlife they had seen since they were young men: oystercatchers, curlews, wild bees, orchids ... the list was pretty endless. They had heard from English friends about this concept of farm clusters, where groups of farms would get together under ecologists' guidance, and then come up with a list of coordinated actions to drag biodiversity levels up.'

Five other farmers quickly joined in, as did the local Forestry Commission, meaning that they had a canvas of around 7,000 hectares on which to paint by the time they were ready to start in early 2021. Importantly, the area comprised multiple different habitat types, all the way from inshore marine to upland forestry. Then three local ecologists worked on a baseline survey and, separately, a habitat survey, so that they were armed with not only what biodiversity was on their own area, but also what was on the neighbouring land, which could then act as a control.

'At that stage, they asked us what species we most wanted to see back, and then produced a very simple plan of action for us to achieve it. It came down to two main activities: habitat connectivity, which we are largely doing by planting alleys of broad-leaved native trees and leaving hedges alone more than we normally would, and then wetland creation.'

Fred sees the wetland work as the main activity for now.

'Basically, we have reversed 200 years of unsuccessful draining down in some low ground. We've reprofiled ditches to take them from vertical to sloping sides, which spreads out and holds bodies of water, and then added wildlife bridges so that mammals can move easier around. Already, a family of otters has moved in, and we've got a few lapwing and curlew breeding. It's early days, but it has so much potential.' He knows he has to give it all time: down south, for example, it has taken the farmers of the Martin Down Cluster in Hampshire five years to get the turtle dove back in town, but now half the farms there are seeing this desperately endangered bird daily. Like most things to do with nature, this is a waiting game.

'Who pays for it all?' I ask, referring to the perennial elephant in the room.

'England is ahead of us on this in terms of public funding,' says Fred, 'so for now we rely on a variety of charitable trusts.' He lists them off on his fingers. 'Working for Waders, Highlands and Islands Environmental Fund, Trees for Life, the Lund Fund. We even got a contribution from DPD.* Money is not the problem; people are really interested in this sort of stuff.'

* A parcel delivery company. Aka Dynamic Parcel Distribution.

It all sounds a little perfect, so I ask him if he has had any pushback, anyone that they had invited to join in but had decided not to.

'Yup,' he says. 'Not everyone is going to be convinced in these sort of schemes until they have established some sort of credibility and record of achievement. The habit of independent action is a hard one to break. We've currently got a large hole in the middle of the doughnut, but it's really not a problem.'

Later on, I sit with Fred on the banks of a large pond at the top end of the family farm, a rudimentary dam speaking eloquently about just which biodiversity engineer lives there.

'Any room for them on the rest of the cluster?' I think aloud. Fred has only just got over laughing at the fact that I fell up to my thighs in a deep bit of pond behind the dam, but he is always keen to talk about his beavers.

'You bet,' he says. 'Where the habitat is right, beavers can be very useful.'

Just how useful, British river systems have slowly been rediscovering for the last twenty years. By regulating the flow of the water, they not only contribute to flood mitigation downstream, but also provide a free tree-thinning and coppicing service, and create a multitude of different ecosystems at different depths behind their dams, which go on to create those vital trophic cascades. Up above, more caddis flies, for example, bring in more dippers who attract more stoats who go on to be eaten by more raptors; down below, more stoneflies feed more salmon who provide meals for more ospreys.

I ask Fred what the problem is with beavers, why the issue has become so divisive.

'It shouldn't have,' he says. 'The problem arises when they are introduced to where they shouldn't be, which happened a lot in the early days. It's not black and white. Nothing is. People just need to understand that a beaver in the right place is a good thing, and that one in the wrong place is bad.'

It seems that the main problem is that humans can put dams exactly where it suits them, whereas beavers will build them where nature directs them to. Also, as is so often the case in Britain, a genuine conservation debate gets informed by emotion rather than science. Anglers talked about beavers voraciously eating their fish (beavers don't eat fish, except in *The Lion, the Witch and the Wardrobe*) or stopping the salmon runs, when, in truth, salmon have been running without let or hindrance past or over beavers' dams since the dawn of time.* But Fred also has sympathy with fellow farmers further south who are losing good trees and prime farming land to an animal they never even invited in.

'Anyway, we need to go on experimenting, and the farm cluster project is going to allow us to do that in an

* And there are, of course, two sides to this story. Down in the Tay Valley farmlands, for example, the beaver is causing serious damage by destroying important trees and undermining river banks. In other European countries, this tends to be dealt with by keeping beavers on relatively unproductive ground, which is carefully zoned, and away from low-lying productive areas. Here, not so.

informed and cumulative way. Just like cattle grazing in the woodland as well as the fields, or the relocation of something like the great-crested newt, it's all about different solutions to old problems.'

We walk back over the hill to the farmhouse, which doubles as my accommodation for the night.

'Farming is the new "F" word out there,' he says, as he pulls the door open and shakes his boots off. 'And I suppose I just want to do my bit to persuade people that, actually, farming is the solution.'

*

A day later, at breakfast at the Cnoc Hotel in Struy, a sturdy biker called Gary walks over to my table in full leathers and hands me a £20 note.

'I heard you telling the waitress about your walk when she asked,' he says, 'and thought that this might help.' For an instant I am knocked off balance, as my life has rarely involved being given cash by passers-by. It occurs to me that this is a habit I could get used to, but then it dawns on me that it's for the charity, and not for me.

Gary is riding his Ducati around the NC500* on his own, as his normal companion is off games with a bad

* The North Coast 500, a 516-mile scenic route around the north coast of Scotland, designed to bring tourist pounds into an area where they are badly needed. Its success in this aim has been undeniable, but the resulting pressure on the small local roads, and the behaviour of some of those visitors (it is now locally known as the 'Andrex 500'), has led to it being as much loathed as loved.

back. He has never consciously seen a curlew, but wants to do something positive if nothing else. I play him the bird's call on my phone so that he can recognise it if he ever hears it in future, and, for an instant, he is transported to another place, far away from his Multistrada bike and his job, helping manage a hospital supply chain in the East Midlands.

'That's beautiful!' he exclaims, and we tacitly agree that he should move his things over to my table so that we can eat our respective breakfasts more companionably. While it reminds me that I haven't seen or heard a curlew for a few days now, it reminds me much more forcibly about the thousand random acts of kindness that have been shown to me, and will go on being shown to me, along the way. From a dab of someone else's sunscreen over a garden fence near Salisbury, to an impromptu cup of tea while I fill my water reservoir from the owner's garden tap outside Inverness, the ancient law of hospitality is alive and kicking.

I have been on the road for over 50 days now, and have slept in 45 beds, most of which have been as a non-paying guest. This has often involved hosts driving relatively long distances towards the end of a busy afternoon to collect me from my path, and then repeating them in the morning to get me back there again. On a few occasions, people had me to stay for a second night, if Covid happened to have struck the next day's house, or if I couldn't find anyone else twenty miles up the trail. Often, we have never clapped eyes on each other before we meet in some moorland car park, churchyard or lonely hillside. For my part, I have always tried to remember to leave my muddy boots in the hallway, and for theirs, they have always granted me the freedom of their fridge. My specialist subject has become the art of navigating my way around strange kitchens, instinctively knowing where the tea is stored, the mugs are kept and the biscuits are hidden.

This has been an adventure built on multiple layers of kindness.

11. A VALLEY LOST IN TIME

Beauly to Alladale and Invercassley:
73 miles; four days
(PRINCIPAL HABITAT: HIGH MONTANE HEATH)

'It is not always easy to be comfortable in the space created by open questions'
MERLIN SHELDRAKE, *ENTANGLED LIFE*

At Contin, near the Ullapool road, my way is barred. To be more precise, the staff of Scottish Southern Energy won't let me walk across the top of their hydro dam at the tail of Loch Achonachie, something that I have been planning to do all day, and the denial of which will occasion a five-mile detour if I can't persuade them. Which I can't. I try, and fail. It seems that they are worried that I might fall in the water, interfere with the turbines, or just become confused. The engineer would let me over if the decision was his, he says, but it's not, and he can't. The supervisor won't come and talk to me, so I can't even offer some suitable bribe, like a heroic mention in my story. I then spot a rowing boat on the southern bank of the River Conon below, and ask the angler if he could take me across. He would if he could, he says, but he only has one life jacket. I say that I don't mind the risk of falling in, but he has the fishing club insurance to think of. Finally, I admit defeat and tread my weary way back down the two-mile track to Marybank and the crossing beyond, through verges of anemones, violets and ground ivy, chewing my way thoughtfully, as I do so, through the healing power of an emergency packet of fruit pastilles.

Obstacles and hazards are part and parcel of a long walk, the daubs of bright colour on an otherwise understated canvas. Over the last few days alone I have encountered a marked bridge that wasn't actually there, a marked footpath that didn't actually exist and a high unmarked deer fence that did; I have been chased by a snarling farm dog ('Don't look scared; it will only make him aggressive!'), majestically ignored by one bull, enthusiastically trotted after by another, and fallen flat on my face in some steep clear-fell forestry; in the hills, I have become a tick magnet, even through my gaiters, and rather impressively, my life has nearly been extinguished by the near silence of a speeding electric car while I crossed the road in the Muir of Ord. To have been removed from the gene pool by an eco car would have been an ironic end to my biodiversity story. Finally, in Beauly, and out of nowhere, or at least out of a hidden side alley, an old lady knocks heavily into me on the pavement with her runaway wheelie bin and then smiles mischievously, as if the accident is neither her fault, nor mine, but the bin's.

But the more I walk, the more resilient I find I have become, and therefore the more that all these inconveniences feed into a general sense of an adventure that I feel rather privileged to be having. My feet are hard, and my shoulders can take just about anything. In the back of my mind is Douglas Adams' elegy to uncertainty: 'I may not have gone where I intended to go, but I think that I have ended up where I intended to be.' It is the very unpredictability of it all that enriches the experience. All those shards of uncertainty that populate my seven- or eight-hour days accumulate, with hindsight, into a vast mosaic pattern of an adventure thoroughly worth having. Even a simple road sign with the word 'Ullapool' or 'Wick' on it cannot fail to delight a man who has walked all the way from where the signs said things like 'Guildford' or 'Chichester'.

In these northern reaches of my home country, I catch the occasional glimpse of the young man I once was, and find myself wondering why, with all that youth and energy available to him back then, he had lived life so cautiously. Besides, if I called my family or friends and complained about any hardships, they would only remind me whose idea it was in the first place, and rightly so.

But for now, I am within 100 miles of my journey's end, and heading back into deep nature.

*

It turns out that deep nature, once you exclude the presiding mountains, has still been recently shaped by man up here to a surprising degree.

And that shaping process has been largely driven by the way the huge sporting estates that make up the area have been managed, which has traditionally been some sort of harvest of death, or of protein, depending on your starting position. I may still be over a hundred miles from Cape Wrath, but the truth is that, with some careful route planning, I could get all the way to the north coast by passing through the land of no more than nine landowners.[1] Actually, if I was really diligent, I could also do it without ever seeing a stand of native trees. The unavoidable fact is that around 23% of Scottish land is devoted to sports shooting of one kind or another and, whichever fringe of the debate you happen to find yourself on, this matters, and is hugely influential. Apart from anything, the sport brings real employment to an area that traditionally is able to offer almost none. Fred's farm cluster may very well be a suitable future model for reasonable farmland, but over 5 million hectares of Scotland is classified as 'less-favoured area',[2] unsuitable for anything more than the occasional sheep or deer. There needs to be a plan for that, too. And, whatever that plan might end up being, it cannot healthily be a continuation of the status quo, where the entire human ecosystem is reliant on the harvesting of a bird, a fish or a mammal, thanks to a few people with extremely deep pockets. Nor can it be endless coniferous plantations.

What also matters is that until very recently it has proved to be almost impossible for anyone other than a super-rich person to own one of these tracts of land, as the living is so tough, and the money drains out of it like its peaty water runs off the largely treeless hills. For all the images we might like to harbour of tweeded lairds knocking grouse out of the August sky from comfortable hillside butts, many or even most of the estates that have recently changed hands have been to the super-rich, many from abroad, who have no intention at all of shooting over them. Apart from anything, why would they, when they will eventually make far more money by playing the carbon offset game? With the lucrative market for green gold now prevailing, it's not for nothing that the chronically depressed price of Highland land has soared recently.* Wouldn't it be much better to rewild the place?

The answer is 'Well, possibly', but there are many pitfalls, not least what your chosen definition of rewilding happens to be. This is where three themes that have been developing in my mind over the last week or so have come to a head. First, in conservation, nothing is as straightforward as anyone claims it is, and there is no 'one size fits all' solution up here, or anywhere else. Secondly, a nation of 68 million hungry people puts full-on rewilding ahead of food production at its own peril. And finally, rewilding is a concept that is as wilfully misunderstood as any apart, perhaps, from regenerative farming. Some estates, like Bunloit on the banks of Loch Ness, are treating the problem scientifically, measuring carbon dioxide equivalent (the standard unit for measuring emissions) and carrying out DNA sampling of the earth to establish what life it actually contains; some that I pass through

* A *Guardian* article from March 2022 ('Lost forest: why is BrewDog's green scheme causing controversy?') estimated that hill ground with natural capital potential had recently doubled in value to between £1,200 and £1,500 per acre.

are ripping out the old Sitka shroud, and planting in its place appropriate native woodlands; some produce glossy, often exaggerated, claims as to just how much carbon they will capture, and how much of the cost is coming out of their own pocket. But the taxpayer is picking up much of the bill, and everything that these estates do affects the daily lives of the people who live and work there, not least by making them financially less attainable as community buyouts. It's all a delicate balance.

Over the course of my walk, I have grown more comfortable around the idea of 're-naturing' than the more fashionable one of rewilding. The idea of re-naturing is to help the relevant local nature flood back in to the borders of even the most intensive of farms and the most desolate of habitats. In fact, I am starting to conclude that the hope I am searching for lies in widespread and routine re-naturing rather than in small islands of biodiversity. 'Bigger, better and more connected', as the 2010 Lawton Report suggested. Two large villages where half the gardens have been left unmown throughout May, linked by unkempt verges and un-manicured hedges, that kind of thing. By the end of my walk, I will come to the uneducated conclusion that possibly 5% of the British countryside is suitable for full rewilding, maybe double that for partial rewilding, and the rest should remain for food production with nature bountifully embroidered around its margins. But that's just a layman's view of an extremely complex subject.

At what is reputed to be one of Britain's remotest houses, Deanich, I meet Innes McNeil, the Reserve

Manager for Alladale, a famous example of an estate whose owner is trying to reinvent the model. I have walked twelve miles to our meeting place, alone but never lonely, and through valleys of the sounds of spring: the clicking of stonechats, scolding of oystercatchers and the endless, invisible sky song of the lark. There are wheatears* everywhere, as there will be from now until the top, and ring ouzels fleeting around the rocks, like clerical blackbirds. The last of the spring snow is clinging on in the lower temperatures of the high hills to either side of my path. After three and a half hours on the hoof in this grand theatre of life, I am rather proud to have arrived only two minutes after I said I would, and only slightly sweaty.

'You're late,' Innes says, with a smile. 'But I've brought along tea and biscuits from the lodge for you, anyway.' This further reinforces a phenomenon that I am not alone among wayfarers in sensing, that the warmth of the welcome in Scotland is often in inverse proportion to the amount you are spending. Go to a four-star hotel, and you will be routinely ignored and patronised; ask for something for free and you will mostly be treated as a long-lost friend. If ever I found a stereotype that should be up for reappraisal on this trip,

* Originally called 'white-arses', for reasons that anyone familiar with them will immediately understand. The prudish Victorians couldn't deal with that, so the name was changed to something completely misleading; but then again, these were the people who bred black Highland cattle to golden brown, because the black version was upsetting their touchy monarch, who didn't like anyone other than herself in the colour.

it should be the highlander's reputation for a certain tightness around the sporran. Out in the wilds, I have been treated like a prince.

Looking around while we eat our pieces*, I drink in one of the most arresting landscapes I have ever seen, a scree-strewn valley sculpted by the forces of nature, maybe the epitome of what John Muir meant when he wrote that 'all that the sun shines on is beautiful, so long as it is wild.'

'It wouldn't be the right thing to go back to how things once were, even if you could,' Innes says, talking about large-scale reforestation. 'The peat is far too thick for it, anyway. What we are doing is accepting a short-term loss for a long-term gain, using native trees as a seed source for the future, and fences as temporary exclosures and enclosures, just until the new trees are big enough.' 800,000 trees have been planted all the same, but native ones, thoughtfully, randomly and not in blocks.

Alladale is famous for its owner's determination to bring wolves and lynx back to the Highlands, in an effort to reintroduce a 'landscape of fear' for the browsers, specifically the red deer, and thus increase fertility by reducing grazing pressure. As has famously been seen in Yellowstone with the reintroduction of that apex predator, the grey wolf, this should lead to a trophic cascade of new biodiversity. But this new approach would need a major shift in the way we think about nature, a shift

* A Scottish packed lunch. Unimprovable, except perhaps with an added Mars Bar.

that slowly puts the natural ecosystem back above man, his livestock* and his pets in the pecking order, or at least alongside them. It would also probably need full area fencing, which could interfere with the legal right of open access for all; and above all, it would need a shift in society's willingness to collectively absorb risk. In other words, it won't happen.

At the time of writing (July 2022), the last fatal wolf attack in the world was three years ago, in Udorsky district, Russia. Wolves *can* kill humans, of course, but the occasions when they do are almost vanishingly rare, especially if there are a million deer knocking about to divert their appetites. (The 'one death is too many' argument, so beloved of health and safety campaigners as a reason not to allow things, is sometimes an easier one to articulate than are the long-term consequences of living with its results.) And experience in Europe over the last decade or so informs us under what circumstances wolves will take out livestock, and allows us to predict roughly how many and therefore plan proper compensation schemes. Meanwhile, dogs kill about four people a year in the UK, and attack thousands more; even bees and hornets kill around five.[3] The likelihood of an informed debate taking place, which balances the known risks against the extraordinary possible environmental

* Studies all over Europe tend to show that, while sheep are very occasional prey for lynx, the numbers are very low (lynx are evolutionarily adapted to hunt roe deer) and the farmer can be properly compensated.

(and therefore human) benefits, is almost tragically small. As a society, it is always easier to walk away from this kind of bold opportunity than it is to surrender the fairytale thought that wolves will be snatching our children from their very cots as soon as the first one sets foot in the country, or that lynx will be queueing up outside lambing sheds with napkins around their necks.

But, for Innes, it goes much further than wolves.

'I was a young stalker when Paul Lister bought Alladale back in 2003. When he first told us that he wasn't interested in shooting things, I wasn't sure that my job would last for long. Either he'd get bored of me, or I'd get disenchanted with what he was doing. But over that time, a combination of his drive and my experience has convinced me that there has to be a new model for the failing Highland estate, one where eco-tourism, outdoor learning and multiple wildlife projects replace the harvest of death in the financial structure. You can still catch the fish and you still need to control the deer, but the business no longer relies on it.'

And control the deer they have, reducing their concentration over that time from over 30 in a square kilometre down to around five. Not all the neighbours are delighted, but that's not the primary aim. Actually, the primary aim is to try to work together with those neighbours, and persuade them to do the same. As with Schiehallion, so here: this has to be done on a landscape scale, and even Alladale's 23,000 acres don't amount to that in this kind of territory.

There is a separate human challenge to all this, but one that I don't hear mentioned often, or not out loud. A keeper on an estate further south tells me privately that a major issue in the move from shooting to ecology as the prime motivator for land use, would be that most employees on sporting estates are extremely low-paid, but make up income from the handsome tips with which rich customers furnish them throughout the shooting season, tips that can make the difference between poverty and comfort.

'Remember this,' he instructs me, in a powerful reminder that many things are not as simple as they might look at first sight. 'Birdwatchers don't tip. Even the rich ones. If you remove the sport entirely, it is the lowest paid who will get hurt the most.' He may be right, but unfortunately he is right in the context of a society that accepts low pay in certain sectors as no more than a routine inconvenience.

Innes and I head north-east up the Gleann Mòr track to a secluded enclosure on a steep wooded bank near the lodge. Each compartment is built around a low tree, and has platforms and shelters to accommodate one wildcat. What strikes me most about my first glimpse of an animal I have hitherto only known in folklore and documentaries is her small size and her unwavering eye contact. Wildcats have not so much been victims of persecution as of dilutions of their former pure selves by the seemingly unstoppable process of hybridisation with domestic cats. Pick any number between 1,000 pure cats left in the wild and none, for no one knows, and you can begin to understand that projects like this one, small in scale though they may be, often remain all there is between a species and its own extinction. In a landscape whose potential progress often seems to be caught in the barbed wire of its own traditions and perceived limitations, experimentation is rife at Alladale; from the hydroponically grown tomatoes to the gradual process of breeding back to something approaching a pure wildcat, they are permanently asking questions.

More questions. More answers. More intervention. More of a chance.

*

'Where are you headed?'

So I tell him, the owner of this gentle voice in the Oykel Bridge Hotel, where I am headed, and where I have come from. It is a day after my Alladale visit, and the voice belongs to a face whose beard seems to contain more than a fair amount of his recent cream of tomato soup, and whose small table is covered in comforting maps. I have spent three sodden hours coming over the hill from Croick through curtains of pouring rain in the forestry rides, one of the rare washout days of my journey. When I look in the mirror behind the bar, there is a faint blue line around my forehead where the baseball cap dye has migrated onto my skin, and I look ridiculous.

'Me too, but the other way,' he says. 'I'm walking from Durness to Dungeness before I get too old. So I've only recently started out. I'm hoping to get home by late August.' If only by a small margin, it's further than I am going, and I am at once impressed and a tiny bit offended. I've grown used to being the person with the biggest journey story around the place and, now that I'm not, it's a bit of a tough surrender.

'I just liked the alliteration of it,' he says, when I ask him how he came to choose the route. 'No other reason that I can think of.' He explains that he is taking each day as it comes, camping where he needs to, and getting a roof over his head where he can. If he finds somewhere he likes, he says, he'll just stop for a day or two and check it out. No sponsorship, and no reason beyond a content-looking person stretching their horizons for a few months. We are both temporary refugees from the pouring rain, and yet not only doesn't he have a clue where he will spend the coming night, he couldn't care less about it. I, on the other hand, know exactly where I am staying, how I will get there, and roughly what time I will arrive. I even know what I am going to eat, shepherd's pie, as my hosts of the night emailed and told me so. I decide that it would be unfair to tell him about that shepherd's pie.

His carefree adventure strikes me as pretty hardcore, and suddenly I feel a twinge of shame about my rather Stalinist programme of events that, each day, has to deliver another twenty miles done, and is always centred around the next comfortable bed and the next tin of digestive biscuits.

We swap our respective motivations, and agree that more than a little comes down to a powerful wish that we both share to avoid becoming one of those embittered old men who look over their garden hedges, pruning shears in hand, resenting the pervading happiness and youth of people passing by. I tell him that I decided long ago to stay as the passer-by as long as I could, until it became ridiculous.

He watches me settle the bill for coffee at the bar, and then haul my soaked pack onto my soaked back. I have become practised at doing this with an ergonomic flick of the pack off my right knee and onto my right shoulder, only this time I have to apologise as it throws a little shower of droplets over a group of forgiving German bikers.

'I'm 71, by the way,' he adds, as I head for the door. 'How about you?'

All the others along the way seem to have been younger than me, and I can't help admiring his energy and ambition. Actually, more than anything I admire his courage at being happy to be flexible.

At the same time, as I walk back out into the torrential rain, it dawns on me that my bones are finally getting a little weary. For some reason, some little wellspring of pent-up emotion suddenly hits me on the sodden road from Oykel Bridge to Invercassley, a sharp pang of homesickness mixed with a rather less easily defined one of irrelevance, and a sliver of eco-grief for good measure. The feeling is threatening to become something altogether harder to shift when a huge white camper van sprays me with water as it speeds past, and I laugh, and get a grip again. A few months ago, I might have offered my middle finger to his rear-view mirror as he sped away, but I find that my brain doesn't think like that any more, so I wipe my face and walk on.

However, even if it has taken 850 miles, the first tiny crack has appeared in my journey. From now on, I sense that I may just be starting to live on borrowed time.

*

As I walk the long solitude of Glen Cassley the next day, escorted by stonechats and cuckoos, I think a bit more about that 'harvest of death' that Innes talked about, and its part in my past.

For a few summers in my twenties, I used to go each August with some friends to a little valley in Sutherland, and walk up red grouse behind pointers or setters on the moors behind the lodge. In fact, the first bird I ever shot burst not out of the heather in front of me, but from under the wing of a crashed German bomber left over from the Second World War. As an exercise in harvesting the surplus protein from the land in a sustainable way, it has few equals; and, although it might be creatively convenient now to criticise my youthful self for doing it, I can neither unlearn the lessons of the natural world that it taught me, nor pretend for a second that it didn't thrill me. While I no longer shoot, I retain a great deal of sympathy with the sport at its most basic, pot-filling level, and for the cultural links it gives us with our past. Our species has been hunting for around 2 million years, and it is probably going to take more than three or four decades to knock it out of the system altogether. Equally, I am repelled by its excesses – as, I might point out, are most of its participants.

For all that the commercial sport of shooting creates the revenue for people to be paid to manage land sympathetically, it has many questions to answer, and a growing disconnect with what the rest of society feels comfortable with, particularly the industrial nature of its 'big bag' days. The effect on their habitat of millions of reared pheasants,[*] only a third of whom ever actually go on to get shot, is hotly debated, but it is highly unlikely that a non-native species that makes up around 40% of its adopted country's avian biomass has no effect at all. The glacially slow move away from lead shot to steel means that any mass route to market through the supermarket chains is still a non-starter, which in turn leads to concerns about exactly where much of this wild, healthy and nutritious meat is actually ending up. And yet it's all too easy to vilify a gamekeeper in the hectic echo chamber of today's press and social media, easy to infer from the shocking minority that every industry contains, that the remainder must also be 'up to something'. But to do so is not only deeply unfair to the professional majority, but also to overlook the positive role a good keeper on a sustainable and well-run shoot can have on the habitat and the biodiversity that lives within it. For good or ill, the keeper is Britain's only remaining apex predator, and there are now 3,000 left from the army of 23,000 who headed over to the trenches in 1914.[†]

The issue of legal predator control, which has cast its long shadow over conservation for many decades now,

---

* 48 million, according to the RSPB, or 35 million, according to the Game and Wildlife Conservation Trust (GWCT), conservation statistics tending to be a function of who is providing them.

† Disclosure: I have been paid to write an account of the re-naturing exercise on a grey partridge shoot in West Sussex, and have spent hundreds of hours with the keeping staff. That is where I found the rough poppy, referred to in Chapter 1.

is at its most emotive when it comes to game shooting, where the inference is that the entertainment of the privileged few trumps the rights of any carnivore species who happen to get in the way. This may be an easy point of view for the neutral observer to get behind, and is certainly an accurate one in the frequent instances when a rogue keeper, say, executes a protected raptor. My experience is that it is generally more complicated than that, even when the control involved has nothing to do with shooting for sport, such as in protecting breeding lapwings and curlews. Predator control is one leg of a three-legged stool for the protection of vulnerable species (the other two being sufficient habitat and a plentiful food source), and the more vulnerable the species, the greater role it plays. I once did some informal research over a beer with a grey partridge gamekeeper on the South Downs and, between us, we came up with no fewer than 36 different predators* that would be lining up as a pair of greys laid their large clutch of eggs on a May morning in a little scrape in the hedgerow, none

* The full list is: magpie; rook; crow; raven; jackdaw, jay; kestrel; sparrowhawk; goshawk; red kite; peregrine; buzzard; marsh harrier; hen harrier; tawny owl; adder; grass snake; rat; hedgehog; grey squirrel; weasel; stoat; mink; polecat; feral ferret; fox; badger; feral cat; domestic cat; dog; human. Then add to that sheep, deer, pheasants and red-legged partridges, who will sometimes break the eggs for calcium or kick them out for no good reason. The gamekeeper had even seen incidents of eggs falling out of the nest into mole holes that had been drilled directly underneath, which might just have been clever weasels using an existing facility to access the nests.

of which would particularly matter if the prey population was at a healthy level. However, the grey partridge is, like the curlew and capercaillie, a red-listed bird and, like them, would certainly go locally extinct without human intervention to protect it. Of those 36 species, only ten can be legally controlled as it is, a figure that comes down to seven (crow, jackdaw, magpie, fox, stoat, weasel and rat) when other practical and local limitations are applied. Ironically, as always, the species that has done them the most harm is the one now belatedly trying to save them.

It is not hard to search out someone who disagrees with me, which I deliberately do, and I walk and talk with Professor Chris Spray to tease out why he thinks I am wrong. I originally met Chris back at Peebles, where he is supervising the re-meandering project as a scientist, but here I am talking to him as a friend and fellow birder who happens to have stronger views on shooting than I do. We both like the discourse that comes from different views, so this works well.

'The problem with predator control for the purposes of shooting,' he says, 'is the start point, that and the activities of a few rogue estates. And that start point is the creation and management of a largely unnatural environment for one aim – to maximise a target species that paying clients want to shoot.'

'They then introduce millions of that target species artificially, an act that totally unbalances any natural equilibrium between predator and prey. Next, they target any predator that comes within a mile of upsetting the financial model, and finally, they claim to be enhancing biodiversity when, often, they are just enhancing one hunted species at the expense of all the others, and shouting all the while about the few species that happen to benefit collaterally.'

'By the way,' he adds, with a nod towards that most basic of human needs, 'I'll happily eat the next pheasant I'm offered, in case you were wondering.'

The issue cuts both ways, of course, and I find myself honestly conflicted, while the debate rages on from within the siloes of each camp. Eventually, there needs to be some sort of consensus. Many of the same people who would support the control of rats and crows with some enthusiasm on a shooting estate, may well baulk a bit at licenses being issued for shooting the relatively uncommon goosander on fishing rivers, and even more so for any amber-listed eider duck who happens to live near a mussel farm. With the exception of the brown rat, whose misfortune is to be un-mourned by most humans in most places when it is locally eradicated, predator species that are currently being lethally controlled are generally just collateral victims of man's wider inability to live alongside the nature he is part of.

In other words, if we looked after the place properly, most of it wouldn't need to happen in the first place.

*

In the wilds below Ben More Assynt, I break out Ordnance Survey's sheet 16, which also officially happens to be their least asked-for map. It is the second-last of the

30 maps I will eventually have used on my journey, and the thought of its rarity delights me.

In recent nights, I have started to see the Cape Wrath lighthouse in the corner of my dreams, but also to slightly dread what lies beyond. 'Always the journey, never the destination',[4] is what I continually seem to conclude, rather than risk thinking about it, because I have thought of little else for over half a year.

That journey has become as much a part of me as my right arm, and is now quite simply what I do. The names on the map, Glenrossal, Duchally, Corriekinloch, are all way marks in the long story of my walk. April becomes May and here, in the far north, the daffodils that are a long-composted memory at home are still in full bloom. In Rosehall, I even find some that haven't quite come out yet. Caroline tells me that the oak under whose half-lit boughs this adventure was born, the one under which I lay all those months ago and all those hundreds of miles to the south, is now in full leaf, and the nesting buzzards back in its canopy. This is in stark contrast to north Scotland, where the oaks are still utterly dormant. If it were ever a race in the first place, I have beaten the greening oaks hands down, and the first one I see in leaf will be in Fort William, on my way south a week later.

Other than the oaks and the late-coming storm petrels, the balance of spring seems to have arrived overnight. It has been a very dry season by Scottish standards, with many reservoirs half empty and the pollinators out in force: hoverflies, thrumming bumblebees, orange tips, peacocks and tortoiseshells. Each new arrival, each colourful stonechat perched high on the yellow gorse, each overflying whimbrel and each grey wagtail bobbing on the pebbles of a stream bed help to fill in the pieces of that vast seasonal jigsaw puzzle that we call the return of spring. I see it mainly through birds, others do so through insects or plants.

But it is beside a lonely inlet off Loch Shin that I am brought up short by a plaintive call that emanates from the far side of some reeds. First one, and then another in reply from a little distance away. I stand stock-still, even though I know exactly what that sound is. Part deranged donkey, part gull call in slowed-down speed, it is an elegy for the wilderness whose echoes leak out from the surrounding mountains straight into my soul.

Indeed, if I had to take one sound from nature to my desert island, it would be the haunting cry of the red-throated diver. That and the curlew.

Right now, it is simply time to stop and listen, and let the moment live itself out.

12. THE LIGHTHOUSE AT THE END OF THE WORLD

Invercassley to Cape Wrath: 88 miles; four days
(PRINCIPAL HABITAT: BLANKET BOG
AND COASTAL DUNE)

'He has married me with a ring, a ring of bright water
Whose ripples travel from the heart of the sea'
KATHLEEN RAINE

And, once again, the sun shines on.

Friends who thought that I was foolish to walk this early in the year, rather than summer, had tutted their concern even when I pointed out to them that spring was traditionally the driest season.

'Just think carefully about it,' one of them had emailed me, fearing for my frostbitten feet. 'You could still be walking through thick snow up in the Highlands.' He added by inference that, if anyone was going to get themselves lost in a snowdrift and thus inconvenience the locals, that someone would be me, and he probably had a point.

As things unfold, this April, which has just given over to May, will turn out to have been the sunniest and the fourth-driest on record, but also to have had the lowest average maximum temperature since 1922,[1] all factors that heavily favour the unheroic walker. The snow is around, but only splashed erratically up on the high peaks like a child's landscape drawing, not blocking the passes and valleys down below. Every inch of exposed skin on my body has become a deep chestnut brown, which is all a bit ironic, as the changing climate is supposed to make things warmer, wetter and windier. I have got through more sun-screen in two months than I generally use in a decade.

Anyway, the truth is that the longer I walk, the less I am affected by the weather, which is simply the reality of my workspace. I have a plan, I have the kit and, most of the time at the moment, nothing gets in the way. Unlike the biodiversity around me, I am relatively sheltered from the long-term effects of a warming planet, even though I, too, happen to be moving slowly northwards, and sometimes uphill. But I cannot shelter my attention from all the other changes that are slowly happening around me, and which my own species has also kick-started, for they are increasingly obvious. While climate change well and truly has control of the microphone for now, in reality it is only one important factor of many that are affecting every layer of our planet: pollution, waste, over-consumption, soil degradation and water contamination, to name but five others. Even the fact that our shrinking world has allowed us and our goods to travel everywhere we choose, has introduced invasive species with gay abandon, and accelerated the progress of diseases that our wildlife then has to live with.

We run the risk of educating a generation of people to think that climate change is the only show in town; and, increasingly, it strikes me as rather uncomfortable that most of us never seem to get round to talking about any of the others. 'Climate change probably won't kill us,' repeated more than one conservationist on my journey. 'Species loss well might.'

*

For a short while by Loch Shinn, I seem to be under a sky exclusively full of eagles, both golden and white-tailed.

The banks below where they soar are an almost shocking acid yellow with the flowers of gorse and broom. Apart from the oaks, whose buds are still nowhere near bursting open, spring has saturated everything around me with colour and life, her bounty continuing to take me by surprise at every turn. The prevailing sense of plenty reminds me that biodiversity is really only the first rung on the stepladder of nature recovery; important enough, and well understood by most people these days. But of course it is really bio-*abundance*, for want of a better term, that we should be retrieving from our generational memory and then aiming for, a return to the days of bounty when it wasn't all an ongoing crisis.

I break out the last map of all (Sheet 09: Cape Wrath) from the pocket of my pack. For a minute or two, I can't quite bring myself to open it up, preferring instead to admire and finger its pristine cover, and allow my imagination to run up the road ahead of me towards the crashing waves and high sea cliffs depicted there. Unopened, a brand-new Ordnance Survey map is a treasure chest of hidden possibilities and beckoning adventure; opened up, it is simply a tool of the trade that happens to be a bit difficult for a clumsy person like me to fold the right way. Besides, just as, when I was a soldier, every operation we carried out seemed to take place on the border of two or more maps, so in my walk, every junction that requires a decision is inconveniently right on the fold.

'That will be you,' I say to my old feet, pointing at the picture on the cover, 'in a couple of days' time.' But the feet keep their silence. They will have their moment.

Hitherto, I have lived in the day, as Satish suggested I should, but from now on it is as if there is a magnetic force reaching out to me from a lighthouse on a cliff, 30 miles to the north, and I finally allow myself to think that I *should* get there, rather than *might* get there. Abandoning the comfort of that protective uncertainty is a more significant decision than you might at first think. In truth, I have done this entire journey on the basis that I will probably fail to complete it; it has been simply inconceivable that something, some awkward moment in just one of those 2 million steps, won't happen to derail it. But now, from the top of the mountain I can see in front of me, I know full well that you can see Cape Wrath, because I climbed it in a past life, and saw from it the hill above the lighthouse.

Even now, the approaching ocean will reveal itself only by degrees, and slowly. First, there is the watershed. It is the final one of the dozens that I have crossed, somewhere on the low pass between Loch Merkland and Loch More where from now on, every drop of rain that falls will head westwards into the Atlantic Ocean, instead of eastwards to the North Sea. But the rain doesn't fall today and, in the resulting dryness, the occasional desultory gull quietly patrols the flatlands around Achfary in the cool sea breeze that begins to have just the faintest hint of salt about it. Then, a little short of Laxford Bridge, mussel and crab shells, dropped by birds onto the anvil of the tarmac road, are joined first by strands of seaweed, and finally by the sea itself.

At Laxford Bay, I take my boots and socks off and paddle my feet in salt water for the first time since Lymington, 930 miles behind me. Those pale, unblistered feet have lasted well, and deserve this small reward in a rockpool left by the ebb tide, alongside the seaweed, the shrimps and the anemones. They are not pretty, but then they haven't really needed to be. Besides, no one other than me has to look at them, and even I don't make a habit of it. Beyond the seaweed, a little flock of eider duck are making slow progress across the water, their voices sounding for all the world like astonished, scandalised stock doves.

I cannot be bothered with paths any more, and so take my chances on the A838, alongside the rented motorhomes, pimped-up sports cars and surprisingly polite bikers of the North Coast 500. It's still early season, so the road is quiet, but there is also a silent coming together of end-to-enders, of cyclists from the south and of walkers off the Cape Wrath Trail, for whom these complex private moments of mental crescendo amount to so much more than the drivers of those passing vehicles will ever know. I have driven past their predecessors myself many times over the years, these pilgrims of endurance, near Lands End or John o' Groats, but only now do I understand that it is only in the final step that the account can in any way be settled. For my own part, I still haven't the faintest idea how I will react when I finish, only that I am becoming a little bit more emotional each passing day, even if only subliminally.

'Good on you, mate,' says a Welshman I chat to on the bridge at Rhiconich who, to my pleasure, is called Taffy. He has cycled all the way from Cardiff, he tells me, but rather curiously has gone via Exeter, Southampton and Manchester, and spent over a year going about it, a year, it seems, largely spent growing a beard of lush magnificence. He is delightful, in the sense that that he simply exudes delight.

'I just get work for a few weeks when I run out of money, and then I move on.'

A lone snipe soars up from a spot right next to where his wheel is resting, squeaking its way across the heather to the east in a series of rapid jerks and dives. I feel like telling him that it is only the third one I have seen all journey, but then desist. Taffy is an adventurer, not a bird man.

'Where next?' I ask. 'I mean, after you get to Cape Wrath.'

'Cape Wrath?' he asks, as if this is a strange and alien concept that he has never really thought about. 'Now there's an idea.'

His beard really is magnificent, and he proudly tells me that he hasn't had a bath since Keswick.

'Leave soap out of the equation,' he explains, 'and the natural oils will do all the cleaning you need.'

My brain is tired, and full of many complicated things, so I think I inadvertently tell him that I love him, rather than the idea of his soapless life. Whatever it is I actually say, he just smiles and hugs me awkwardly over the handlebars of his bike. 'Go well, man,' he says. 'Go well, yourself,' I say in return. I think I even say 'man', too.

Then, leaving a vibrant waft of those natural oils in his wake, he pedals his heavy-laden old bike northwards up the long hill, only very slightly faster than I am walking. Only long after he has gone out of my sight do I realise that, as much as anything, what I really love about him is the liberation that he represents.

My plan is to get to Durness tonight, fifteen miles distant on the north coast, visit the oyster farm there, and then take the little ferry across the coastal inlet of the Kyle of Durness the next morning, before walking the final few hours to the lighthouse to complete the journey. It is a good plan on paper, but becomes rather less so a few hours later when I call the ferryman from my bed-and-breakfast, only to hear that he has arbitrarily decided to go shopping in Inverness the next day.

'Then I'll have to wait till Thursday,' I say manfully, struggling to hide my disappointment.

'Too much weather on Thursday and Friday,' he says. 'Next crossing will probably be at the weekend.' It never really occurred to me that you could have too much weather, but this has been a voyage of discovery all along, to which this gem can now be added.

Anyway, it is immaterial. By the weekend, I need to be 200 miles south, on a cruise ship, contracted to talk about seabirds in what is part of my planned reintegration into polite society. I need a new plan, and quickly. For eight weeks, I have pretended to myself and anyone who would listen that Durness would do as a final destination if I couldn't get over on the ferry; but, now that it is a live prospect, I see it for the baseless fiction that it always was. It is Cape Wrath or nothing, as it always has been. So I make a cup of tea and lay the map out on the bed to make a new plan. Making cups of tea has become my go-to activity in times of crisis, as automatic a reflex as swatting a fly away from a summer picnic.

There are two options left to me, one of which is to go down to the south end of the Kyle and then work my way around the estuary until I get to the other side of the ferry crossing. For various reasons, this doesn't excite me. The other, and my preferred option for various reasons, is to go up the coast from Kinlochbervie, over the bridgeless rivers and pathless bogs of the final day of the Cape Wrath Trail which, annoyingly, also means backtracking all the way to Kinlochbervie before I do it. Worse, I jettisoned my sleeping bag southwards a few days ago, so the option of sleeping out is no longer on, and I will have to get from Kinlochbervie to Cape Wrath and back in one day. There is also the small matter of this being a naval live firing range, which will close the entire area if it is in use. I know that it will be open tomorrow because I checked in advance, but have no idea whether those naval guns are planning to grind back into action over the following days.

Just when I don't want the expenditure of one extra joule of energy, I have to commit to finishing on the route that all the locals have warned me to avoid. And just when I need a day of sunshine, the forecast for the following few days is, indeed, atrocious.

It is quite a time for the long run of luck to go missing.

*

For days now, weeks even, I have passed through lands largely without people, walked down tracks without waymarks, so it is something of a relief to find Don O'Driscoll the next day, exactly where he said he'd be, by the side of the road in one of Britain's outermost villages. As the local hooded crow flies, I have under 1% of the journey left, and I have decided to leave that last bit until the following day.

'That's a decent walk you've been on,' he offers, eyeing me up and down for a moment. As it turns out, Don is as keen to talk poetry as he is biodiversity, although strictly speaking I am here because he is warden of mainland Britain's northernmost nature reserve, Sandwood Bay.

'Have you heard of Kathleen Raine?' he asks. I've been expecting him to talk about machair* or sand

* One of Europe's rarest habitats, coastal machair is a low-lying strip of species-rich grass and dunes, based on lime-rich shell sand. Influenced over the centuries by grazing and low-intensity rotational farming, it is a habitat that occurs only in north-west Scotland and western Ireland.

dunes, so I assume that she is an academic, or some PhD student working on her ecology project. I give a neutral, negative reply, but enthusiastically write her name down in my notebook to show willing, or at least not to look stupid, planning to look her up later. She probably wrote a paper on machair or something, I decide.

'"There is stone in me who knows stone,"' he says slowly, in his soft Irish brogue, looking away down the four-mile track that leads to Sandwood Bay. '"Substance of rock that remembers the unending simplicity of rest." I love that. She wrote it. She was the one who indirectly gave the phrase "ring of bright water" to Gavin Maxwell.' This strikes a chord, and I tell him so. *A Ring of Bright Water* is one of the few pillars left standing from the years that have eroded so much of the architecture of my boyhood reading.

As we set out towards Sandwood Bay united by the love of that 60-year old story, we talk as we walk, and as if we have been talking all our lives. Of how the rocks came. Of faraway people who have always seen this place as a problem, not a joy. Of how debate is damagingly polarised up here on sheep, deer, grouse, beavers and land ownership. Of the goldeneye on the lochan and how the curlew no longer breeds in the high moors here. Of how he likes to leave most of the skin and bones from a deer carcass on the hill, so that the nutrients return to the ground that first sustained them, for the eagles and others to feed off. Of heather burning and white-tailed sea eagles. Of the sadness of the Irish troubles. Of where we both were in the summer of

1986, and what it means to once have been on opposite sides of an argument. In the normally taciturn world of conservation, the two of us had much to cover.

'See the lichen on this stone,' he says, pausing and bending down to pick a large pebble off the well-maintained path. 'The acid from the lichen will slowly break down that stone for the next thousand years or so, until it is part of the earth beneath us. No one really thinks of stones as transient things. But they are.'

This comes as quite a revelation when, all these weeks, I have been seeing myself as the temporary trespasser through a permanent landscape, here today, gone tomorrow. But he is right. Born out of fire, the tallest rock is still only there at the behest of the wind, ice and rain around it. Every last atom is transient.

Don's patch extends to nearly 5,000 hectares of both wild and crofted* land, with the beautiful Sandwood Bay as the jewel in its coastal crown. With its wet peatlands, saltwater lagoon, dune grassland, shifting dunes and machair, it is an exquisitely precious area for countless reasons, and is under the strongest of legal protection. On this spring day, it is almost painfully beautiful.

Birdsong is everywhere, and all around us insects are making loud use of the lengthening northern days. That same spring alongside which I started at Lymington has finally arrived here with all its energy and change. It

* Crofting is a form of land tenure and small-scale farming and food production that is widespread in the Highlands.

runs from the hills, bursts from the heather and seeps out of the very fissures in the living rock.

'We maintain the four-mile path to the beach,' he explains, when I ask what the John Muir Trust's main work is here, 'with groups of volunteers who might come from anywhere in Britain; and you might not think we'd need to, but we also have to organise regular beach cleans.' Later, I will see what he means, on a shoreline punctuated in patches by the very unorganic detritus of a fishing industry that hasn't so much as heard of this place, let alone cared about it. 'We maintain culverts and bridges, paint the building at the road head, and monitor the wildlife.' If the maintenance work is the hard landscaping of his role, he sees the less tangible side as equally important: facilitating access to one of the great beaches in Europe, reducing collateral damage by keeping walkers on the path, and helping to interpret the landscape in a way that compensates for the loss of ecological literacy from which we all maybe suffer.

These are the routine jobs to be done, and very important for all that, but I sense that there is much more to Don's relationship with Sandwood Bay than what he is paid to do. He is imbued with the deepest sense of place that only somewhere with the rawness of these peat flows and dark pools can bestow, and a cultural inquisitiveness that goes far beyond its natural history; he has married into it both physically and metaphorically. Like the red squirrels at Dundreggan, it is as if he has been translocated to a new habitat that is instantly home. I get the feeling, as I have elsewhere on my journey, that many of these professional conservationists live not so much in the job, but in order to secure the stories of the land and pass them on, and thus make sure that there are enough people in future to carry the flame forward. Every time I walk away from one of these encounters, I find that what remains when everything else has been sifted away by the passage of time are those stories. Adult or not, that bit of the child in us we never lose. And the truth is that, adult or not, each one of the footprints we make in the course of creating our own life story is either helping or harming the nature around us. Nothing here is neutral any more, if it ever was; nor can it ever be again.

And it is the children that are a focus of Sandwood, as they are for the Trust that owns and manages it. Don describes how he helps to run 'Hill to Grill' sessions for the local Ullapool schoolchildren, where they learn to camera-stalk a deer using the wind and the folds of the land, to read signs of damage in the heather and to learn about venison. They even do a foraging walk, to sample pine needle tea, rowan jelly, gorse flowers, sorrel and wild garlic. 'Sometimes I cull a deer before they arrive,' he says, 'and then they sit around and watch me butcher it. It's a brilliant little lesson in anatomy, and in the magical process by which a grazing animal converts sunshine and vegetation into protein. We end with a barbecue where the teachers are legally allowed to eat the venison, but the children aren't.'

We exchange weary smiles. We have both raised children in a world that increasingly seems to want to protect them from natural realities, while at the same time being content to feed them lethal salts and sugars, and expose them to all the darkness at the far end of social media.

However, I can't help but ask how the vegan and vegetarian children get on with the sight of a fallen deer being worked on.

'Fine, actually. Some just turn away from time to time, and a few don't want to see it at all, but there seems to be a fascination in how an animal that has recently been running free goes through the process of becoming recognisable food.' He acknowledges that there may be a difference in attitude between a child raised in Ullapool and one from a southern inner city, but asserts that children tend to complicate these things much less than the adults who are raising them.

For the first time on my long journey, I can actually arrange to re-meet someone I am with a couple of days later, because what has been linear for 55 long days is now finally circular.

Cape Wrath is only a dozen hard miles to the north of me and, as Satish Kumar advised me all those months ago, I can finally focus on the destination. For a second or two, the prospect of getting there terrifies me, and the sense of imminent bereavement outweighs the satisfaction I should feel.

Then Don and I stand for a moment in silence, listening out for curlews.

'Never more,' he says quietly, when we fail to hear one, and then adds mischievously: 'That was Edgar Allan Poe, by the way.'

*

When I look out of the window on the following morning, the soaked car park under a leaky and leaden sky confirms yesterday's pessimistic weather forecast.

'Just today,' I tell my pack as I haul it on to my back. 'Then it's done.' That Osprey pack has become my replacement friend now that the sunshine has gone, and my shadow has shrivelled away into my feet. I have rather taken the achievement of every individual day's destination for granted for the last two months, but not now. The confidence of two days ago, when I gazed out at Ben Stack from the watershed at Merkland, when I knew that I was more likely to make it than not, has receded like a forgotten political promise. Today, I will be out on the open moors in thick cloud, compass in hand and trying to stay out of the depths of the peat bog. I will be pushing a weary body rather harder and further than it had expected to go, doing once again what the taxpayer was funding me to do over four decades ago when I was an infantry soldier.

Don is standing in the rain at the Sandwood road head with a cheese and pickle sandwich and a couple of bananas for my lunch, and I take comfort from the fact that the prospect of my walk amuses rather than concerns him.

'Man up, I thought you were a soldier!' he says, when I stare balefully out at the dreech.* 'Anyway, there'll be venison in the pot for you at my house this evening,' he says. 'And whisky. Obviously whisky. Lots of whisky. That goes without saying.'

Once I have retraced the easy four-mile track to Sandwood Bay, and just when the minor challenge ahead of me calls for calm, I go slightly mad, as if the whole weight of the last 55 days is pushing down on the next four hours, and plasticising it into some sort of impossible challenge. On that manic walk out, all I can think about is the fear of personal failure, and I start to notice a version of me that I neither like nor trust, a version that has already decided to go clean through the red flags of the military danger area regardless of whether or not they are flying.

The obsession with that lighthouse has become so intense that I neither stop nor drink nor eat anything at all, and I suspect that I never notice that the danger flags aren't flying anyway. To stop even just the once, or so my addled brain decides, is to jeopardise the whole adventure, so I never stop at all. I just hold the compass in the flat of my right hand, and follow the arrow through the wet mist to where it leads me. At a time when I might reasonably be basking in the coming aura of a job well done, all I can think of is how to explain

* Scots word for damp, grey weather, and which has no English equivalent except damp, grey weather.

away my potential failure to do it. My family had previously offered to come and walk the last day with me, and I am now glad that I put them off, not least because this is not the heroic version of me that I would like them to see. For four or five hours, I become the person that I have managed not to be for the last 50 days.

So I just press on into the damp gloom, compass held out in front of me, picking landmarks at the limit of the 50-metre visibility, and then resetting to the next one as I arrive. The reality of crossing a peat bog is that walking in a militarily straight line is out of the question, subordinated instead to hundreds of little switches to the left or right to avoid ponds or high hags, and then a compensatory switch the other way. It's a job that requires competence rather than skill, in that if I go too far to the right, I will eventually come to the Durness road, and if I go too far to the left, I will reach the cliffs of the Atlantic, and presumably stop. I have become quite adept at reading land while out on the trail, and gradually find that the route I have chosen is a good one, and that I am reaching each waypoint at roughly the time I had planned to.

On the ridge at Cnoc a' Ghiubhais, the cloud clears momentarily, enough for me to make out two figures in bright waterproof jackets up ahead in the middle distance, working their northwards way through the bog. From my vantage point, I can also see that they are about to disturb a herd of twenty or so red deer, and I watch the latter trot their easy way down a valley towards the sea, away from danger. The sight of the pair partially reinstates the quiet adventurer in me in place of the recent maniac, and I quicken my pace over the ground so that I can at least ask to walk the final few miles in the fellowship of other pilgrims of endurance. I have always understood deep down that a memorable journey is entitled to a respectful conclusion, if only to acknowledge that the changes that it has brought along are real ones, and not transitory. Besides, I am only just managing to subordinate the emotional child within whose soul a whole year of hope and effort has so recently been boiling over the sides, like a saucepan of unattended marmalade.

Running them down across the ditches and hags of the peat bog is the work of no more than fifteen minutes of quick progress. They are zoology graduates from Sheffield University, two lads on the final stages of the brutal Cape Wrath Trail.* They are exhausted from a shorter but rather tougher assignment than mine, and their feet are in a terrible state, but the embarrassing thought nonetheless still dawns on me that all I really want is to be parented by someone other than me after my weird morning. They may be 40 years younger than me, but it turns out that they are more than up to the job.

'You must be buzzing,' says Sam, when I tell him where I have come from.

* Britain's toughest trail by far, the CWT is a 230-mile hike up from Fort William to Cape Wrath, distinguished by the fact that there are hardly any paths to follow. All the completers I met at the time had three things in common: their feet were wrecked, they were proud as hell of their achievement, and none of them had enjoyed it.

'I guess,' I say, still without commitment. Right now, whatever else I am doing, it is not buzzing. In behaving as I have behaved this morning, I actually feel that I have contaminated the purity of the walk, even if just by a tiny bit.

'That's amazing, what you've done,' agrees Gareth. I decide not to tell them about the comfortable beds and large suppers of my nights along the way. They have camped out every night, and they look it.

'Surely you are going to celebrate?' adds Sam, when I tell him that I forgot to pick up the miniature of Dalwhinnie malt that I had been carrying for the last ten days, but had left in the room.

'Eventually,' I say, almost under my breath, knowing that I have still got a five-hour return journey to deal with.

After a while, we reach the track up the length of which I would have walked if the ferry had been running, about a mile from the lighthouse. I have thought about this time for long enough over the last few days to respect it and enjoy it for what it is, a tiny moment of near-grace before the almost inevitable anti-climax that will follow. Equally, I don't want to prioritise my achievement over theirs, just because mine has taken longer. I couldn't have done what they are just about to complete. If I had expected a kaleidoscope of emotions after being on the move for 50 or so days, I discover to my surprise that I am instead just focused on the immediate matter of getting the job completed. Once I am touching the sturdy wall of the lighthouse, I will work out what to do next. Also, in a journey of a thousand conversations, I find that I want to finish it not in silence, but by having the thousand and first.

For the first time in hours, the rain has let up, and a watery sun throws three faint shadows in front of three human sundials as the path bends round to the north, and the dark top of the lighthouse finally comes into view.

Four hundred feet below, the grey sea swells collide softly with the cliffs in an abyss that I can't quite make out through the spray and mist. White fulmars ride the breeze in rapid searchlight sweeps across the vertical rock face and, to the north, maybe a couple of miles out to sea, a little yacht runs before the gentle breeze under the shroud of high cloud, heading for the Orkney Islands and beyond. For an instant, something deep inside me insists that I should be doing the same thing, not stopping here but moving ever north until there is no more north left, that those feet in the water at Lymington were only at the very beginning of something much, much longer than this. Until today, I seem to have managed just to move by slow degrees up the map, never really thinking about the significance. Standing here, it is as if north has mutated from being a direction to an obsession. Part of the journey is driving me on to completion, while another part, quiet but insistent, wants to hold me within it for ever. I have walked this far, and now a little part of me wants to walk on for eternity.

'You first,' says Gareth, breaking the silence. 'Give me your phone, and I'll record the moment for posterity.'

I hand him the phone and walk on down the final few yards to the lighthouse.

PART 4

Full Circle

13. DOG DAYS IN SHAKESPEARE LAND

Fairford to Stratford-upon-Avon, July 2022:
60 miles; three days
(PRINCIPAL HABITAT: ARABLE)

'On a finite planet, there must be some limits to material expansion. A rising population with insatiable material aspirations sits uneasily with the finite nature of our earthly home'
TIM JACKSON, *PROSPERITY WITHOUT GROWTH*

A sliver of bog pine and two white-tailed eagle feathers were all that remained on the bedroom floor, once I had shaken the pack upside down until it was empty back at home, and put everything back in its place.

Both had been given to me by Don when I had got to his house that last Cape Wrath evening. He never said why he wanted me to have them, and I never asked, which was how so much of the journey had gone. People were spontaneous, especially once they knew and understood what I was up to. If you discounted the two extra holes that I had had to put into the inner bit of my belt, one in Hebden Bridge and one in Pitlochry, to compensate for my changing shape, they were also the only physical souvenirs that I brought back with me, apart from a vegan sausage that Trevor had humorously secreted into my pack in Fort Augustus while I wasn't looking.

Back in the little Ozone Café in the lighthouse at Cape Wrath, where I had bought the 68th and final flat white of my trip, there had been general surprise and concern that I was doubling back on myself and returning to Kinlochbervie the hard way the same day, and in deteriorating weather.

'You probably shouldn't,' said the only other hiker there, glancing up through steamed-up glasses from his hot chocolate. 'Not in this weather. Not really at ...', but then he stopped. It didn't matter. The start of some sentences reliably predict their endings, even when they are unstated. We could all tell where this one was going, anyway: 'Not really at your age.'

In the event, this old man's walk back had been a good deal easier and calmer than the way out. The weather had indeed closed in again, but I was still able to count back all the landmarks of my outward journey, a wet Theseus making his way out of the labyrinth by following and reeling in the imaginary strands of cotton that he had laid on the way out. I'd even made the time to sit by a tiny lochan halfway back to Kinlochbervie, and done no more than just watch a pair of amorous teal and see the ripples from their progress breaking almost noiselessly against the reeds on the edge, for a quarter of an hour. I had been readmitted to the house of adulthood after the madness of the morning.

What with the role of guest speaker on the cruise ship, going home took a further fortnight and, with a backlog of work and general catching up, it was late July before I was ready to go and walk those missing Covid miles in the Cotswolds. The cheapskate in me wondered just for a moment whether I really needed to, but then I remembered that I had walked partly for the sponsorship that I could earn for Curlew Action, and hundreds of people had trusted me to do it with many thousands of their own pounds.*

Also, in the event, purity turned out to be a hard habit to break. Ultimately, there was no point to any of the journey unless I walked every inch of the way.

*

So now, these are the dog days, and this is a thirsty land.

It is high summer and the north pole is just starting to retreat from its maximum tilt towards the sun when I finally return to Conygree to begin my walk again. The thin grass is already up to the bellies of those dainty little Herefords in their paddocks. It seems odd to be walking away from them into a heat haze on what is officially still my spring journey. I walk with Caroline, so that I can share a little bit of the adventure with her.

* https://www.curlewaction.org/donations/donate/ Just in case you feel similarly moved.

Back in the spring, it was all about hope and growth; here in the Cotswolds, at least for the time being, it is about abundance. It is for this season that the Romans devised the idea of cornucopia, the horn of plenty. The infinite jigsaw puzzle of nature has shifted again, and the world is a very different one.

Right now, the language of the fields is harvest, and it is spoken in the rich, dusty dialects of wheat, barley, straw and beans. Sometimes, we are silent as we walk. We can hear for ourselves the wind whispering towards us over the ripe barley, see the brave red dots of poppies in the unmown margins of the ochre stubble fields and feel the heat of the day on the back of our necks. Where, four months ago, I walked by barely budding hedges, now they are a faded sage green, fringed by rosebay willowherb, giant hogweed and yellow ragwort; on the blackthorn trees are the first sloes of the year, earlier than ever, and from the brambles we can pick the first succulent blackberries to supplement our meagre lunch. At one point, a cloud of marbled whites rises up out of the margin of wildflower mix as our knees brush against a section of knapweed. Beside those hedges, we can see the noisy goldfinches dipping in and out of the thistle-down and, in a tiny pile of debris at the foot of an old oak tree, some broken white woodpigeon eggs speak of a second or even third clutch for one pair of this most fertile of birds in this most fertile of summers.

As we set off down the hill from Farmington, 100 acres of lucerne on our right-hand side quite literally sings out to us like medieval plainsong leaking out of the open windows of a nearby abbey, in the buzzing of bumblebees and hoverflies in its purple flowers. On the northern headland, we spot maybe 40 beehives tucked in a neat double-decker row along the hawthorn hedge: 2 million honeybees each visiting 500 flowers a day in 100 billion acts of free pollination, on which our own ecosystem depends utterly.

A few fields later, we see two recently fledged hobbies screaming out the ecstasy of their new-found freedoms, as they fly endlessly around an isolated ash tree in a vast field of beans. Their time will come soon, and then they will feed on the pipits, who feed on the grasshoppers who feed on the leaves of the lucerne that we have just come through. Everything is connected to everything else.

Where we lie against a fallen tree with our sandwiches in the dappled shade of someone's private high beech wood to escape the noonday heat, we are gradually lulled to sleep by the sound of a tractor going about its work in the valley below, and by the beautiful monotony of the calling of a nearby stock dove. Far away across the woods and fields, my shallow dream is interrupted by the peal of bells that is being rung out of the tower of St James's, Longborough. Those bells will chase us in *diminuendo* across ten more fields before we eventually lose them. All these things are the changeless gifts of a changeful world that, nearby, is changing out of all recognition. For a second when we resume our walking, I become slightly overcome with it all; I lean over a rusty old gate and pinch myself at the knowledge that it is all here, and all free. That butterfly, these blackberries and those hobbies, they carry me back to some remote but powerful childhood sensation of a spiritual order of things, anchored somewhere between a Ravilious watercolour and an old Ladybird book I had, called *What to Look for in Summer*.

It is a thirsty land, but we have just seen the very best of it. This is what it can be like, but so often isn't. By a process of huge fortune, the farms that have lined the various footpaths that we travelled have been ones where nature is on an equal footing to food production. A couple of miles either side, we might have been passing through large chemical fields. A passenger jet passes overhead on its way from Birmingham to Spain or Portugal, and a little part of me finds myself wondering why anyone would want to be anywhere else.

Then, on the last day of July, at Stratford-upon-Avon, the circle of my journey is done.

Out of a sense of propriety, Caroline and I walk the final miles along the Shakespeare Way, compressed though it is by development into a scruffy shadow of what someone on a Shakespeare pilgrimage might want it to be. From where it sidles rather sheepishly into the town, via a diversion and a footbridge, it is all Shakespeare, every last thing: his church, his school, his friend's house, his inspiration, his favourite Starbucks, everything. His endless gift to the local traders is a vast self-licking lollipop of financial opportunity that is enthusiastically being sucked on each day. It is Edinburgh all over again, only more so, and you either get into the spirit of things, or you don't.

As it happens, we don't. It's not why we are here. But it doesn't matter: we are happy just to spend an hour among the crowds and in the sunshine, happy to sit on the grass by the river enjoying the view and eating our sandwiches; happy to make appalling Shakespeare puns; happy to be waiting for the Sunday evening bus to take us south to Chipping Norton, and our car.

As the bus rattles on through lanes that have been quietened by the long, hot day and the prospect of a huge evening football match at Wembley, I drop in and out of a shallow sleep, my head on Caroline's shoulder. When a branch of ash thuds against the front of the roof just above our top deck front seat, she notices that I am awake again, and asks me what I am thinking.

'Children,' I say. 'That's what was missing.'

In three days of walking on national trails, through what is the heart of England and in the middle of school summer holidays, we have hardly seen a single child, indeed precious few people even under twenty. Given that children are the down-payment on the achievement of our future hopes, and that their passion will be its eventual currency, this seems a bit of a missed opportunity.

After all, hope is what I had set out in search of all those months ago.

*

And did I find it?

Of course, I found it. I found hope everywhere. Hope turned out to be the easy bit.

Humans don't have to seek permission to hope; hope is the very thing that defines them. Hope is why forests are planted by people who will never walk through them, and cathedrals built by people who will never pray in them. It is why people survive concentration camps, and why man set foot on the moon. Hope is why many of us try to deploy the lessons of the past to create what we think will be a better world. Hope is why I had walked nearly a thousand miles, and why so many people had proudly shown me the projects they were involved in. Hope is threaded through the fabric of the entire conservation world. It enables those of us who wish to, to subordinate our 'eco grief'* below our determination to get off our backsides and do something about it all. It is no less than 'a human survival trait', in the words of Jane Goodall, 'and without it we perish.'[1] Greta Thunberg told my generation that she 'doesn't want my hope', but I'm not sure that she is right: without it, and hers, nothing will happen.

I found it in every farm and field, every stream and shore, every beech wood and bog where I watched these people actively working to make things better. If you aggregated all the hope I found, and then factored it up by the 99.9% that I never even knew about, let alone saw, you would have an ocean of it. And if that ocean

---

* Eco grief is increasingly accepted as a real psychological condition. It is the sense of loss that hits people when they experience or learn about environmental destruction. I have certainly experienced it myself.

of hope could change things on its own, then stories like this would probably not need to be told. And up to a point, it can: by the example of what has already been achieved, and by the inspiration that flows from the daily work that these people do, things get better and more and more of us get involved. Someone sees the hedgehog box that their neighbour has sited, for example, and emulates it in their own garden, and creates a gap in the fence through which the animals can freely commute. A farmer gives up the unequal struggle of his high-input intensive indoor dairy business, halves the herd and sends them out into the fields once again. Hope is urgently seeking to be heard.

But only up to a point is it breaking through. All those projects that I had visited were only tiny and often unconnected islands of virtue among 24 million hectares of land and 68 million of us scratching our heads and simultaneously trying to make sense and a living out of it. The otter that flopped back into Hamish's Eddleston Water still wouldn't enjoy life much in the Lea, Britain's most polluted river, where raw sewage and levels of chemicals and phosphates that are 'off the scale' flow their way down to a sunless sea to the east. And pity the nesting curlew who powerlessly watches the threshing blades of the silage-maker heading towards her nest early one May morning a couple of farms away from the Heseltines at Malham. We are a desperately de-natured people, and nothing will really change in our grand ecosystem until that fact changes. Britain's nature is in a truly shocking state, but the evidence from my walk screams out to me that it really doesn't need to be. What I had just spent these last few days walking through demonstrates that.

What I learned was really no more complicated than that, to restore biodiversity, we most often need to do nothing more than stop killing it, especially on our farmland. The vast majority of it is depleted, for sure, but it's still there, and most of it is resilient, so it's not like we need to invent new devices and technologies to save it; we just need to allow natural processes to seep back in. And to stop killing it, often we need to do no more than remove our boot from its throat and perhaps give it a little helping hand, something that we can contribute to as individuals by simply practising a small number of slightly different behaviours. Rewilding may be part of the answer, but it is not the pretty catch-all solution that it is often credited with being. National food security is still a very real need, and as the Game and Wildlife Conservation Trust notes, 'farming is not just what people do, it is who they are. Being told by outsiders that you are "unproductive" and that the land that your family has nurtured for generations should be re-purposed for some other use is unlikely to be a good footing for building engagement.'[2] For nature to be restored, good farmers need to be, and to feel they are, a central and valued part of the solution, rather than the perpetual bad guys.

So what are we supposed to be doing? First, I suppose, embracing rather than avoiding the fact that we need to consume less, and in a fairer way, and learn to enjoy our new moderation, so that it is not just temporary virtue signalling, not just some finite process that we can give up when it is all alright again. There are uncomfortably many of us on these islands, indeed on this planet, but there can't suddenly be fewer of us, so we need to learn to live more in harmony with the rest of its creatures. It is just not in the gift of our planet, let alone morality, to go on supplying us with the growing extravagances of the first world, or letting us add yet more to the 10.5 million full shipping containers that pour into Britain's docks each year.[3] The ceaseless search for growth at all costs is really no more than a dangerous illusion, perhaps best caricatured by our expanding waistlines and contracting mental robustness, so we need to find the secret of prosperity without growth. We have to relearn what our grandparents knew about good housekeeping, and waste much less, especially food: as mentioned earlier, we in Britain consign around a third of our food to landfill one way or another (which amounts to about £65 billion of the stuff each year,[*] or roughly the GDP of Kenya). Avoiding this habit could change farming for the better at a stroke, with no policy change required at all.

Next, we have to learn to try to mimic nature rather than ignore it, to go with and not against its grain: nature doesn't 'grow' plastic lawns, plough deep furrows into its own soil or drench fields in herbicide; it doesn't

* Based on taking a third of Statista's estimate of the £205 billion annual value of Britain's grocery industry.

scrape out the living layer of its own seabed with the bottom of nets, release infected farmed salmon to wreak havoc in the wild population, or dump industrial quantities of effluent into its own rivers. It doesn't accelerate growth by using hormone injections and antibiotics, or cover trees with nets so that birds can't nest in them. It doesn't even provide strawberries in deep midwinter, or a burger that comes from a cow for whose food a little patch of rainforest has been trashed 5,500 miles away.

But we already know all of this. I have written nothing new and original here that has not been written a thousand times before, so it is not the knowledge that is missing, so much as the will and the urgency with which to change course. Governments need to get real with us. The age of 'nudge' has failed.

Therefore, because so much of the future damage is out of our immediate hands, we also need to learn to lend our votes and hand over our spending money very carefully, and only to people and companies who we have reason to trust to be on the same side as us. My July walk took place against the depressing background of the Conservative leadership campaign, and far from either of the final two candidates to be our next prime minister even mentioning a world of 'enough', all the talk was still of tax cuts and the endless pursuit of growth. For an environmentalist, it was like watching a slow-motion train crash that was also entirely deliberate. At some stage, some senior politician is going to have the metaphorical balls to ignore their activists and tell us in plain language that the party is over, and that we simply can't go on like this. As for Greta Thunberg and climate change, so for the beleaguered curlew and the rest of our declining biodiversity, we need more activists lying in front of the metaphorical bulldozers.

Finally, we need to get our children back out into nature, to imbue in them its central importance to our lives, from the very start of their own. This means all of them, and not just the comfortable ones already living in the countryside. This takes planning and commitment and extra money, but the reward lies in tomorrow's stewards of our nature being of a consistently higher commitment and ability than ours.

Nature is not some amenity. It is our home.

EPILOGUE

A Bog in Macclesfield

There is always a 'however'.

Instead of going south to Sussex from Stratford-upon-Avon at the end of my walk, I go north to Macclesfield, only this time by car.

On the southern edge of that peaceful Cheshire market town lies a beautiful 100-hectare raised peat bog that I particularly want to see, and which I have thought about often during the walk. It is called Danes Moss, and it is a remnant of a much larger peat bog; but below it is still maybe 1.25 million cubic metres of peat (holding about 70,000 tons of carbon), and above it over 600 observed species, including rare orchids, butterflies and a small population of Britain's fastest declining red-listed bird, the willow tit. Around its pathways are great stands of birch and sallow, second only to the oak in their capacity to host invertebrate biodiversity, and bordering its pathways are orchids, willowherbs and a host of beneficial fauna, with banks of angelica fringing the woodland in an intoxicating insect heaven. Above all, it is a delightful oasis of green into which the townspeople can plunge at will for their fix of nature, where they can walk their dogs and inspire their children. If nature can help heal us in these troubled times, it is great to know that Macclesfield has this abundance right on its doorstep. It would be a jewel anywhere in Britain.

No wonder the local council are proud of it. No wonder they would do anything to protect it.

Only they're not, and they won't. On the contrary, what they are actually seeking to do is build a development of 950 houses over at least half of it, with a huge through road across its middle, plus a supermarket, warehouses and even a small primary school. It is not being done in answer to any statutory need, as the five-year house-building pipeline is already at the required level, and any possible benefit in terms of affordable housing is being watered down before the town's very eyes, from 30% to 11% to a probable 5% when and if it is actually completed. We need to build many houses, for sure, but we certainly don't need to be building executive homes in a bog.

At best, the scheme is a bastard child of an ill-thought-through relationship between the 2017 Local Plan and the 1947 Town and Country Planning Act, the gist of which means that all farms are protected, and all waste ground, into which category the jewel of Danes Moss apparently falls, should be ripe for development. Either way, it is hard to see who, aside from the developer, can possibly gain. In fact, it is quite difficult to find anyone local who admits to supporting it at all, let alone with enthusiasm, but still it ploughs on. It has even been rechristened the South Macclesfield Development Area, which I guess is at least a philosophically easier place on which to build nearly 1,000 houses than somewhere called Danes Moss. Never underestimate the power of changing a name.

Even the various impact surveys have been carried out in an unusual and deeply disturbing way, with the insect survey being conducted, bizarrely, in November, and then coming up with a recommendation to do a full invertebrate survey that was ignored. Stranger still is the cloak of secrecy hanging over the Assessment of Peatland Carbon Status report for whose disclosure no fewer than three Freedom of Information requests have been refused, with a complaint now lodged with the Information Commissioner's office. But then, when an environmental report recommends that it would be 'acceptable' to destroy the peat so long as 10% is retained for conservation, which it does, you'll get a dim understanding of why its sponsor might want to protect it from drifting into the public gaze. For the record, 23 species on the site are protected under UK law.

Ecological considerations aside, there is an immediate hint as to the general unsuitability of the terrain for development when I get there to meet the team from Save Danes Moss, an informal but highly professional local pressure group who have come together to fight the scheme: our conversation is drowned out by the noise of a piledriver on a next door (but unrelated) plot, where the developer is having to build each new house on a series of 20-metre piles to ensure that they don't sink into the peat.

'Once the peat dries out and shrinks,' says Tony Hothersall, a leading light of the group opposing the scheme, 'it will be like the houses are sitting up on stilts.'

We walk deeper on into the Moss along the main path in dappled summer sun, stopping often to look at passing nature: a toad here, a commuting dragonfly there.

'Even the management of the redundant landfill site next door are formally worried,' says Gordon Richardson, a retired ecologist. 'Because, by drying out the peat here, it cannot fail to start to dry out the peat next door, which could destabilise the structure of the old landfill site, and then release large amounts of methane and other gases.'

A bullfinch flits across the clearing we are standing in; somewhere overhead a mewing buzzard calls out reassurance to its unfledged chick.

'Look at this over here,' calls out his colleague, Diana Moss. There, on a trackway, in high summer and in the middle of the third month of the longest drought for 40 years, is thick, wet, oozing peat with planks laid across it for walkers. 'In a country of dried-out peat bogs, it's one that is actually still doing its job, holding thousands of tons of greenhouse gases within it. I mean, why would you want to build anything on that?'

Given that Cheshire East Council has undertaken to become carbon-neutral by 2025, and is running a hydrogen project to help reduce carbon in their vehicle fleet, and given that they have committed that all 'new development will be sensitive and sustainable', it seems counterintuitive to be doing something at Danes Moss that could well release an extra quarter of a million tonnes of CO_2 straight into the atmosphere, let alone the damage that will be inflicted on both the variety and abundance of the resident species. Our community leaders have a responsibility to engage in, and not duck, these issues. They may be politically inconvenient, but they will define the future of our nature.

All through the writing of this book, I have seen the need for nuance in discussing the issues in nature that divide us – and yet here, right at the end, I have arrived at a scheme that seems beyond nuance. It is as if the working lungs of a beautiful town are going to be quietly removed and then replaced by mechanical ones. Indeed, it is so strange that it may well not happen. It is highly likely that it eventually will be called in by the Secretary of State, or be subject to a judicial review.

Whatever the outcome, that is the point. Remove this ill-thought-out proposal, and suddenly there is a great opportunity for the town, where a historical landscape of regional importance can be retained within the context of a modern town, free for everyone to walk through, be in, learn from and enjoy. 'This life has been in that bog for the last 5,000 years,' said local campaigner and writer, Mark Cocker, when I talked to him about it. 'It's not just our bog, it's theirs, too. All those species also happen to be British citizens.' If Tony, Diana, Gordon and their colleagues prevail, this will eventually be no more than a bad memory. Without them, it would probably already be under construction.

There are no bulldozers to lie in front of yet, so the work of a group like this takes place in the background, continual and relentless, a network slowly growing within the community: writing briefing notes, submitting formal objections, meeting community leaders and conducting their own surveys. Money has to be raised for a fighting fund* and a vision created for what the bog could be once the shackles of the threatened development have been thrown off. And all the time, they keep the campaign in the public eye through social media and via their stand at the monthly Treacle Market. Because the truth they know is this: that all the incremental gains for nature of the kind that I have walked through in my entire journey are cancelled out by just a few of these. This is about much more than Macclesfield.

Standing with them under the alder canopy, they look less like a group of rebels than a trio of walkers of a certain age out for a summer's ramble. Scratch the surface, though, and they are calm, well-briefed, well-connected and, above all, relentless campaigners. Without people like them, projects would be rising up, unchallenged, in inappropriate places all over the country. On the one hand, they simply take their place in the small army of people who have given me their time and patience on this long walk of mine, explaining what they are doing to keep our natural world as varied and abundant as it can possibly be, enabling all of us to at least be hopeful about the future. On the other, they embody the dominant sentiment of my last few months; which is that, in the fight to protect and enhance what we still have, none of us can be neutral any more.

If you want it, then, for now, you must fight for it. We all must. Every inch of the way.

---

* It is likely that a judicial review would cost the group around £60,000.

BIBLIOGRAPHY

The Natural Health Service, Isabel Hardman, Atlantic Books, 2020

The Great Melt, Alister Doyle, Flint, 2021

The Oak Papers, James Canton, Canongate Books, 2020

Walking Home, Simon Armitage, Faber & Faber, 2012

Pilgrimage for Peace, Satish Kumar, Green Books, 2021

Coastlines, Patrick Barkham, Granta Books, 2015

Hurricane Lizards and Plastic Squid, Thor Hanson, Icon Books, 2022

Britain's Habitats, Lake et al., Princeton University Press, 2015

Greenery, Tim Dee, Jonathan Cape, 2020

Raptor, James MacDonald Lockhart, Fourth Estate, 2016

Invasive Aliens, Dan Eatherby, William Collins, 2020

The Nature of Nature, Enric Sala, National Geographic, 2020

Our Place, Mark Cocker, Jonathan Cape, 2018

Regeneration, Andrew Painting, Birlinn, 2021

Rebirding, Benedict MacDonald, Pelagic Publishing, 2020

Forecast, Joe Schute, Bloomsbury Wildlife, 2021

Goshawk Summer, James Aldred, Elliot & Thompson, 2021

The Wild Places, Robert Macfarlane, Granta Books, 2007

Cornerstones, Benedict Macdonald, Bloomsbury Wildlife, 2022

Restoring the Wild, Roy Dennis, William Collins, 2021
Land Healer, Jake Fiennes, BBC Books, 2022
Regenesis, George Monbiot, Allen Lane, 2022
The Book of Hope, Jane Goodall, Penguin Viking, 2021
Prosperity Without Growth, Tim Jackson, Routledge, 2016
The Hidden Universe, Alexandre Antonelli, Witness Books, 2022
Sixty Harvests Left, Philip Lymbery, Bloomsbury, 2022
Forget Me Not, Sophie Pavelle, Bloomsbury, 2022

ACKNOWLEDGEMENTS

Research

Tim Birkhead (Sheffield University)
Philip Warren (Sheffield University)
Nicola Hemmings (Sheffield University)
Joanna Dobson (Sheffield Hallam University)
Satish Kumar
Mike Smart
Charlie Mellor
Russell Wynn (Wild New Forest)
Marcus Ward (Wild New Forest)
Jonathan Brunyee
Mark Cocker
Mark Beevers
Dr Jill Edmondson (Sheffield Hallam University)
Maxwell Ayamba (Sheffield Environmental Movement)
Sarah Deakin
The Swift family (West Clunes Farm)
Liz Auty (John Muir Trust)
Don O'Driscoll (John Muir Trust)
Luke Comins (Tweed Forum)
Rachel Coyle (Tweed Forum)
Hamish Robertson (Tweed Forum)
Professor Chris Spray (Dundee University)
Doug Gilbert (Trees for Life)
Ash Watts (Derbyshire Dales District Council)

Emma Mortimer (Derbyshire Dales District Council)
Phillip Neal (Hartington Wildflower Meadow Project)
Janet Bray (Hartington Wildflower Meadow Project)
Liz Broomhead (Hartington Wildflower Meadow Project)
Chris Ellis (Royal Botanic Garden, Edinburgh)
Leonie Alexander (Royal Botanic Garden, Edinburgh)
Neil and Leigh Heseltine (Hill Top Farm, Malham)
John Meadley (Pasture for Life Association)
Will Boyd-Wallis (The National Trust for Scotland)
Simon Winton
Sir John Lister-Kaye (Aigas Field Study Centre)
Roy Dennis (Roy Dennis Foundation)
David Sexton (Isle of Mull)
Stuart Gibson (Isle of Mull)
Christina Taylor (RSPB)
John Miles
John Aitchison
Kate Plumbridge (Peak District National Park)
Diana Moss
Sally Hunter
Ed Oxley
Christina Taylor (RSPB Geltsdale and Hadrian's Wall)
Susan Standring FRCS
Mary Colwell
Julian Hector
Diana Moss (Danes Moss Action Group)
Tony Hothersall (Danes Moss Action Group)
Gordon Richardson (Danes Moss Action Group)

Philip Lymbery (Compassion in World Farming)
Alexandre Antonelli (Royal Botanical Gardens Kew)

Hospitality

Bryn and Emma Parry
Mhairi Coull and Jim Smith
Sue and Paul Chuter
Hume and Davina Jones
Richard and Chick Paget
David and Cindy McFarlane
Michael and Gina Bochmann
Alasdair Ogilvy
Mark Firth
Christopher and Deborah Wolverson
Richard and Mandy Plant
Sarah Colwell
Janet and Andy Bray
Charles and Kitty Noble
Sheila Hammond and Ali Hall
Stuart, Carla and Alex Blake
Bert and Kit Hollings
Duncan and Luzaan Allison
Angus and Fi Macdonald
David and Pat Smyth
Simon and Alex Winton
Chris and Sarah Boles
James and Carol Hall
Don O'Driscoll
Matthew and Rachel Canwell
Jonathan and Katy Townsend-Rose
Colin and Carol Gilmour
Hugh and Wendy Stewart
Chris and Sue Hopkinson
Chris Mitchell
Charlie and Camilla Drax
Rob and Fiona Rattray
Fred and Kitty Stroyan
Tom and Katie Orde-Powlett
Nick Walmsley and Nicola Taylor

APPENDIX 1

The Route

Total 57 days: 51 days walking; 6 days off; 977 miles.

Most of the planned route worked well, providing strenuous days at the start that became rather less so as I gained fitness. The general plan of covering twenty miles each day on the relative flat, and sixteen or seventeen on hilly ground, worked well. As a rule of thumb, the further north I went, the longer the days' walks were between stops (dictated by where the accommodation was), and the freer I felt to walk long stretches on roads that were still pretty empty in April. Surprisingly often, marked footpaths turned out not to exist as any more than a memory through the undergrowth. With full open access in Scotland, a willingness to climb over 1.8-metre deer fences and to hop over wide but bridgeless burns generally made for a shorter route, as well as a more adventurous one. While canals, disused railway lines, reservoir service roads and transmission line service roads were all extremely useful, walking through clear-fell forestry is well worth avoiding. For safety's sake, but only when I was out in the open country or on high and exposed ground, I always told the next day's hosts where I was coming from and what route I was planning to take. Mileages are measured on a device, not the map, and include any small diversions etc.

In 977 miles, I was offered unsolicited lifts by four people, five if you count the abusive taxi driver in Crossgates: one that Yorkshire gamekeeper, two foreign, and one of them more than a little drunk. Sadly, the purity of the route prevented my accepting any of them, but I like to think I persuaded the drunkard to sleep it off safely in the layby on the pretext that I might come back and find him later.

Day 1. Lymington to West Wellow; footpaths; 22 miles
Day 2. West Wellow to Newton Tony; 22 miles
Day 3. Newton Tony to Pewsey; 17 miles
Day 4. Pewsey to Barbury Castle; mainly Ridgeway; 19 miles
Day 5. Barbury Castle to Fairford, via Swindon; mainly small roads; 21 miles
Day 6. Fairford to Lower Slaughter; footpaths; Monarch's Way; 22 miles
Day 7. Lower Slaughter to Chipping Campden; Heart of England Way, Monarch's Way, 20 miles
Day 8. Chipping Campden to Stratford-upon-Avon; Heart of England Way, Monarch's Way; 16 miles
Day 9. Stratford-upon-Avon to Meriden; footpaths, Grand Union Canal; 24 miles
Day 10. Meriden to Tamworth, via Shustoke; 21 miles
Day 11. Tamworth to Woodmill (Yoxall), via Alrewas; 22 miles

Day 12. Woodmill to Rocester, via Uttoxeter; 22 miles
Day 13. Rocester to Tissington, via Wooton; 22 miles
Day 14. Tissington to Chelmorton, along disused railway line; 14 miles
Day 15. Day off
Day 16. Chelmorton to Edale; 18 miles
Day 17. Edale to Torside; Pennine Way; 16 miles
Day 18. Torside to Diggle (Standedge); Pennine Way; 14 miles
Day 19. Diggle to Hebden Bridge; Pennine Way; 13 miles
Day 20. Hebden Bridge to Ickornshaw; Pennine Way; 17 miles
Day 21. Day off
Day 22. Ickornshaw to Malham; Pennine Way; 17 miles
Day 23. Malham to Horton-in-Ribblesdale; Pennine Way; 15 miles
Day 24. Horton-in-Ribblesdale to Hawes; Pennine Way; 14 miles
Day 25. Hawes to Keld; Pennine Way; 13 miles
Day 26. Keld to Middleton-in-Teesdale; Pennine Way; 23 miles
Day 27. Middleton-in-Teesdale to Lanehead (Weardale); 17 miles
Day 28. Lanehead to Slaggyford; part Pennine Way; 15 miles
Day 29. Slaggyford to Greenhead; Pennine Way; 16 miles
Day 30. Day off
Day 31. Greenhead to Steel Road; 26 miles

Day 32. Steel Road to Hawick; disused railway line and road; 20 miles
Day 33. Hawick to Innerleithen; drove roads; 24 miles
Day 34. Innerleithen to Cowdenburn; along the River Tweed and Eddleston Water; 18 miles
Day 35. Cowdenburn to Edinburgh; across the Pentland Hills; 23 miles
Day 36. Day off
Day 37. Edinburgh to Kelty, via Cramond and the Forth Bridge; 22 miles
Day 38. Kelty to Dunning, via Kinross; 22 miles
Day 39. Dunning to Amulree, via Glenalmond; 21 miles
Day 40. Amulree to Keltneyburn, via Kenmore; 17 miles
Day 41. Keltneyburn to Kinloch Rannoch, via Schiehallion summit; 20 miles
Day 42. Kinloch Rannoch to Balsporran, via Loch Garry (A9); 19 miles.
Day 43. Day off
Day 44. Balsporran to Kinloch Laggan, via Dalwhinnie; 16 miles
Day 45. Kinloch Laggan to Melgarve bothy via Sherramore; 12 miles
Day 46. Melgarve to Fort Augustus, via Corrieyairack; 16 miles
Day 47. Fort Augustus to Tomich, via Torgyle; 22 miles.
Day 48. Tomich to Aigas, via Struy; 16 miles
Day 49. Day off
Day 50. Aigas to Contin, via Beauly; 17 miles
Day 51. Contin to Aultguish Inn, via Garve; 16 miles

Day 52. Aultguish Inn to Croick, via Loch Vaich; 20 miles

Day 53. Croick to Invercassley, via Oykel Bridge; 20 miles

Day 54. Invercassley to north end of Loch Shinn, via Duchally; 22 miles

Day 55. North end of Loch Shinn to Rhiconich, along the road, via Laxford Bridge; 25 miles

Day 56. Rhiconich to Durness; 14 miles

Day 57. Kinlochbervie to Cape Wrath and back; 25 miles (977 miles)

APPENDIX 2

Kit List

The slightly daunting-looking kit list below actually only weighed 15 kg (or 13 kg once I had drunk the water by the end of each day) and covered all bases that I had envisaged. Clearly, if camping, it would have also included a tent, a mat, a cooker and some food, which would have added about 7 kg more. The small pack allowed sufficient space, was comfortable and, above all, prevented me filling it with further weight. Walking in spring meant that my water use was easily covered by 2 litres, although having run out one blisteringly hot day in the Pennines, I carried purification tablets from then on. In terms of safety, the fact of there being a survival bag in my pack allowed me to be more ambitious in bad weather, and gave my family reassurance that I had an ultimate Plan B available; stuck in a snowstorm high up on the Pennine Way, I was mighty pleased to know it was there, even at 400 grams extra weight. The pretty basic first aid kit remained sealed throughout, which discloses the surprising news that I didn't once need paracetamol or ibuprofen or that, if I did, I forgot I had any.

However expensive, I was also pleased that I had chosen to buy paper map coverage of the entire route to supplement the Ordnance Survey app; the latter is good, but it needs some form of signal (which I often didn't have) and quickly drains the battery. In the event, I used it for confirmation only. I sent packs of four or five maps ahead, so that I wasn't carrying half a library's-worth on any one section. For all the boasts of the mobile phone companies, I reckon that I had a workable signal for only a little over half the route, so it is worth planning on being out of touch. Having said that, my phone was arguably second only in importance to my feet in its multitude of uses on the journey.

The boots were excellent, although there is a clear choice to be made between the light boots that I chose, and which were suitable for 85% of the route, and the heavier ones that would have been better in the boggy and rocky sections; the price was just two days of soaked feet. I wore the gaiters the entire time, partly because they offered considerable protection against ticks that might carry Lyme disease. I still spent at least five evenings twisting ticks out of my body. Because it was an unusually dry spring, my expensive Lhotse jacket only got used on two days, but I remain glad that I brought it along. Suncream, on the other hand, which I had only taken as an afterthought, I used on well over half the days. Having originally planned to do my laundry on days off, I ended up washing clothes whenever I could, which gave flexibility in planning, and meant that I smelled less like a polecat. As a side note, washing merino wool is an art: at £20 a pair of socks, and £70 for a base layer, you only make the wrong-setting-on-the-washing-machine mistake once.

My proudest boast, actually my only boast, is that, after sleeping in 50 different places, I still had the same phone-charging cable at the end that I had started with.

Finally, you are either a walking pole person, or you aren't. I am not proud of the fact, but it turns out that I am not. One pole fell unseen off my pack in Pewsey, the other near Uttoxeter, and I never gave them another thought. I hope that whoever found them is using and enjoying them.

Kit list

Items in italics didn't get used

Backpack

Osprey Aether 50L
Waterproof pack cover
Osprey 2L water reservoir
3 waterproof bags

Safety

Survival bag
Sleeping bag (for part of route)
Head torch
Flashing light (for use on dark roads)
First aid kit

Navigation

Silva compass
Subscription to OS app

4 x OS maps (remainder sent on to various stopping points)
Waterproof map case
Map measuring wheel (vital aid to judging times, arranging meet-ups etc.)

Footwear/walking

Meindl boots (plus a second broken-in pair sent ahead to halfway point)
Gaiters
5 pairs Bridgedale hiking socks
1 pair Sealskinz waterproof socks
1 pair trainers
Walking poles

Clothing

Woolly hat
Baseball cap
2 x merino base layer (sleeveless)
2 x merino base layer (long-sleeved)
1 x light fleece (mid-layer)
1 x medium fleece (outer layer)
1 x T-shirt
4 x underwear
2 x hiking trousers (one ultra-lightweight; one lined)
1 x pyjama bottoms
2 x pairs light gloves
1 x pair light shorts

Weather gear

1 x Patagonia lightweight top (shower- and windproof)

1 x heavyweight Lhotse jacket (foul weather)
1 x pair Gore-Tex over-trousers

Cleaning/medical
Spare glasses
Antiseptic cream
Paracetamol, ibuprofen, Gaviscon, etc.
Water purification tablets
Tick removal kit
Mini pot shampoo
Toothbrush
Toothpaste
Insect repellent
1 x can Runners Rub
Factor 30 suncream
Deodorant stick
Mini roll loo paper
Nail clippers
Face mask
2 x Covid test kits

Electrics
iPhone 12
Phone charger
Battery pack
3 x memory sticks (presentations given en route)
Ear pods

Miscellaneous
Accommodation list plus addresses

Bank card; Covid card; driving licence
2 x notebooks
2 x pens
1 x paperback (swapped for new one each time finished)
Spork

Food

A couple of Mars Bars and cereal bars for emergencies
A few more Mars Bars for non-emergencies
An energy shot that I really wouldn't have known what to do with

APPENDIX 3

A Manifesto

'If you think you are too small to make a difference, you haven't slept with a mosquito.'

AFRICAN PROVERB

From my notebook, then, a reminder that I wrote to myself in quiet moments and on wayside stops, by way of a personal manifesto for living better with nature. Very many naturalists, all of them far more qualified than I am, consciously and subconsciously input these thoughts in a thousand conversations along the way. The trick is to do it incrementally, not all at once, and then to make it fun, and keep it fun.

1. **Species loss is every bit as urgent as climate change. Speak up for it now.** Our own species' killing off of the nature around us needs all of us to engage, and now. Quite apart from the moral obligation we have to protect other species, we need plants, animals and functioning ecosystems to survive ourselves.

2. **Learn more**. Make an effort to understand the basic functioning of ecology,* and how human activity affects it. Apart from anything, it will be a hugely rewarding adventure that will enrich the rest of your life. But above that, introduce nature to children at every opportunity, whether as small as an evening walk to the local canal, or as big as encouraging them to study for the new Natural History GCSE.† Sit in a bird hide with an expert. Peer into a lump of soil with a magnifying glass. Spend an evening watching bats fly up the road. The best things in life are often free. Try to understand the real baseline, not any artificial one. The generational memory of what has been lost in the last 100 years is vital, and it is about *past abundance* just as much as it is biodiversity.
3. **Volunteer**. Get involved. Get stuck in. Everything works better if you are involved, especially if your labour is regular, and comes for free, even just a couple of hours a week. The projects described in this book are the tip of a vast iceberg. Take part in 'citizen science' surveys (e.g. the Great British Birdwatch; Pollinator Monitoring Scheme; National Plant Monitoring Scheme); the information that

* A great introduction is *The Nature of Nature*, by Enric Sala, National Geographic, 2020.

† Tirelessly campaigned for over many years by writer and film-maker Mary Colwell, with whom I help run the charity Curlew Action.

comes from them really helps set policy and allocate priorities and resources better. Join a local natural history society, and immerse yourself in the world that they introduce you to.

4. **Become an activist.** Not an activist for every green cause going, which just confuses and bores people, but maybe for one or two things that you feel really strongly about, learn about, campaign on and politely hold people to account on. Pick a hill, and then be prepared to metaphorically die on it. Lie in front of bulldozers, but only if they are being driven very carefully by well-trained drivers with good eyesight. Make positive suggestions for change at your workplace, and then help implement them rather than expecting others to do it. Persuade your golf club to sign up to the GEO Foundation for sustainable golf by resigning if they don't.
5. **Get political.** Well, at least a little bit political. Most MPs start by wanting to make the world better, but then get sucked over to the dark side by whips, lobbying and the smell of money or promotion. Vote for the person, not the party, and then hold their feet to the fire if they get in. If you get a rubbish answer, sharing it with your local newspaper normally does the trick. If they do good things, publicise it, and thank them. Bully your local council into not obsessively cutting verges. Always, always formally oppose planning consents that will damage biodiversity, and get your family and friends to

do the same. By the same token, actively support the good ones. Finally, campaign for state funding of political parties, so as to quieten the corporate lobbyists for ever.

6. **Pick something small to love and then love it.** Try to support one small wildlife charity as well as any larger one, and then support it well. Pick one that ticks all the boxes for you, and then give them a standing order for what you can afford, even if it seems to you a tiny amount. Charities, particularly small ones, are really helped by regular donations, however small. Remember them in your will, because most people won't. Check the CEO's salary* as a vaguely useful guide as to how carefully the money gets spent. And remember, good charities are actively saving wildlife every day of the year.
7. **Be a tricky customer when you go food shopping.** These days, your wallet is even more powerful than your vote, so use it. Be happy to ask questions, like 'Does this have palm oil?' Don't just not buy unsustainable farmed salmon, for example, but also politely tell the shop staff why you aren't, and won't. Ditto with fake honey; ditto with factory chickens. Ditto with drink in plastic bottles. Buy local when you can and never, ever, buy

* www.charitycommission.gov.uk. The average CEO salary for a charity with staff is £52,000 per year. Above £60,000, they are required to disclose this in the accounts.

food that has indirectly trashed a rainforest. (See point 1, about the importance of learning.) Other countries' biodiversity is just as important as ours; more, even.

8. **And then waste less**. It's not a high bar to jump when a third of all the food we produce goes into landfill. Plan better, buy less and, to a large extent, ignore sell-by dates. Wildlife gave its life so that you could eat that loaf of bread. Also, turning lights off when you are not in the room and not running water straight down the plughole are examples of tiny disciplines that, when aggregated across all of us, make a significant difference.
9. **Just buy fewer things**. Reuse, repair, recycle as much as you can. A million square feet of new online warehouse on a pretty greenfield site is simply a reflection of our species' inability to know when to say 'enough is enough'. A hedgeful of sparrows eradicated so that someone can have a new charger for their phone slightly quicker. To avoid waste, buy just-in-time rather than just-in-case. Rent clothes for that special event, rather than buying them; try to avoid non-organic cotton. Ditch schemes like Amazon Prime that tie you to one lazy supply chain for all the purchases in your life at the click of a button. Embrace the old and tatty.
10. **Live less chemically**. Be imaginative about what damage your fancy cleaners and cosmetics do downstream of your life, and use organic agents

like vinegar for surfaces, and plain soap instead. Also, just be less obsessed about cleanliness.

11. **Eat less meat,** and then make sure it is grass-fed, humanely raised and as local as possible. Give up meat, if that's what you really want, but don't be bullied by bad science into not eating it at all. Farmed correctly, livestock are important biodiversity engineers in their own right, who make the land they walk over better.
12. **Travel less often, less expensively and less far.** The excessive moving around of humans, and the extraction and burning of fossil fuels don't just cause climate change; they harm wildlife directly. The chances are that you haven't even begun to fully know all the delights of your native land, even your native county. If you do fly, offset your carbon using the best scheme you can find. (Note: there are plenty of bad ones!)
13. **Try to avoid buying single-use plastics,** directly or indirectly as packaging, even if it means making tedious compromises, or not getting exactly what you set out for. Each household chucks out 66 pieces of plastic packaging a week,[1] on average, so try to drop it by half. Micro-plastics kill or harm wildlife every day of every year, and every piece of plastic ever made is still in existence in some form, somewhere.
14. **Pick up five pieces of someone else's litter a day,** every day of the year, and then put them in the right sort of bin. Roadside litter is a nightmare for small mammals such as bank voles and wood mice;

riverbank and seaside litter is a nightmare for just about anything.

15. **Become a greener gardener**, and ditch pesticides and herbicides for organic substitutes, or none at all. Only buy peat-free composts. Instead, grow what wants to be there naturally, tolerate weeds and lose the lawn habit. Tidiness is the enemy of biodiversity, so stop being so tidy. Life below your soil will improve, your invertebrate count will soar, and birds and mammals will move in and delight you. Leave rotting logs for burrowing animals and invertebrates. You will also spend less time slaving away and more time enjoying the flowers and nature around you. Influence your neighbour to do the same. Switch off outdoor lights, except when you really need them: light pollution affects birds and insects badly. If you aren't lucky enough to have a garden, get on the waiting list for an allotment; they are hard work, good fun and nearly almost always more species-rich than the surrounding area. And never, ever buy a plastic lawn.
16. **Shove up a nest box or two**, whether you have a garden or not. Do it in the right way, and in the right place. Over 50 species of British bird can be attracted through an appropriate nest box.[*]

* https://www.bto.org/how-you-can-help/providing-birds/putting-nest-boxes-birds/putting-nest-box

17. **Become the best pet owner you can be.** Think carefully before buying: feeding a Labrador-sized dog for a year is responsible for the same level of emissions as 6,000 miles in a large car.[2] If you have a dog, keep it under control during the nesting season. If you have a cat, attach a bell to it so that the local birdlife knows it is coming. If you have a bird in a cage, you probably shouldn't.
18. **Invest ethically.** If you are lucky enough to have investments, make sure that they respect and reflect your values. If you are part of a pension scheme, be very interested in what holdings they have, and ask to bail out of companies that are damaging your world, or someone else's for that matter.
19. **Use the internet, not trees.** Apart, of course, from buying books!
20. Finally, **just stop and stare** from time to time. The madness of the modern world is predicated on us being busier than is good for us so that we earn more money than we need so that we can buy more and more stuff that we don't actually want, to impress people who don't even know us, and wouldn't care if they did. Breathe deep, and drink it all in.

NOTES

Chapter 1

1. Higher Education Staff Statistics: UK 2019/20 HESA.
2. *The Hidden Universe*, Alexandre Antonelli, Witness Books, 2022.
3. *Cornerstones*, Benedict Macdonald, Bloomsbury Wildlife, 2022.
4. *The Hidden Universe*, Alexandre Antonelli, Witness Books, 2022.
5. *Biodiversity Intactness Index*, October 2021.
6. From 'On a Monument to a Pigeon', Aldo Leopold, 1947.
7. *My First Summer in the Sierra*, John Muir, 1911.

Chapter 2

1. www.kew.org
2. 'The state of UK peatlands: an update', Artz et al., peatlandprogramme.org, 2019.
3. 'More than 75% percent decline over 27 years in total flying insect biomass in protected areas', Hallman et al., paper for *PLOS ONE*, October 2017.
4. RSPB figures.
5. *The Struggle of Existence*, Georgyii Gause, 1934.
6. *Aurochs and Auks*, John Burnside, Little Toller Books, 2021.
7. *Fortune* article, March 9th, 2022.

8. *Forecast*, Joe Schute, Bloomsbury Wildlife, 2021.
9. *Hurricane Lizards and Plastic Squid*, Thor Hanson, Icon Books, 2022.
10. *Nature's Calendar*, Woodland Trust, 2021.
11. Darwin Tree of Life project.

Chapter 3

1. *This is your Mind on Plants*, Michael Pollan, Penguin, 2021.
2. *The Nature of Spring*, Jim Crumley, Saraband, 2021.
3. *The Oak Papers*, James Canton, Canongate, 2020.
4. 'Individual variation in the phenology of oak trees and its consequences for herbivorous insects', Crawley et al., *Functional Ecology*, 1988 (2).
5. www.actionoak.org
6. Game and Wildlife Conservation Trust (GWCT) briefing note.
7. GWCT.
8. Hampshire and Isle of Wight Wildlife Trust article, January 2019.
9. *The Slow Death of the New Forest*, article by Brice Stratford, *The Critic*, May 2021.
10. *Threats and Opportunities in the New Forest National Park*, National Park Authority paper, 2018.
11. University of Exeter research, quoted in *New Scientist*, May 23rd, 2022.
12. 'Assessing habitat disturbance: the case of Salisbury Plain military training area', article in the *Journal of Environmental Management*, Hirst et al., October 2000.

Chapter 4

1. AHDB data analysis, June 9th, 2022.
2. UK Flour Millers briefing paper, May 24th, 2022.
3. UK Government Family Resources Survey: 2019–20, March 25th, 2021.
4. www.businesswaste.co.uk article, January 2022.
5. www.cotswoldmarketgarden.co.uk
6. 'What size is the average farm?', Dodds, paper for Macintyre Hudson, 2019.
7. *Land Healer*, Jake Fiennes, BBC Books, 2022.
8. 'Sheep attacks and harassment research', paper for Scottish government, December 2019.
9. 'Significance of *Neospora canium* in British dairy cattle', Davison et al., paper for *Science Direct*, August 1999.
10. www.graywolfconservation.com
11. 'The botanical education extinction and the fall of plant awareness', Stroud et al., paper for *Ecology and Evolution*, July 2022.

Chapter 5

1. RSPB report.
2. 'Contribution of non-native galliforms to annual variation in biomass of British birds', Blackburn et al., paper for *Biological Invasions*, 2021
3. 'What's the Damage? Why HS2 will cost nature too much', Wildlife Trusts report, 2020.
4. www.urbangreennewcastle.org
5. www.hartingtonvillage.com
6. www.caringforgodsacre.org.uk

7. 'Urban cultivation in allotments maintains soil quantities adversely affected by conventional agriculture', paper for *Journal of Applied Ecology*, Jill Edmondson, 2014.
8. 'Health Equity in England: The Marmot Review 10 Years On', The Health Foundation.

Chapter 6

1. Dr Tim Leunig.

Chapter 7

1. Woodland statistics, Forest Research.
2. www.bbc.co.uk
3. *Rebirding*, Benedict Macdonald, Pelagic Publishing, 2020.
4. Forestry Investment Zone (FIZ), North-East Cumbria Pilot, 2020.
5. 'Subarctic afforestation: Effects of forest plantations on ground-nesting birds in lowland Iceland', Palsdottir et al., paper for *Journal of Applied Ecology*, June 2022.
6. 'The state of UK peatlands: an update', Artz et al., 2019.
7. 'UK natural capital: peatlands', ONS paper, July 22nd, 2019.

Chapter 8

1. *Phytophthora austrocedri.*
2. *Gyrodactylis salaris.*

3. https://commonslibrary.parliament.uk
4. Anecdotal: Maxwell Ayamba, Sheffield Environmental Movement.
5. *Hurricane Lizards and Plastic Squid*, Thor Hanson, Icon Books, 2022.
6. *The Great Melt*, Alister Doyle, Flint, 2021.
7. '75 years of the influential Great Tit study at Witham Woods', Oxford University press release, April 2022.
8. 'Great tits may be adapting their beaks to bird feeders', article for University of East Anglia, October 2017.
9. 'Climate change projections for UK viticulture to 2040', Nesbitt et al., paper for *OENO One*, July 2022.
10. *The Hidden Universe*, Alexandre Antonelli, Witness Books, 2022.
11. *The Press and Journal*, December 10th, 2021.
12. 'Understanding the decline of the Common Cuckoo', Jeremy D. Wilson, British Ornithologists' Union article, June 2018.
13. 'UK River and Flow Regimes', National River Flow Archive.
14. *A Gazetteer and Bibliography of Water Meadows in Scotland.*
15. 'The Eddleston Water Project', Tweed Forum.
16. 'Factory farming is turning this beautiful British river into a sewer', George Monbiot, *Guardian* article, June 2022.
17. Article in *Bird Guides* magazine, July 10th, 2022.

18. Interview with the *Guardian*, April 16th, 2021.
19. Nature Recovery Network: www.gov.uk

Chapter 9

1. *Greenery*, Tim Dee, Jonathan Cape, 2020.
2. Salmon Scotland.
3. From Mowi's 2021 annual report.
4. BioMar report, 2017.
5. 'The Protein Puzzle', Henck Westhoek et al., paper for Netherlands Environmental Agency, 2011.
6. 'Impacts of lice from fish farms on wild Scottish sea trout and salmon: summary of science', www.gov.scot, March 12th, 2021.
7. Gov Scot, Marine Scotland.
8. Scottish Land Commission Report, 2019.
9. Forestry and Land Scotland report, August 2021.
10. 'Deer in a changing climate – how do wild deer affect carbon sequestration in Scottish woodlands?', Christopher Hirst, paper for *Climate Change*, March 2021.
11. Campaign for Real Farming article, November 20th, 2021.
12. 'Public Perception of Deer Management in Scotland', Hare et al., paper for *Frontiers in Conservation Science*, December 2021.
13. *Regeneration*, Andrew Painting, Birlinn, 2021.

Chapter 10

1. *Science Focus* article, February 2022.
2. *Property Week*, September 20th, 2019.

3. HS2 website.
4. 'Davos 2020: People still want plastic bottles, says Coca-Cola', BBC article, January 21st, 2020.
5. F1 website article, November 12th, 2019.
6. Airportwatch blog, November 2015.
7. 'Phenological trends in the pre- and post-breeding migration of long distance migratory birds', Lawrence et al., paper for *Global Change Biology*, October 2021.
8. 'Sweden's forests have doubled in size over the last 100 years', article for World Economic Forum, December 2018.
9. 'Water Quality in Rivers', House of Commons Environmental Audit Committee paper, January 5th, 2022.

Chapter 11

1. 'Who Owns Scotland?' property map.
2. www.gov.scot
3. Mortality statistics reported in Data Blog.
4. Sir Simon Rattle.

Chapter 12

1. Met Office press release, April 30th, 1922.

Chapter 13

1. *The Book of Hope*, Jane Goodall, Penguin Viking, 2021.
2. GWCT blog, August 2022.

3. Department of Transport, UK Port Freight statistics, 2019.

Appendix 3

1. The Big Plastic Count, 2022.
2. *The Hidden Universe*, Alexandre Antonelli, Witness Books, 2022.